MORE ADVANCE PRAISE FOR *A FABULOUS DISASTER*

"I'm completely absorbed in this book right now—it's impossible to put down. It's not just the life story of one of thrash metal's greatest icons, it's also a detailed account of the birth and evolution of the entire genre. Gary Holt's raw energy and insane talent have kept thrash alive and kicking for decades, cementing his status as a true pioneer. The guy's an absolute legend, but what makes him stand out even more is how humble and genuine he is. I'm lucky to call him a friend."

—Adam Nergal Darski of Behemoth, author of
Confessions of a Heretic

"Gary is one of the most fiery and wickedly recognizable guitarists of thrash metal, and he was one of the first musicians to welcome me into the Bay Area when we debuted Megadeth there in 1984. He's a thrash metal OG—he's lived it, he helped build it, and his name is firmly on the door of our genre. This book is not for the faint of heart, as it tells it like it was, warts and all, of a young man who learned the ropes of our business from the ground up and became a true superstar."

—David Ellefson, cofounder of Megadeth and
author of *My Life with Deth*

"It's very rare to find someone in the music business so willing to expose themselves through vulnerability, humility, and purity of spirit in order to share their truth. Especially when that someone is a creator and pioneer of a history-changing musical genre that no one saw coming and is now impossible to deny. Gary Holt's story is uncompromising and unique in its brutal honesty and willingness to display all of the warts and scars that ultimately lead to redemption. With an unmatched work ethic, he's traversed the minefield of making (and not making) music for a living, and all the triumphs and tragedies that go along with that, to ultimately find himself become the man he was always meant to be. I've always had mad respect for Gary as a musician, and I've always really liked him as a person. Now I love him!"

—Dave "Snake" Sabo, Skid Row guitarist

"One of the best books I've read in years from cover to cover. I could not put it down. It's a must-read."   —John 5, Mötley Crüe guitarist

A FABULOUS DISASTER

A FABULOUS DISASTER

FROM THE GARAGE TO MADISON SQUARE GARDEN, THE HARD WAY

GARY HOLT
WITH ADEM TEPEDELEN

GRAND
CENTRAL

New York Boston

Hachette Book Group supports the right to free expression and the value of copyright. The
purpose of copyright is to encourage writers and artists to produce the creative works that
enrich our culture.

The scanning, uploading, and distribution of this book without permission is a theft of the
author's intellectual property. If you would like permission to use material from the book
(other than for review purposes), please contact permissions@hbgusa.com. Thank you for
your support of the author's rights.

Grand Central Publishing
Hachette Book Group
1290 Avenue of the Americas, New York, NY 10104
grandcentralpublishing.com
@grandcentralpub

First Edition: April 2025

Grand Central Publishing is a division of Hachette Book Group, Inc. The Grand Central
Publishing name and logo is a registered trademark of Hachette Book Group, Inc.

The publisher is not responsible for websites (or their content) that are not owned by the
publisher.

The Hachette Speakers Bureau provides a wide range of authors for speaking events. To find
out more, go to hachettespeakersbureau.com or email HachetteSpeakers@hbgusa.com.

Grand Central Publishing books may be purchased in bulk for business, educational, or
promotional use. For information, please contact your local bookseller or the Hachette Book
Group Special Markets Department at special.markets@hbgusa.com.

Print book interior design by Amy Quinn.

Library of Congress Control Number: 2024950720

ISBNs: 9780306834011 (hardcover); 9780306837739 (signed edition); 9780306837746 (BN.com
signed edition); 9780306834035 (ebook)

Printed in the United States of America

LSC-C

Printing 1, 2025

Dedicated to the memory of my father, Bill Holt

CONTENTS

PART III: REDEMPTION: 2003—PRESENT

FOREWORD

BY KIRK HAMMETT

GARY HOLT HAS SOME STORIES TO TELL, BUT THIS ONE'S MINE.

I met Gary when Exodus played the gym of Richmond High School. He was friends with Tim Agnello and Tom Hunting. Tom lived right across the baseball field from Gary. And right from that initial introduction, I could tell Gary and I were very like-minded when it came to music and that we shared a similar taste in the dark, heavy aesthetic.

Not long after that very show, I invited Gary to go with us to see Ted Nugent, with the Scorpions opening. I can recall to this day that I really wanted to impress Gary when he came over to the house, so I had a huge bucket of Michelob beer on ice sitting on my kitchen floor. I told him I was excited to show him some stuff and proceeded to play him all the Uli Roth Scorpions songs because he wasn't familiar with the earlier, ballsier version of the band. I told him he'd love it because it was even heavier.

I was impressed he had good taste in music. He was into the Nuge, Sabbath, Deep Purple, Rainbow . . . all the great '70s hard rock was the common ground for us, so there was a lot I could play for him. Over the next few weeks, I played him albums by UFO and Iron Maiden, and we both really got into the NWOBHM scene happening in the UK. Gary loved all of it.

He took it all in, and that was part of what brought us together. It was kind of amazing how much he learned and how fast he learned it. At one point, we were practically inseparable, just hanging around listening to music.

Gary had four older brothers, but Chuck, who was a total punk rocker, was closest to our age. He was obsessed with punk rock and British punk rock, and he was always throwing things at us to listen to. "Listen to this," "Hey, check this out," "You gotta hear this. . . ."

I remember Gary stealing Chuck's pin for the band 999 and turning it upside down so he could wear it as 666. We always got a big laugh out of that.

But Chuck was a big influence on Gary and me in terms of looking to other places to find aggressive, hostile, cerebrally therapeutic music, which is what we needed in those days. It was all about music, and back then, I always had a guitar in my hand, which I guess I still do to this day. Whenever I'd put my guitar down, he'd pick it up and pretend he was playing. And I was like, "Hey, man, you know your way around the guitar a little bit." And he was, "Nah, I'm just going for it." But then I would show him little parts of songs and solos, and I could tell he had potential and a feel for the music we both loved so much. And what he was doing when he was just going for it made sense, so I showed him a few chords and asked if he wanted to be my guitar tech. And without any hesitation, he just said, "All right!"

So he became my guitar tech. At this point, Tim Agnello had left the band and Exodus were a power trio. And during that whole time, I was teaching him things. I was constantly showing him riffs and licks here and there, different chords, and when I played, he really watched me. He was progressing quickly, and I knew with some solid practice he'd be able to become a decent rhythm guitarist in a very short time.

I loved it, because for years I had played with John Marshall, but John and I differed stylistically. I felt I had finally found someone who was the perfect foil for me, and from that point on, we were a guitar team just like the bands that we worshipped at the time. And sure enough, after a couple of months, he became Exodus's second guitar player.

Gary would just go for it—rhythm, solos, everything. I love that about him. He just full-on charged. I loved his energy, and he was a funny guy, and by that time, we were good friends. We were hanging out all the time and, of course, getting into trouble all the time. Chasing girls, doing petty crimes, playing guitar, listening to heavy metal. Just having the time of our lives. We were doing what one should do when you're at that age. The average age of the band members at that time was seventeen!

And we were totally turned on by the raw aggression of music that seemed to be coming at us from all sides—through hard rock, through British punk rock, through the college radio stations that would play new Bay Area and SoCal hardcore punk bands, and from the NWOBHM. It was a proficient time for the music we liked, and we could both see the tide turning toward a new type of musical aesthetic that was hyperaggressive and energetic and had somewhat of a poignant message attached that Gary and I both recognized: this was the music of our generation, and Gary and I were heeding the call.

I remember exploring a whole range of different sounds with him, different techniques on our instruments to find a new heaviness that was different from Zep or Skynyrd or whatever was playing on FM stations at the time. It was so important to us because this music was still underground, and we felt it was our job to put it out there to anyone else who would listen to this amazing new music that was being created. We did not realize it at the time, but we were a part of a movement, and it's weird how you never see how one can be involved; you only get an idea of it once years have passed and you have the luxury of looking back at the bigger, greater picture of how things came to be.

We were so invigorated by our new lives as musicians, and the music was just *so* good to us back then. It was a special time; you could almost call it the moment heavy music turned on itself just to influence us and set us on a path to develop a new genre that would eventually take over the world!

But we had other adventures as well.

Gary and Tom lived in a gnarly-ass neighborhood, and I lived in a neighborhood that was maybe slightly less gnarly. Jeff Andrews lived in a somewhat nicer area, but still, it was a great solace that the four of us could hang out at Gary's garage and make music together. I mean, it wasn't like a war zone, but still the streets of the East Bay were dangerous at that time, especially the San Pablo area, but somehow, we managed to fit in.

We were mischievous and underprivileged, and we were passionate for our music and for that lifestyle, so we found ourselves in a lot of trouble a lot of times. I mean, we ran the whole gamut in terms of delinquency. We chased girls together . . . we chased a lot of girls. We went for it. We all did. We were young and male, so of course we would.

Gary and I became close right away because we had a similar sense of humor, similar tastes in music, literature, and horror. Also we even had the same height stature. I loved that. We knew we looked good together, playing guitar side by side. As a young adult, you look for stuff like that, and we were still kind of insecure about our appearances.

We were always looking for things that looked cool and would add to the experience of playing in a band or seeing a band. And I loved how Gary and Jeff and I looked together. We looked great. We just needed to find a singer, and we found one. Oh boy, did we find one in a certain Paul Baloff. But that's another story, and one Gary can probably tell better.

But you know that over-the-top excitement that's so needed in heavy metal, and the strength of the scene and being there to support other bands and members of the heavy metal conglomerate? I knew for a fact how important that was to Gary and how much he understood that from the very get-go, the need to support the local scene and even police it against the poser element that always seemed to threaten to dilute the message (i.e., Mötley Crüe–type "glam" people, who were not generally accepted by the scene at the time).

Gary was always right there, making the scene stronger, bringing people together, and adding and contributing to it. All the guys in Exodus contributed a lot to the development of the '80s Bay Area thrash metal scene, making it something that really became historical and influential. And a lot of it started right there, in that high school gym, at least for Gary, Tom, and me.

Look, I know Gary.

I know his heart.

He is an excellent musician.

Excellent songwriter.

Exceptional lyricist.

Amazing friend and loving partner.

Yes, I know how batshit crazy he is, and how passionate he is about life in general.

I am batshit crazy, too.

And this is one of the many reasons we are still friends today.

His observations on life have always been interesting, and his commentary on life has always been entertaining. Gary's a very intelligent person, a very smart guy. And he has fucking good street smarts as well. He knows how to conduct himself in any situation, even if sometimes those situations call for less-than-excellent behavior. But I don't care. I love him unconditionally.

I can honestly say he has never, never, ever been boring, so I know he has a lot of really great stories to tell.

PLATINUM ROSEBUD!!!!!!

Kirk Hammett
May 2024

INTRODUCTION

Nineteen eighty-two was no Summer of Love in the San Francisco Bay Area. In fact, it was pretty much the polar opposite. Fifteen years earlier, the hippies espoused peace and love through their folk-influenced psychedelic music, but the sound gestating in the backyard parties in the Bay Area suburbs and at clubs like Ruthie's Inn, the Stone, Old Waldorf, and Mabuhay Gardens—the music my friends and I were playing—was angry, violent, aggressive, and fast as hell. This was no Summer of Love, but our music was just as revolutionary.

Heavy metal, since its birth in the late '60s and early '70s, had—for the most part—been a fringe dweller in the commercial music world, with a few exceptions. Bands like the Scorpions, Judas Priest, Rush, Rainbow, and UFO could sell records and turn out big crowds when they toured in the '70s, but they rarely found their music played on mainstream radio. Their audience was devoted, but metal was looked down upon as unsophisticated music for cavemen. The kids knew, though. It was a young generation of metal musicians/fans in the UK in the late '70s, who grew up seeing the rebellious, DIY spirit of the first wave of punk, that showed that heavy metal was just as legitimate, creative, and diverse as any other form of rock, and there was potential to sell as many records (or more!) as any band on the planet. This movement was called the New Wave of British Heavy Metal (NWOBHM) and produced Iron Maiden and Def Leppard, as well as dozens of less commercially well-known but no less influential bands like Venom, Diamond Head, Saxon, and Angel Witch.

I'd grown up in the '70s on a steady diet of the commercial hard rock that my older brothers fed me—AC/DC, Ted Nugent, Nazareth, Montrose, Molly Hatchet, Lynyrd Skynyrd, the Outlaws, and Blackfoot (still one of my favorite bands of all time)—but when my friends and I heard that first Iron Maiden album and those early Angel Witch and Venom seven-inch singles in 1980 and '81, everything changed. This music was heavier, darker, rougher, (at times) faster, and eviler. Though some bands from the NWOBHM were signed to major labels, nothing about Iron Maiden's seven-minute epic "Phantom of the Opera" on their debut or Angel Witch's "Angel of Death" suggested they would ever be played on the radio—or sell millions of albums. Our love of this music not only inspired us to form bands and create our own similarly aggressive music, it connected us with other like-minded musicians who were discovering the same sounds simultaneously. This is where my musical story begins, giving birth to a genre, thrash metal, that had a huge impact on the music world.

In 1982, we obviously had no idea that this music would make it beyond the backyard parties or the Bay Area clubs. In fact, it seemed really unlikely. As far as we were concerned, we were making music for a small minority—the tape traders, the hardcore devotees, the true headbangers—with no concern for what was going in the mainstream. This was music that shared DNA with the hardcore punk that was developing on both coasts and creeping out of the UK, and it was similarly staunchly independent. We knew major labels didn't want any part of this, wouldn't even know what to do with it, so we made zero concessions in our music, lyrics, and artwork. We just wanted to be heavy as fuck, and I'm pretty sure that no major record label saw that as a marketable attribute.

Nonetheless, with that goal as our guiding principal, we made music that took all our heavy metal and hard rock influences, added in some punk aggression and attitude, and pushed everything into the red. It was faster, more brutal, and more geared to incite a violent pit than the previous generation of metal. So how did thrash metal, and some of the foundational bands of the genre—like my own group, Exodus—find not only worldwide fame but become some of the biggest and most influential metal bands on the planet?

Well, that's my story, because I was there when Exodus and a handful of other bands—Metallica, Megadeth, Death Angel—built the ground floor in the San Francisco Bay Area scene in the early '80s, and I was also right in the mix when one of the biggest bands of the genre, Slayer, ascended to the top echelon with sold-out headlining shows at places like Madison Square Garden and the LA Forum on its final tour in 2019. In between, there were decades of rampant drug- and alcohol-fueled insanity in my life. That I survived and ultimately thrived and am today considered an elder statesman of thrash metal is no small miracle.

But the reason why is simple: I love this music I helped create. I do what I do because I genuinely love it. It's my life. It always will be. That's why I'm able to play it with such conviction and a level of fury, because I'm not faking it. At sixty, I still feel like I've got shit to prove. I still feel like I've gotta prove myself. I've gotta prove that I can keep up and do this, because I love to do this. Thrash metal, it's not a joke to me. It's who I am.

PART I
DESTRUCTION
1964—1992

CHAPTER 1

WELCOME TO SAN PABLO

T HOUGH I WAS BORN IN RICHMOND, CALIFORNIA, IN 1964, I CAN thank my father, William "Billie" Charles Holt, for the hint of a Southern accent I somehow acquired from him and never lost. He came to California from Oklahoma, where his family had lived for generations, and he didn't leave his accent behind. He was born in a tiny rural Oklahoma town called Asher, where prospects for work after high school were meager, so he joined the army, which eventually brought him to California. After arriving in the Golden State in the early '50s, he was shipped overseas to serve in Okinawa, Japan.

The army offered him three squares a day and the opportunity to see the world. While he never talked much about it, family lore had it that he just missed serving in the Korean War while serving in Okinawa. He was apparently en route when the conflict ended. Apart from that near miss, my dad loved his time in Japan. He never really drank much around the home, but later in life, around the holidays, I'd bring him a sampler pack of Japanese lagers, as he'd developed a taste for them when he served in Okinawa.

When my father's time in Okinawa ended, he returned to the Bay Area and was stationed at the Presidio army base (now a national park). In 1961, he met my mother, June Bernice Earnest, who herself had moved to California from Wisconsin in search of work. My mother's initial experience in California, though, had been markedly different from my dad's. She'd gotten married young, had four children—three boys and a girl—in rapid succession, and her first husband had abandoned her. So when she met my father, she was a single mom of four living in San Anselmo in Marin County, an area she most definitely couldn't afford to live today on her own with a house full of children!

It must have been true love, because my young father, fresh out of the army, stepped up and married my mother and, like the man of great character that he was, raised her children—Kathi, John, Donald (whom we called Butch), and Steven—as his own. Finished with his military obligation, he got a union job as a forklift operator with Nabisco, bought a lot on Nineteenth Street in San Pablo—an enclave city in Contra Costa County—and built our family home from the ground up with help from my uncle and some other family members. The house still stands to this day, and my mother still lives there, so I guess he did a good job.

In the '50s, San Pablo was the kind of place in the Bay Area where a young family could afford to buy a lot and build a home. Located in the East Bay, a fifteen-minute drive north of Berkeley, it was a small, lower-middle-class city that a couple of decades later, when I was a teenager, could best be described as a barrio. It was definitely the armpit of Richmond, which encircled it. But when my parents and older siblings settled there, it was filled with other young families—a mix of races and ethnicities—trying their best to get by. By the late '70s, though, it had the unfortunate distinction of having one of the highest crime rates per capita in the US.

Once settled in San Pablo, my parents decided to add to their already large family. My brother Charles came along in 1962, and I followed two years later. The three-bedroom, one-bathroom house my father built was soon stretched to its limits. And my poor mom had a household full of boys—all nightmares—save one daughter. We were, as the saying goes, though, one big happy family. My father raised and treated us all the same. We were siblings, not step- or half siblings—just brothers and sisters. It never even occurred to me until many years later that my four older brothers and sister still had their father's last name, Earnest, rather than Holt. Had times been like they are today, I'm certain my father would have legally adopted them and given them his last name. Back then, it wasn't something that anybody ever thought to do. So four of us are Earnests, and myself and my brother Charles are Holts. My father was our hero and role model. For anybody who wants to know what it means to be a real father, it was my dad.

My mom was the glue that held the family together. She had so much love for all of us kids and for so many other people. In her own way, she tried to pay forward the fact that she was helped out of a very difficult situation as a single mother with four young kids. Years later, she ran a day care center out of our house, helping other single mothers. So, being as I was the youngest, in addition to my five siblings, I was raised along with six or seven or eight *other* kids at any given time. She treated those kids (and their mothers) like part of our large family. Some of my best friends were the day care kids my mom was looking after, who were my age. That was the life I knew—kids everywhere and a mother who loved them all.

I had a good childhood, and we were a close family. But as older siblings tend to do to the youngest, I was picked on a lot, mostly by my brothers. I had a horrible lisp when I was little, and when I said an *s*, it sounded like a grunt. My brothers teased the shit out of me and would mock and imitate me. I was like, *Fuck you guys. You're gonna pay for this shit someday.* (I'd remind those assholes, with a laugh, of these transgressions many years later when they were looking to get guest list spots for Slayer or Exodus shows. "*Sorry,*" I'd say, "I don't think I can get you a *spot* on the *San Francisco list,*" emphasizing every *s*.)

Surprisingly, we weren't a musical family at all. At some point, my parents bought a piano because one of my brothers wanted to learn to play, but it ended up as little more than a mantel with photos on it. We used to just beat on that thing until my mom would yell at us to stop. My parents bought other instruments, like trumpets and saxophones and shit, because we had to take some sort of music in school. But no one ever stuck to it, and the instruments inevitably ended up in a closet. My parents didn't think I would keep playing either, so I wasn't exactly encouraged to take up an instrument.

Which was fine, because my passion as a kid wasn't music, it was dinosaurs. Well, it was more like my obsession. All I wanted to do was be a paleontologist when I grew up. Until my early teens, that was the only thing I ever considered for a career. I wanted to dig up dinosaur bones. And as much digging as I did as a kid, I never found any dinosaurs in San Pablo.

My aunt Neva, Dad's sister, who lived with her husband, Lawrence Nolan, one street over from our house in San Pablo, eventually moved to a farm in tiny, rural Winton, California, where I could do a lot of digging. To be honest, though, when I was staying there for weeks at a time in the summer, my cousins Dean and Brian and I were digging foxholes to play army, not looking for dinosaur bones. We would get shovels and dig a four-foot-deep foxhole and put an old camper shell from a truck over it. We even made "guns" that shot rubber bands. It was fucking awesome. I looked forward to it every year. What I wouldn't give for another couple of weeks on that farm. My uncle sold it many years ago, after my aunt Neva passed, but it's still there, in spite of the housing developments that have grown around it.

Another benefit of my aunt and uncle's farm was a little side hustle I had. Uncle Lawrence grew sweet potatoes and red onions, and every so often, he would drive his old fucked-up red truck two hours north to San Pablo to do a couple of things. First, he'd haul all the scrap metal that he'd collected to the scrapyard for cash, and then he'd bring me a delivery of sweet potatoes and red onions to sell. I was probably about ten years old, and I would load them up on this red wagon I had and bring along a bathroom scale. I knew everybody on the block, like you did back then, and I'd cruise the neighborhood with my wagon, selling onions and sweet potatoes, a little OG hustler, making some money. I'd later put these hustling skills to selling weed and meth, but it all started innocently enough with produce.

That was San Pablo. It was blue-collar, but it was a cool place to grow up. We were a working-class family; my dad was a member of the Teamsters, who only ever drove a forklift his entire working life. San Pablo suited us. Its makeup now is largely Latino, but it used to be a good blend. I grew up with a pretty well-rounded group of friends of all different nationalities and races. We were super well integrated growing up. Even Exodus in the early days had people of color in the band. Some of my best friends as kids ended up in lowrider gangs as young adults, but we were always friends. I'm proud of the city. It's a shithole, but it's *my* shithole. The most notable attraction now is the casino, which they had to knock down the bowling alley and a bunch of trailer parks to build.

I sometimes hear other dudes in metal bands talking about where they came from and how tough it was, and I'm like, *Motherfucker, I could take you to San Pablo right now, drop you off two blocks from the house I grew up in, and you'd hide and call someone to come get you.* They'd be terrified.

Welcome to San Pablo.

CHAPTER 2
GRAVY KIDS

I THINK I BECAME ACCUSTOMED TO MAYHEM AND CHAOS AT AN EARLY age, a skill that would serve me well in navigating the music industry. Growing up with five siblings in a three-bedroom, one-bathroom house was fucking challenging. Think of that: one bathroom for eight people. There were many times I'd have to piss in the garage sink because there was someone taking a shower and I had to fucking piss. And if there was somebody already pissing in the garage sink, I'd go *behind* the garage and piss. You did what you had to do.

Amid the insanity, however, was an underlying stability. My parents never divorced, we didn't move around a bunch, and the Earnest and Holt kids all went to the same schools from kindergarten through high school. I knew people who went to like ten different schools, their parents constantly moving for work or whatever. I had solid roots. I'm still friends with people from kindergarten and people from junior high and high school, like James Maxwell and James "Moose" Mangrum, who are some of my best friends to this day. My first school, Dover Elementary, located a block from my childhood home, is still there. I walked to and from school every day because it was so close. I actually got hit by a car coming home from Dover as I was crossing the street one day. A drunk driver in a Volkswagen ran right into me, and I ended up flying over the car and landing on the pavement behind it. I was lucky. The impact could have killed me, but shockingly, I only ended up with stitches in my lip and pretty gnarly road rash. Otherwise, I was okay.

My dad was a lifelong, passionate Oakland A's fan, so another way he was involved in our lives growing up was as a Little League coach for all my older brothers. As much as we were a baseball-centric family, though, I was more interested in BMX (bicycle motocross) and skateboarding. That was all I wanted to do in the mid-'70s when both sports took off in California. We didn't really have any BMX tracks nearby, so I was more of a street rider early on. Eventually, a track was built in Vallejo, north of San Pablo across the Alfred Zampa Memorial Bridge, so my father would take Ronnie Schwartz (RIP) and James Maxwell— two of my best friends from kindergarten—and me up there. We'd throw the bikes in the back of the pickup and go to the track on non-race days. The whole goal of BMX racing is to stay on the ground for the fastest possible laps, but we wanted to get air. We thought those dudes rolling over the jumps were lame. We would just go nuts, aiming for big air over speed.

When it came to skateboarding in San Pablo, it was pretty ghetto. We were just street skaters. I got every issue of *Skateboarder* and read it like it was the Bible. The whole Tony Alva Dogtown thing down in Southern California, that meant everything to us. But we were Northern California kids, in an area where nobody had pools. Skating in a pool? Fuck, I wish I knew someone who *had* a pool. There were no swimming pools in Richmond and San Pablo to skate. My dad would sometimes take us to the Newark skate park, but mostly we just skated banks, schools, parks, and the occasional drainage ditch. A local water ski store, Mello's Water Ski Shop, had a skateboard shop in the back, and that's where we bought all our gear. They built a half-pipe in the back, and we used to skate that. It was the only ramp in existence in our world. It had a really, really tight transition because of space limitations, so it was hard to skate, very steep. You just dropped and plummeted. But my buddy Tim Head used to skate it with ease. He was really good.

As the youngest of the five boys, I was picked on a lot by them, though I also discovered that there were plenty of advantages to having older brothers, especially such cool (and crazy) ones who offered me a measure of protection navigating through Walter T. Helms Junior High School and Richmond High School. My brothers ruled the schools, so I had an easy adjustment into each subsequent one. When I was a freshman at Richmond High, the seniors who knew my brothers would forgo putting my head in the toilet or whatever freshman torture they were into, because it was like, *It's fucking John Earnest's brother—leave him alone*, or *His brother's good friends with my older brother; they're fucking best friends, so I'm not gonna fuck with him*. And my brother Charles was a certified lunatic in school. He was the guy people would fuck with, and then he'd fucking hurt 'em, like bad. You didn't fuck with Charles. All my brothers were super popular, so I was able to have an easier time than most because of who they were. As far as I was concerned—and I still feel this way—my brothers were cool as fuck, and I looked up to all of them.

Two of my brothers even owned lowriders. Steve had a lifted front-to-back '64 Impala, and Butch had a lifted front-to-back '75 Monte Carlo. Lowrider culture was huge in San Pablo, and they were fully immersed in it. Twenty-Third Street was the main street in town, and the lowriders would cruise along there every Friday night. It was the place to be, so my friends and I would ride our BMX bikes there and watch the lifted cars jumping up and down the street. It was fucking cool. They would be stopped all over the place, the owners hanging out. It was just part of growing up in San Pablo. I still to this day want a lowrider of my own.

The most important influence all my brothers had on me growing up was shaping my musical tastes and earliest musical influences. I looked to them and their record collections and tastes to guide me in discovering the music that ultimately made me want to play guitar. They were all rockers, so I had the benefit of listening to the music they did at a really young age. They had the cool record collection, and all this fucking amazing early '70s hard rock—Deep Purple, Mahogany Rush, Robin Trower, Peter Frampton, Les Dudek, Nils Lofgren, and a million others—was right at my fingertips. I kind of just emulated listening to what they liked because that's what I was surrounded with; that was my environment. In the sixth grade, once a week we'd have record day, where you got to bring a record in to play for the class. I borrowed one of my brother's—maybe Montrose or something like that—and I got shot down. I got vetoed on playing what I wanted to hear. The other kids—because it was kind of a democracy, I guess you'd call it—got to decide what was going to be played, and they didn't like what I brought in. We ended up listening to the Bay City Rollers or some shit like that.

My brother John brought home the first Rainbow album, *Ritchie Blackmore's Rainbow*, in 1975 when I was eleven, and I was immediately mesmerized by it. I consider the band's 1976 second album, *Rising*, to be the greatest rock album of all time. Guitarist Ritchie Blackmore (ex–Deep Purple) would take you on these adventures in melody, like the sounds of Egypt were coming out of his guitar. It just moved me. It was epic. I've always said if you wanted to abandon me on a deserted island, all I need is Rainbow *Rising*. I don't even need a second album; just give me that one. Or give me "Stargazer"—just the one song will do. Or give me UFO's *No Heavy Petting* or *Lights Out* or *Obsession*, or any one of those albums with Michael Schenker playing guitar, and I would probably go years and not get sick of it because they're still my favorite albums. There's a lot of great music being made today, but no one will ever make records that good, myself included. They're just masterworks. They stand the test of time against anything.

By the time I got to Richmond High, I was fully part of the rockers' clique. We were the so-called gravy kids, the white trash rocker fucking losers. We hadn't climbed on the potato yet, as we used to say. I don't exactly know where the term *gravy* came from, but we were totally gravy. (If you were *really* gravy, we would yell at you to stop fucking around and climb on the potato!) For us, it was all about hard rock. AC/DC and Ted Nugent—they *ruled* our high school. And then, of course, we liked Nazareth and Montrose. We loved Southern rock, too; Molly Hatchet was huge at our high school, Skynyrd, the Outlaws, Blackfoot. We liked Aerosmith and Van Halen. These were all my early heroes. I've always said that I'm just a hard rock guitar player on meth. And for a lot of my life, I literally was.

This is probably when the idea of actually *playing* guitar started for me. None of my older brothers (or sister) had played or taken lessons, so there wasn't a guitar gathering dust in the closet. Being in a family of six kids, none of whom stuck with any instrument, I think my parents thought I would also eventually lose interest and they'd have a guitar in the closet, too. I had to grab the next-best thing: a tennis racket. I played air guitar for years, just raging in my bedroom with that racket. It would be the middle of the afternoon, and I'd have Ted Nugent's *Double Live Gonzo!* on and I'd be drenched in fucking sweat, just rocking out. Then my mom would walk in, and it was like I'd been caught masturbating. It was that embarrassing: *Uh, I'm just looking at this tennis racket, Mom.*

No surprise, this is also when I discovered marijuana. Until high school, I'd never done a drug in my life, under threat of an ass whupping by my older brothers, who were all total stoners themselves. I'd been an honor student through junior high and was the one in my family who was supposed to go to college. So they were like, *You're not gonna fuck up, or we're gonna beat your ass*—that is, until I started smoking weed, and they were like, *All right, whatever, let me show you how to roll a joint.*

I went from being obsessed with dinosaurs and having a lifelong dream of becoming a paleontologist to smoking marijuana, listening to hard rock, and going to concerts. It was a fucking amazing time to grow up in the Bay Area if you were into rock and roll. The local FM radio stations played nothing but pure hard rock, and the Day on the Green concert series brought some of the biggest and best artists in the world to the Oakland-Alameda County Coliseum every summer. You could go see a bunch of legendary bands—Aerosmith, Van Halen, UFO, AC/DC, Ted Nugent, Thin Lizzy—for like fifteen bucks. We'd head out to the Coliseum at 7:00 in the morning with a quarter pound of weed and a mini pony keg of beer and have a fucking good old time. One of the highlights for me from this era was definitely seeing Styx with my brother Steve at the Cow Palace. They were one of my favorite bands and still are to this day (*The Grand Illusion* is an all-time classic). Synth solos, two guitar players, dual leads, rocking songs, ballads—they had it all! That show fucking blew my mind. I was like, *This is the music for me. I don't give a shit about anything else. That other shit's all garbage.*

I kind of felt like maybe this gravy kid had found his calling.

CHAPTER 3

HIGH IN HIGH SCHOOL

AN PABLO IN THE LATE '70S WAS KNOWN FOR ITS HIGH PER CAPITA crime rate, and it's safe to say that my friends and I contributed to that. We were ghetto kids and behaved accordingly. I used to ride around on my BMX bike and steal car stereos and shit with my little group of hoodlums who lived on Brookside Drive, across Davis Park from my house. Occasionally, when we rode past one house on Brookside, we'd hear someone in there playing drums. I'd never heard a guy actually playing drums before, like in real life, so it definitely caught my attention. Even though the house was just across the park from my own house, I had no idea who lived there.

It could have been someone at my high school for all I knew, because I wasn't really attending classes much anymore. The lure of hanging out all over the East Bay with my buddies, getting baked, was greater than my interest in schoolwork. We used to get on the BART train and go to

San Francisco and roam around the Palace of Fine Arts or the Explor-
atorium all high as fuck. Then we'd return home in time to pretend
we'd been at school all day.

Once, I showed up in my high school English class for the first time
in a month and a half, and my teacher gave me shit, like, *Who are you?*
He was busting my balls. It was the same day we had a school-wide
reading comprehension test, and I ended up placing in the top four or
five students in the whole school. All the class nerds were up in arms
because they thought it was a lie and the fix was in, like I'd cheated. But
it was easy for me. I could show up in math class one day a week and
do the whole week's work. I wasn't like the book-smart nerds. I was a
fuckup who was naturally kind of smart and really good at doing the
work. But there's that thing called *attendance* that you need to have.

There were periods of time where all my friends would make their
semiannual attempt to start attending class, and I would be alone, with
no one to cut class with. I would just go spend the entire day at the public library. I'd sit there all day reading books, and then I'd head home
about the time school was supposed to get out. I'd do that five days a
week. I had my parents convinced I was attending class. I gotta be honest: By the time I got to high school, my parents weren't paying real close
attention. They had six kids, so when it came to me, the youngest, I had
them pretty fooled that I was keeping up on my schoolwork.

There was one rare instance where I was glad I hadn't skipped school.
It was actually life-changing. I was friends with a guy named Tim
Agnello who played guitar in a band with a few dudes from De Anza
High School over in El Sobrante. On this day, Tim's band, called Exodus,
were invited to jam in Richmond High's band room. Tim mentioned it to
me, so I was eager to see him play and hear what they sounded like.

Exodus was formed in 1979 by guitarist Kirk Hammett and drummer Tom Hunting, along with Tim and a bassist named Carlton Melson. They originally came together jamming in their high school music

room. Some of these early music room sessions even included bassist Les Claypool, who went on to Blind Illusion and later Primus (and many other projects). Exodus briefly had a lead vocalist, Keith Stewart, but eventually, Tom took on most of the lead vocal responsibilities, with Kirk and Carlton chipping in as well. Even though Kirk and his bandmates were in high school, they made a name for themselves locally performing mostly covers—AC/DC, Scorpions, Judas Priest, among others—on the active backyard party scene, where Claypool's Blind Illusion were a big draw, too.

This band room performance at Richmond High was the first time I ever laid eyes on Kirk Hammett, and it was the first time in my life hearing electric guitar right in front of me. It was magical; I couldn't believe how awesome it was. I'd obviously seen many concerts by then, but here I was listening to and watching someone my age playing through a little 2×12 combo amplifier, right in my own element. It made me think, *This is something I could do, too.* Before that, my heroes were rock gods, and I couldn't fathom doing what they did—like, *Wow, they're not even human. They're a whole other race of being.*

But these were just kids playing a bunch of cover songs. Kirk singing "Another Piece of Meat" by the Scorpions was pretty fucking hilarious. His singing was awful, just terrible. The riff, though, was so killer, and seeing them play was spellbinding. At the time, I thought it was the best guitar tone—hearing it loud, right in front of me—but they were all probably just playing on cheap gear. Tim was a big focal point of the band at that time. He had more stage presence than any of the other guys, and he played this badass black Les Paul Custom guitar. My fascination and love for Les Pauls, especially the Custom, is all directly linked to his guitar. Seeing it two feet away, it was like, *That's a beautiful instrument. It's like a Stradivarius.*

Apart from the mind-blowing musical experience, this was when I befriended the other three guys in Exodus who went to De Anza. Tom, as it turned out, lived right near my house, just across Davis Park. He was the person I'd heard drumming over on Brookside when I rode by on my BMX bike. Tom was a year younger than I was and had gotten kicked out of a couple of schools, so he ended up at De Anza, which was a good five miles away—might as well have been the next state, from my point of view—where he met Kirk. Unfortunately, I proved to be a negative influence on young Tom, as he was arrested for shoplifting at the Alpha Beta grocery store the first time we hung together. We were stealing beef jerky and caps, the kind you use in a cap pistol. We'd smash a whole roll of caps with a brick, and it sounded like a cherry bomb. I waited outside for him, not knowing he'd been nabbed, but when he didn't come out, I bailed. I only found out later that he got caught and they called his mom to come get him. Tom's mom still loves me to this day, despite the fact that the first time her son ever spent time with me she got a call from the cops. She says she prays for me, and she's the only one who does that and I'm not offended by it.

As a teenager, Tom was a big, burly guy, about six three or something like that. He was always just happy-go-lucky, with a big fucking smile and goofy charm. And his legs never stopped moving. It'd drive you insane when you were sitting on a couch with him because he was constantly drumming, and the whole couch would be like a fucking giant vibrator. And he'd always be singing. No matter what song's on, you'd have to listen to Tom sing it—whether it's fucking Rush or Daryl Hall, it didn't matter, Tom was gonna sing along. He's just always been an upbeat guy.

I also got to know Kirk better when he and I went to see the Scorpions and Ted Nugent on May 23, 1980, at the Cow Palace. It was the first time we'd spent a day or evening together, and we just hit it off as best friends right away. Before the concert, he invited me over to his house for some preshow partying and played one of the Scorpions' earlier Uli Roth–era albums, *Virgin Killer*, which eventually had a huge influence on me as a guitarist. I had never heard early Scorpions until that day, and it changed my life! While in line to enter the Cow Palace, security took away the beer Kirk was holding, and he took a half-assed swipe at them. Surprisingly, they just sent him in anyway. Different times! Back then, Kirk used to wear these big thick-framed glasses, even onstage playing his Gibson Flying V, which definitely gave him a unique look.

After getting to know Tom and Kirk, I started working at their shows as a roadie. I use the term loosely, because I was just hanging out because they were my friends. Being a roadie meant that I carried gear, smoked hella weed, and got wasted. They'd print their own tickets, rent out a hall (or set up in someone's backyard) and provide obscene amounts of alcohol to anybody, regardless of their age. We had names for the different gigs. One was called "the Ripper," because we had ten kegs. Then we had another called "Jug Night," which is still legendary among the Richmond / San Pablo people who were old enough to have been there. We provided fifteen or twenty kegs of beer and we had like ten or fifteen half-gallon jugs of whiskey—all you can drink until it ran out. There were probably countless DUIs that night, dudes spinning tires, wasted in their hot rods out front. It was just crazy times. I don't think any of us were old enough to buy the alcohol; we either knew a liquor store that would sell to us illegally, or we had someone else who was old enough to buy it.

Exodus were kings of the local backyard parties. It sounds crazy to say it, but there was a great music scene in San Pablo. There were a lot of bands. Rock was prevalent, and all different styles were being played. Some played more like Southern rock, but Exodus were the closest thing anyone had seen to a *metal* band.

Attending classes at Richmond High became less and less important to me when all my extracurricular activities—keggers, smoking weed, concerts—started increasing. A lot of my issue with high school was just boredom, because it was the same work I'd been doing in junior high. I still have my final report card, which was all Fs, because I wasn't going to class. It's burned around the edges because I started to set fire to it, but thought otherwise. If you look at the number of days missed, it was *all of them*. My friends and I had moved beyond pot and beer and were now doing hallucinogens and amphetamines, like Black Beauties. We'd bust the capsules open, crush up the little balls inside, and snort them. It was gnarly shit, way gnarlier than snorting meth, which we discovered later.

So for a while, I figured out a scam to prevent my parents from discovering I was no longer attending classes. The rule at my high school was that if you had overdue library books, they withheld your report card. Like that was some kind of punishment! It was a benefit to me! I didn't want that thing coming home. They eventually sent it anyway. My mom was like, *Gary Wayne!* I knew if my middle name was being used, I was in trouble.

"Gary Wayne, what is this?" she asked, probably knowing full well exactly what it was.

"Well, Mom, I haven't been going to school," I admitted. No use in lying when she was holding the receipts.

"You're either going to get your GED, or you go back to class," she insisted in no uncertain terms.

"I'll take my GED."

Once the jig was up and I no longer had to pretend I was going to class, I watched a lot of fucking soap operas, because all my friends were still going to school. I watched *Days of Our Lives* and *The Young and the Restless* all the time. I'd walk over to the park, smoke a joint, and then it was soap time. There was nothing else on then, no cable TV with a million channels; I had five channels to watch. I got addicted to that shit and, to this day, am still a fan of trashy, escapist TV. I got my GED, but I knew that that wasn't going to do much more than satisfy my parents.

Going to college wasn't on the horizon. My brother Charles and I were the only two children of the six who didn't finish high school. Some days, I look back and wish I'd graduated from high school. I feel like I missed out on something. But everything happens for a reason. Had I done any of that and kept my shit together in high school and kept my grades up, I wouldn't be writing this book. I'd be out in the fucking Badlands, digging up a fucking *T. rex* skeleton for no money at all. I'd be happy, living my own *Jurassic Park* dreams.

CHAPTER 4
EXODUS BOOKED

Kirk Hammett. A Montgomery Ward guitar. A handful of chords. Some Rolling Stones song I can't remember. That's how my career as a guitarist started. I know what you're thinking: *We're four chapters into the memoir of a world-renowned thrash guitarist and he still hasn't picked up a guitar?!* Well, I was a late starter. Though I'd *thought* about playing earlier, I didn't actually put hands on a guitar until I was seventeen.

One day when I was hanging out at Kirk's parents' house in El Sobrante, in an area called Sherwood Forest (all the streets have Robin Hood–related names), he offered up his piece-of-shit Montgomery Ward guitar and asked me if I wanted to learn how to play. Fuck yeah I did! You can imagine the quality of this catalog-bought guitar, though. The strings were a mile off the fretboard, there was no intonation to speak of. It had a melted Strat-looking body, but it was way smaller than a Strat. It was black with a tortoiseshell pick guard. Kirk got out that legendary Gibson Flying V of his and showed me some chords and a random Rolling Stones song to start with. After my first lesson, he let me take it home to practice. Kirk Hammett's first guitar became my first guitar. It was junk, but I was able to practice the fingering of the chords, and it didn't matter if it sounded good. It gave me something to work on. I initially started playing it without an amplifier, but at some point, Kirk loaned me a little tiny five-watt amplifier, along with a distortion box.

My brothers weren't impressed by my skills, or lack thereof, and they gave me a lot of shit: "Ah, Gary's playing that thing again. God, he sucks!" But a couple of weeks later, they'd changed their tune to "Gary sounds okay." Two months went by and it was "Little brother is fucking *good!*" After I'd mastered the basic chords and whatever Rolling Stones tune Kirk taught me, he showed me some basic lead licks. He gave me the building block of all solos—the pentatonic box—and that made sense to me. And harmonies made sense to me, too: You hit this big E-minor chord, then every note in that chord is a harmony. I picked it all up really quickly.

Completely coincidentally, my friend Tim Agnello had been fired from Exodus (he had a new outfit called Outrage), and Exodus were now practicing in a storage container—one of those metal shipping containers—in Richmond. There were a couple of other bands practicing in neighboring containers as well. The remaining Exodus trio was despondent over their lack of gear, and like any bunch of kids from the ghetto would do, they plotted to steal better equipment. A plan was hatched, and even though I wasn't in the band—I'd only been to their storage container once or twice just to watch them jam—I eventually became an accessory.

Exodus's ill-conceived plan was this: They staged a double theft. They ripped off the band in the neighboring unit's gear and made it look like their *own* gear had also been stolen at the same time. Soon after this, they moved their ill-gotten booty out of the storage container and started practicing in my parents' garage. Any easily identifiable gear they stole was disguised or disposed of, including a guitar cabinet that had belonged to the Greg Kihn Band at some point. It still had the stencil of the band's name on it, so they took it out to Point Pinole on the pier and threw it in the water. A cop rolled up just as they tossed it.

"What are you kids doing out here on the pier?" he asked, eyeing them suspiciously.

"We're, uh, just throwing rocks," they lied as the cabinet they'd just chucked was floating like a dead body in a Hollywood movie before slowly sinking to the depths before the cops could see it.

Not long after—and I still wasn't actually in the band—the police contacted my parents because Exodus had been rehearsing in our garage, and I once again got the *"Gary Wayne!"* treatment. Out of the blue, my dad showed up at an Exodus concert in Alvarado Park I was attending, which I knew was not a good sign.

First thought when I saw him: *Who died?* My dad would *never* track me down like this for something that wasn't serious. On second thought, he looked more mad than sad, so it seemed like something else was up.

"Come with me. We're going to the police station," he said.

This brought up the inevitable question: *What'd I do?*

Honestly, I'm pretty sure any number of things ran through my mind as possible reasons the Richmond, California, police might want to talk to me, but having my dad actively hunt me down seemed more serious than—just throwing out a hypothetical here—possession of marijuana might have required. Something weightier was clearly on law enforcement's mind. I had the sinking feeling this wasn't going to end well.

My dad took me straight to the Richmond police station for questioning. Since the gear was stolen prior to my involvement in the band, I told them I knew nothing about it and said, *I'm totally innocent.* They believed me. Just to be on the safe side, however, the first thing I did when I got home was to transport the rest of the stolen gear out of our garage and over to the garage of Tim Redding, another friend. Transportation of stolen property officially involved me in Exodus's crime. Someone eventually ratted us out to the cops, though we never found out who, and since I had moved the gear from my garage and since Kirk's older brother, Ricky, had traded me one of the stolen guitars—a Gold Top Les Paul Standard copy—for a skateboard, I could no longer claim innocence. Rumor had it that Tim Agnello was the snitch, thus earning his band the nickname, courtesy of Ronnie Schwartz, "Rat and the Hamsters." It was just a rumor, but the rivalry between Exodus and Outrage was real, like the white trash party scene version of David Lee Roth versus Sammy Hagar.

Exodus and I were busted, and the stolen gear was taken away. My sentence? I had to do a month's worth of work-detail weekends (as did Tom) shoveling mud over the winter, and I ended up spending one night in juvenile hall, because I missed a day of work detail. Juvie was a nightmare. I was in a cell overnight with a teenage white supremacist, which didn't put me in good standing (guilt by association) with the Black and Hispanic kids in there. I spent my day washing trucks (coincidentally) within a hundred yards of my brother John's wife's family nursery, which was located close to the detention center.

Kirk and Exodus's manager, Mark Myrick, were adults (eighteen-plus), and they just had to pay hella fines. I still have a clipping of the story that appeared in a local newspaper that had the headline "Cops Bust Band, Get Booty." It named Kirk and the other adults involved, and then said "other unidentified juveniles," which were Tom Hunting and me. Not long after the bust (but before I started my punishment), I was watching Exodus rehearsing, and they were going over the part of their set where they played covers. They were a three-piece at this point, with Jeff Andrews replacing Carlton Melson on bass and vocals. Kirk looked over at me and asked if I wanted to play a song using his guitar, without him, since there was only one guitar and amp there. We played "Grinder" by Judas Priest. I guess that was my audition, because after it was over, they asked me if I wanted to join. Fuck. Yeah. I was thrilled to death. That song is near and dear to my heart to this day because of that. And even after all the trouble with my parents and the police this band caused me before I'd even joined, I can't say I didn't know what I was signing up for.

My parents were surprisingly chill about my involvement in Exodus's stolen gear heist. They actually supported me being in Exodus. Since the police had taken back all the stolen gear, and I was without a guitar, my dad bought me a Hondo Strat copy (the same one I'm playing in the picture on the back of *Bonded by Blood*). I mean, if anything's supportive, it's your dad replacing a guitar the police took. That's pretty fucking supportive. He also bought a Peavey combo amp for me. And since I was a member of the band now—no longer a "roadie"—my parents let Exodus practice in their garage again. Probably just so they could keep a closer watch as to what we were getting up to. Regardless, I owe it all to my mom and dad for that support, and to Kirk for asking me if I wanted to learn how to play.

I officially joined Exodus a mere six months after Kirk first sat me down with that piece-of-shit Montgomery Ward guitar and gave me my first lesson. During that time, I didn't really take any proper lessons beyond what Kirk showed me. My mom had insisted I take some junior college courses once I got my GED, so I took a beginning classical guitar class at junior college. It turned out it was more like a beginning guitar class, like, *Here's how you tune a guitar.* So that sucked. My teacher noticed that I knew more about playing than the other people in the class, and he suggested I take his electric guitar workshop class. He was a very good classical player, but a very basic electric guitar player. I'd show up with my practice amp at overdrive, and I'd sit there and start ripping. There was nothing he could really teach me. But I did take a music theory class, and I learned a little bit of stuff from that. That's the extent of my lessons.

I was just able to pick things up quite easily, which helped me in joining Exodus and getting quite proficient so quickly. I was able to retain information easily. If someone showed me something, I could look at their hands, and I didn't have to sit there and go over it a hundred times and be like, *Play it slower. Now just show me the left-hand fingering.* I could kind of watch it and see it and replicate it. The guitar made sense to me, so I learned quickly. Notes made sense. The whole purpose of scales made sense. The guitar has a limited number of notes; they just travel up octaves. That made sense to me—E to E to E. When I first started playing in Exodus and people found out I'd been playing guitar for less than a year, they thought of me as some sort of young prodigy hotshot. Even though Kirk was the driving force in the band, I got a lot of attention for how quickly I became so good. But for as quickly as I got good, I should be a lot better now!

In addition to being guitar partners, Kirk and I were the best of friends. He was a couple of years older than I was and had gone to a different high school, but we found that we had a lot in common— similar musical influences and a love of psychedelics, which were plentiful in the Bay Area. He and I had a whole summer hanging out together in the early Exodus days that we refer to as the Summer of Love. Once or twice a week, we'd start our day with a trip to Rasputin Records in Berkeley where we would sell some of his dad's classical record collection. Next, we'd go to the fabled People's Park and buy a hit of acid. The last stop was a nearby liquor store for a twelve-pack of beer. We'd be high as fuck for the next eighteen hours. It was awesome. We did that shit all summer long—mushrooms, acid, it didn't matter. We'd go to a show and do a hit of microdot or windowpane or whatever we had. We loved acid. It was the best buy in the drug world. You'd spend three dollars and you'd get so high for so long that your face would hurt from smiling. We were having fun; we loved that shit!

We'd get high and go climb power towers—stupid, dangerous shit. We liked to climb. We knew this one place where, to enter it, you had to duck down and crawl through like a tunnel in the hedges, created by animals, that was only about three feet high; it seemed like it went on forever. It probably was only twenty yards, who knows, but it seemed longer when we were tripping balls on LSD. It opened up into this clearing with a huge oak tree. We'd get high as fuck and climb that tree for hours, hanging off branches like frying monkeys. One time we went there, high on mushrooms, and Tom Hunting got freaked out by the tunnel. He ended up turning around and sitting in the car by himself, tripping away, for at least a couple of hours while Kirk and I were swinging away on the branches and laughing our asses off.

CHAPTER 5
UNDER THE INFLUENCE

MAYBE THE BUMP OF COCAINE I DID BEFORE GOING ONSTAGE AT MY FIRST Exodus gig wasn't the best idea. I was nervous as fuck already—I'd only been playing guitar for six months!—but it was New Year's Eve 1981, the place was packed with about three hundred people, and I was in the mood to celebrate. The venue was the Montara Bay Community Center, in the Pinole–Tara Hills area, that we had rented out for the occasion. We'd even built a stage and had these homemade light boxes made out of different-colored patio lights. It was rad. We felt like we were building our own clubs, so to speak, and selling them out.

Once we started playing, the nerves were gone, and I felt like, *This is what I am destined to do.* I had *zero* stage fright. It was killer. At that point, our set still included about half covers—Judas Priest, Scorpions, Def Leppard—and early originals like "Gotta Get Away" and "Death and Domination." By the way, I can still play those songs (and even remember some of the lyrics), much to Kirk Hammett's amusement, because he has no clue how they go, and he wrote them!

Through a couple of years of this type of DIY scene building—from backyard parties to community centers and such—Exodus had created a loyal following in our area. Granted, we were big fish in a little pond, but we were distinguishing ourselves not just by the out-of-hand, booze-fueled ragers we threw but because we were slowly differentiating ourselves from the pack musically with our repertoire and growing influences. Our friend Merle Hall spotted Iron Maiden's 1980 debut album in the import section in a Berkeley record store, and based on the sick-ass front cover and the picture of the band on the back, he bought it. He played it for us, and we thought it was the greatest thing ever. It changed our lives and our entire outlook on heavy metal, and it was our first introduction to the New Wave of British Heavy Metal. We even started covering songs on it, like "Running Free," "Iron Maiden," and "Prowler," and people thought they were our originals. They all became staples of our backyard party set.

The first Maiden album was just one part of the equation when it came to developing the distinctive Exodus sound. There were several factors at play that not only influenced us a bit later when we moved beyond the backyard parties but also every musician in the Bay Area who was paying attention. The impact that local college radio station, KUSF, from the University of San Francisco, had was transformative, with much credit going to two DJs in particular, Ian Kallen and Ron Quintana, who had a program called *Rampage Radio*. Their late-night Saturday show introduced Bay Area listeners to bands that most of the United States had never heard of and wouldn't for another few years. They were exposing everybody to all the great NWOBHM bands and much more.

Courtesy of *Rampage Radio*, we heard live Mercyful Fate bootlegs before the band ever recorded anything, and all these other bands that people who profess fondness for that era of metal probably don't even remember—Legend, Silver Mountain, and Sweet Savage, before anyone knew who Vivian Campbell (later of Dio and Def Leppard) was. What other radio station in America was playing Angel Witch, Diamond Head, Venom, Motörhead, Saxon, and early Iron Maiden? We were spoiled. But this exposure played a major role in the development of the Bay Area sound. Ron Quintana's *Metal Mania* fanzine, which covered all these bands, as well as documented the burgeoning Bay Area scene, was also key. There was a lot of support for heavy music in this fertile time, and no one was more attuned to this than a twenty-one-year-old kid named Paul Baloff.

Kirk was the first member of Exodus to encounter Baloff. Kirk was at some hall show in Berkeley, and back then, you would strike up a friendship with someone based on their vest. It isn't like now where you see a fucking Kardashian wearing a Morbid Angel T-shirt. Back then, if you were cruising down in Berkeley and saw a guy with *Motörhead* hand-painted—because they didn't have back patches back then—on the back of his vest, you went and talked to him. Kirk saw Paul and thought he was cool and said, "We're looking for a singer." Paul was interested but wanted to see firsthand what we were doing, so he came to one of the Alvarado Park outdoor parties that we played. That was the first time he and I met. The second time proved to be more fortuitous.

Paul showed up at my parents' place on a day when we would normally practice, ready for his first rehearsal with Exodus. I heard a knock on the door, and Baloff was there when I answered it. I was puzzled. Then I remembered that we'd told him when we practiced, but no one had bothered to tell him that this rehearsal was canceled.

"Oh no. We didn't mention there's no practice today?" I said. He didn't seem too put out.

"No, but we can still hang out," he offered.

Feeling bad that he'd made the effort but we couldn't jam, I said, "Yeah, cool. Let's go hang out at Davis Park." I lived three houses away, and it was where we frequently went to get high.

We hopped in his car and drove to the park's parking lot. That was the first time I'd really hung out with him one-on-one, with no one else there. We sat and smoked weed, and he lined up some blow while we listened to metal and talked. It was fucking rad; he was turning me on to a lot of stuff I'd never heard. He was an educator in his own way. He was a professor of all things European metal. He was a little older than we were. I was seventeen, and he was twenty-one—and when you're young, four years older seems like hella old. But he possessed this knowledge and wisdom that came with his "advanced" years. It was like, *Wow, he knows the world; what a wise old sage he is.* That day, he introduced me to Angel Witch, which is like my favorite band from the entire NWOBHM, as well as Venom, Sweet Savage, and much more. He introduced me to a lot of music that influenced what Exodus eventually became. I knew Paul was our guy right then and there.

Paul came to Exodus with zero experience singing for a band, but he also came in sounding like no one we'd ever heard before. Yeah, he wasn't all that textbook, but he sang more traditionally in the early days of Exodus because the songs were more melodic and more Priest/Maiden-ish, with a little bit of rawness. That early material with Baloff was maybe like the first Maiden album, which was very raw. As the songs got faster and heavier, he gravitated toward the Baloff we all know and love. He just developed that style on his own as the songs developed. The difference between "Gotta Get Away" and "Exodus" naturally required that his vocal approach would change, because he was singing to more aggressive music. It wouldn't work if he were bellowing out some high-range, power metal vocals to it.

Paul's first gig with Exodus was about how you'd expect: It was epic. It was at the Ducal Palace pizza parlor in Alameda. He looked like a guy who was destined to destroy. In the middle of the gig, he left the stage—by "stage," I mean it was like a foot tall—and was on top of the tables. It was *just like* the scene when Ron Burgundy is playing the jazz flute in *Anchorman*, where he starts walking on the tables and shit. Baloff was doing the same thing. He was on the tables, rocking on them and trying to break them and just fucking going off. I remember watching and thinking, *This guy's fucking the real deal! Never sang before in his life, but look at him go!* His first show, and I was so nervous, and he's breaking things. It was fucking amazing. And we knew he was the guy from then on.

Paul had a larger-than-life presence in the Bay Area before he joined Exodus, but we definitely helped further that legend. By the time we met him, both his parents had already passed, and the stories he told us about them were beyond belief. He owned a pet wolf (maybe half wolf?) called By-Tor—named after a Rush song—and he claimed that he and his parents and his sister had emigrated out of Russia on horseback when he was a kid and that his father was a rocket scientist for the Kremlin. He assured us his given name was Pavel Nikolayevich Balakirshicoff (don't ask me how he woulda actually managed to spell that!), and for the entire time I knew him, I called him Pavel. We didn't know if any of what he told us was true, because all that we knew about Paul was what he wanted us to know.

While Paul became one of my closest friends and a huge influence on my and Exodus's music, his wasn't the sole influence that helped shape our developing sound. Around this same time, my older brother Charles got really heavily into the punk scene, heavy enough that in the very early '80s, he went on a pilgrimage to England with a friend of his just to be immersed in it. Bands like Sham 69, the Exploited, GBH, Anti-Nowhere League, and a million others—that was my brother's jam. He had this massive record collection of all these legendary bands.

I started listening to this stuff, even though I was a gravy boy hard rocker, and it was like, *This shit's speaking to me.* It was a new language, and all of a sudden, I was understanding it. Then I heard Discharge, and that changed everything—it made me want to play faster. There was a certain fury in these bands' music, just charging full ahead. And the guitars on the early Discharge records are still some of the best-sounding guitars I've ever heard. It's hard to replicate something that thick and dense. Listen to "The Possibility of Life's Destruction," "A Hell on Earth," and "The More I See" and you hear that influence all over thrash metal, especially Exodus and Metallica. (I'm still angry to this day that Metallica covered "The More I See" before we ever did. Tom and I jammed on it for years, and then Metallica put it out on *Garage Inc.*)

The tempo, the speed of that UK punk was addicting. We all loved it in Exodus. The Bay Area music scene was one of the first places where punk and metal crossed over. I don't care what anybody says about New York or any of this: Metal and punk kids were going to each other's shows in the Bay Area already. This influence changed everything for me. I needed to go fast; I needed to sound more like "A Hell on Earth" by Discharge and less Iron Maiden–ish. Or let's do both, why not? Who says you can't? We wanted to do dual-guitar harmonies, like Thin Lizzy, Iron Maiden, and Judas Priest. And we wanted to do epics, like what Rainbow was doing. We just fucking put it all together and then voilà!—another branch of the metal tree sprouted out: thrash metal!

You could argue that the seeds of this branch had been planted in the previous decade by bands like Deep Purple ("Speed King"), Judas Priest ("Exciter"), and Queen ("Stone Cold Crazy"), but these first steps lacked the aggression and attitude that the punk influence added. German band Accept, who'd also been kicking around since the '70s, probably came closest to creating an early blueprint with the first song on their 1982 album, *Restless and Wild*, "Fast as a Shark." It had the double kick, it had the grinding riff, it was heavy, it had the riff breakdown and then the most epic guitar harmony section. Everything you wanted in a thrash song was in there, with a monumental chorus.

No one called it *thrash metal* back then, however. That would come later. As far as we were concerned, we were just playing metal—a faster, more aggressive version. Bands in the Bay Area, thanks to KUSF and the cool record stores like the Record Vault and the Music Exchange, which carried the British and European imports we heard on KUSF and read about in *Metal Mania*, were being exposed to and influenced by a wide variety of heavy, raw, and fast music, and we were assimilating it into our own sound. Little did we know, however, that there were other musicians, not far away, following a similar path.

CHAPTER 6
WARLORDS

WHEN I'D JOINED EXODUS IN 1981, IT WAS STILL SOLIDLY KIRK AND Tom's band. Basically, Kirk wrote all our originals, but I was like, *I can write riffs, too, motherfucker*. My contributions were welcomed, but he was still steering the ship completely. As a result, most of the originals we were playing at the time were very influenced by the New Wave of British Heavy Metal. There were songs like "Ender," "Pillager," and the aforementioned "Gotta Get Away" and "Death and Domination."

With Baloff in the band, though, some of the lighter stuff started to get weeded out and replaced by heavier tunes like "Whipping Queen" and "Warlords." Up until this point, despite our dominance in the East Bay backyard party scene, we'd never recorded anything. We obviously had originals, but we hadn't committed them to tape. That changed in 1982 when we had the opportunity to do our first proper demo. We were super well rehearsed, because as kids, we'd rehearse five days a week whether we needed to or not; it's just what we did. Getting together and jamming was our favorite thing to do on earth.

That turned out to be to our advantage, because that first recording wasn't a traditional demo done in a studio. We set up our gear in a nightclub in San Francisco that had an eight-track reel-to-reel setup patched into their PA system, and we played three tracks—"Whipping Queen," "Death and Domination," and "Warlords"—live. There were no overdubs, so all the solos and vocals were done in one take. My gear was still pretty meager then. I was playing my white Hondo guitar through the Peavey combo amp, and I had a little overdrive pedal, an all-plastic piece of junk. I'd upgraded the Hondo a bit with a DiMarzio humbucker pickup, installed for a beefier sound. I was still using the stock bridge in the Hondo, but my friend Tim Redding's dad was a machinist, so he tapped out the thread hole in the bridge so I could have a larger-diameter, longer whammy bar installed, like Uli Roth of the Scorpions. My amp had a built-in phase shift, and I used that on some solos, like on "Warlords." That was pretty much it for my gear.

I have a lot of fondness for this demo, because it was my first time recording—and hearing myself recorded—and I think it came out really well. It doesn't exactly sound like the Exodus we became, but you can nonetheless hear the intensity that we would further hone coming through. It was a start, and the tape traders of the day saw to it that it would find its way out into the world, despite its sonic limitations. Demo traders in '82 weren't expecting (and probably didn't want) something slick and polished; they wanted intensity and conviction, and on those fronts, we delivered.

This demo did, however, expose the fact that we, as a band, didn't have the best gear. If we were going to move up in the Bay Area music scene, we'd need better everything. This is where Baloff's addition to the band (and his family inheritance) was a godsend. He financed some serious upgrades for Exodus: I bought my first Marshall half stack; Tom bought his first real all-matching Rogers drum set; and Kirk bought a Kramer Voyager guitar and an Acoustic 4×10 cabinet. These were loans, however, and to pay him back, Kirk, Tom, and I (along with a bunch of our friends) all got jobs at Kenco Paints in Berkeley. They were hiring under-the-table workers because the machinery that filled their paint cans had shorted a warehouse full of cans. Weights and Measures Department says if you're buying a fucking gallon of paint, it should have a gallon of paint in it. If it's coming up five ounces short, you're fucked. We were hired to top up all these cans. We had sticks that we put across the can that had a screw driven through them and you just had to add paint to the can until it hit the screw. That was the correct level.

However, we didn't exactly stick to the job description. Mostly, we ran roughshod and terrorized the building, because we weren't closely overseen. We even had a code word for when one of the supervisors was coming: "Flanagan!" That's what we'd yell and we'd all know to get back to work. In the meantime, we'd have paint fights, and we'd use the handles of the paint cans to make slingshots. We even had pallet jack races. We were going fucking crazy. I shot my friend Mika Kouvenen with one of those industrial-size copper staples used for sealing boxes. Those things will kill you if they hit you right. I got him right under the eye, just missing his eyeball by about a half an inch.

Somehow we managed to not get fired and actually complete the job! Believe it or not, we actually did work sometimes. The Kenco supervisor even offered a couple of us to stay on, including me, like we were exemplary workers. Truthfully, I was no better than the other guys who weren't extended that same offer. But I'd paid for my half stack, so I declined. *I'm out!* Kenco was my first job and only job for a long time.

With better gear, a demo in hand, and a growing repertoire of original material, Exodus were ready to test the waters outside the East Bay. Even though we were technically a "Bay Area" band at this point, the reality was that we'd only ever played in the *East* Bay and, for the most part, at gigs we'd set up ourselves. San Francisco was a world away, and though we knew about the bands playing there and the metal scene that existed, we'd never ventured beyond our little pond to play in those deeper waters. I was actually kind of intimidated by some of the San Francisco musicians because they were supergood and super talented— they also dressed better and had a certain air about them. Back then, because traffic wasn't as bad, you could drive to San Francisco from San Pablo in twenty minutes, but it was a world away for a gravy kid who didn't even drive.

On November 29, 1982, we made that twenty-minute trip to our first, and a very auspicious, San Francisco gig at the Old Waldorf, opening for a Los Angeles band called Metallica. I fucking knew nothing about this band because we were a bunch of little poor kids from the working-class ghetto and San Francisco was this other world. Metallica had already played San Francisco, but I wasn't there; I'd never heard of them. But they were the out-of-town band and had a track on the recently released Metal Blade Records compilation *Metal Massacre*, so they got the headlining spot, their first in SF.

Since most of us in Exodus were still teenagers, we were just thrilled—if not a little intimidated—to be playing a proper nightclub in San Francisco. It definitely felt like we'd moved up a notch, even though we probably came in dressed like shit and didn't have as nice equipment as other SF bands. It was intimidating, but it was fucking awesome, too. We were playing a real venue that had a real bar and real bartenders. We didn't have to pour in with truckloads of kegs to keep people drunk. There was real staff and a real dressing room. It was a different world. This gig was so momentous for us, even my mom— who has always been my biggest fan, from day one—came with one of her best friends, Joan, and my brother John. The Old Waldorf was right next to the Punch Line comedy club in San Francisco, and they showed up—completely out of their element—trying to find the venue. They approached some young dude for help.

"We're looking for the Old Waldorf," my mom told him.

"Oh, I think you want the Punch Line," he replied, knowing the Old Waldorf was sporting a metal bill that night. "It's right there."

"No, no, we're coming to see Exodus," Mom explained.

He looked dumbfounded. "Okay, it's right there." As he walked away, my mom heard him say, "I'd never bring my mom to this place."

Joan, in her excitement at seeing me perform with Exodus, made a further impression at her first thrash metal show. When we went on, she put her arms up in the air like, *Yay, Gary!*, and her hand came down right into some six-foot-four behemoth's pitcher of beer. He just looked down at her and smiled.

Though this first meeting, so to speak, between Exodus and Metallica was momentous, the reality is that neither band were the juggernauts we both later became. Metallica's lineup at the time—guitarist/vocalist James Hetfield, bassist Ron McGovney, drummer Lars Ulrich, and lead guitarist Dave Mustaine—was still fairly untested; they had gone through some different lineups since Lars and James formed the band in 1981. Lars was still definitely learning to play his drums at that time, and even though James was the vocalist, Mustaine did all the talking onstage. James never really said anything between songs. And when Mustaine broke a guitar string, he stopped the whole show to change it. This would *never* happen with Exodus. We were more professional than Metallica back then, even though Lars claimed otherwise in a fanzine at the time. I had a backup guitar, bro!

As for our performance, we went out and fucking rocked. It was killer. The show was epic. The crowd fucking went off. Going off back then didn't mean stage dives and everything, but we were welcomed from day one, and we became known as a San Francisco band, even though we never had a San Francisco–raised member in the band until

Lee Altus joined in 2005. We were East Bay guys. But San Francisco ended up being our scene. We played San Francisco clubs, went to San Francisco parties. That's where we spent all our time. As soon as we started playing there, it was like, *That's where we're at now.*

And despite Metallica's guitar string issues at our first show with them, I was like, *Wow, this band is fucking rad!* They were very Motörhead-ish in the way they played then, and it was totally killer. I specifically remember an interview with Lars back in the day, in one of the old fanzines, where he was talking about meeting Exodus for the first time, and he said the same thing we said: *It was like a mirror image, our band into the same stuff, playing a similar style of music that we didn't know about yet.* We definitely felt like kindred spirits at the time. For all the great metal bands that were in the Bay Area back then, in the early club days—and it was spectacular—there was no one else like Exodus and no one else like Metallica. But there was never any rivalry. I always said the only difference between Metallica and Exodus in the early days—because we all loved the same bands—is that they heavily took their main influence from Diamond Head and some of the other NWOBHM bands. Exodus loved Diamond Head, but we *really* loved Venom and Mercyful Fate. We gravitated toward the bands that praised the Dark One a little bit more. If you listen to "No Love," I've always said we probably owed royalties to Mercyful Fate for their influence on that. Same with "Deliver Us to Evil." And then you factor in that I'm a son of hard rock. That's what I grew up on, what I still loved. So it's just a hodgepodge of all those ingredients mixed together, like the killer hard rock from Ted Nugent, AC/DC, and Aerosmith and Nazareth and Frank Marino and everything else, Blackfoot, and then mixed in with Judas Priest and Black Sabbath and Iron Maiden and Motörhead.

And on a personal level, we hit it off with Metallica right away. We recognized that what we were doing was going against the grain, and it made more sense to be allies than competition. I mean, it was

competitive enough just to get gigs for the kind of music we were playing; we didn't need to be beefing with a band that was in the same boat.
One time we played with a band out in some hall in Danville, California, which is not known for its concert venues; it's known for expensive
homes and shit like that. The band had a song called "Pink Steel," so
you can just imagine what that's about. Anyway, the fans of that band
viewed us as a full-on punk rock band. So we were already competing
enough for people to accept us, because at the time, our music was hor-
rendous to other people who weren't part of that initial thrash wave.
We were just awful noise, a bunch of guys who played too fast. The
"Pink Steel" rockers had big, high vocals, and meanwhile, Baloff's up
there bellowing away. To those people, we were the worst thing they'd
ever heard. Metallica, too. Both our bands were just trying to find an
audience that appreciated what we liked and especially where we were
taking the music, which was more and more extreme.

CHAPTER 7

STRIKE OF THE BEAST

I DON'T WANT TO GIVE YOU THE IMPRESSION THAT THE SAN FRANCISCO metal scene somehow began with the first inklings of thrash in 1982. The fact of the matter is, the Bay Area had been, as long as I could remember, both a source of great metal bands and supportive of touring talent. When we started regularly playing in San Francisco, as well as attending shows, we were exposed to a wide variety of heavy bands. None of them were exactly doing what Exodus and Metallica were up to, because some of these bands had been around longer and were older, but we definitely discovered a vibrant scene that we East Bay gravy boys didn't previously know existed. There were so many bands. You could go to a different club in the greater Bay Area every night of the week and not see the same band twice.

Our first SF gig with Metallica at the Old Waldorf opened some doors for us in the city. Before long, we were playing Mabuhay Gardens, the On Broadway, the Stone, as well as the Keystone Berkeley on the east side. Metal Mondays at Old Waldorf, though, was where it was at; every Monday, they had a metal show. There was also the Best of Metal Mondays shows, so as we got more popular, we started playing those, which were on Saturday nights. It was fucking good times. At these shows—where it was the best of the best, so to speak—we were meeting guys in other bands who were just phenomenal players, with professional levels of guitar tone and stuff like that, as exemplified by Anvil Chorus.

Anvil Chorus were the kings of the San Francisco metal scene, and I thought they were going to be the biggest band on earth. Everybody in the band was just so massively talented—across the board, just the best musicians. Their guitarists, Thaen Rasmussen and Doug Piercy, were two of the best guitar players I've ever seen to this day. They were doing really cool shit with guitar harmonies. Obviously, Iron Maiden and Thin Lizzy were writing the book on that sort of thing, but Thaen and Doug were doing it in a whole other way, like full guitar-solo harmony sections. Seeing them opened up a lot of doors creatively for me on what I could possibly do with this thing called a fucking guitar.

Another top-flight act was Vicious Rumors, who are still playing to this day. And you had bands like Harvey—an all-Black band—who were awesome, and Thunderhead with Jon Torres (later of Heathen and many other SF bands), may he rest in peace. Then you had bands that weren't quite as heavy, but I thought were going to be the next multi-platinum phenomenon, like Head On. Frank Wilsey was their guitarist, and he was like Aerosmith's Joe Perry. He had big black hair and a low-slung guitar. Their singer, Mark Berglund, was this kid—really young, but fucking awesome vocalist—and they would sell out the Best of Metal Mondays constantly. I thought they were gonna be huge. They were a glam rock band with a really good look, and they had musical chops. Another great band was Violation. One of their guitar players, Paul Harris, was the only guy in the Bay Area club scene at the time who had a professional Nady wireless, and he used to rent it to me for next to nothing for a lot of shows. He was like the Bay Area's own version of Michael Schenker.

It was amid this fervent Bay Area metal scene that Metallica set their sights on an East Bay bassist by the name of Cliff Burton—a Castro Valley guy—who played for Trauma. Metallica had seen Trauma play in LA in late '82 and made every effort they could to get him to join, including bowing to his condition that they move to SF. In fact, the first time I saw Trauma with Cliff, it was at the Keystone Berkeley and Metallica were all there. It was insane. I'd never seen someone do that shit on a bass. Here was this guy with big bell-bottoms and a flannel shirt just ripping on his Rickenbacker with a wah pedal. He was shredding like he was a guitar player. I remember standing there with James Hetfield and everybody watching Trauma—all the thrash guys kind of hung out in the same alcohol-soaked posse—and we all knew why Metallica were there. The worst-kept secret in the Bay Area thrash scene was that Cliff was going to be the new guy in Metallica.

The first show Exodus played with Metallica with Cliff in the band—March 5, 1983, at the Stone in SF—was, unfortunately, the last gig Kirk played with Exodus. After parting ways with guitarist Dave Mustaine in April while preparing to record their debut album in New York for new label Megaforce Records, Metallica asked Kirk to join the band, so he headed east to rehearse in preparation for their May recording sessions. Metallica had become close friends with Mark Whitaker, a Bay Area guy who went on to manage Exodus and produce *Bonded by Blood*, and it was Mark's recommendation that they check out Kirk, like, *He's the guy you should get.* They'd obviously seen him play, but Mark's recommendation helped seal the deal.

When Kirk decided to take the Metallica gig, I was mad for a minute. He called me up and told me. We were all mad for a minute. But then, after that minute passed, we were happy for him. We went to the Old Waldorf in San Francisco after Kirk left the band—but before he left town—and we went out and partied and celebrated with him. In true Exodus fashion, we wouldn't let him get away that easily. We brought a stack of our promo photos with us and cut him out of all of them. Then we stuck the pictures of him in the girls' bathroom stalls— Kirk with his Flying V, looking all sultry!—and he was going around trying to chase them down and pull them down. Later that night, we ended up back at his house in El Sobrante and had a food fight. We partied and we were happy for him. We never looked back. Obviously, none of us did.

In fact, Kirk leaving worked for me; I was happy. It was like, *The band is mine now.* Kirk presented it to me. The baton was passed; do with it as you will. This meant a lot, because when I first joined the band, Kirk wrote everything. The first riffs I contributed were a couple of parts to "Hell's Breath." My first forays into riff writing, Kirk would want to change them a little. I think the only riff that ended up on *Bonded by Blood* that I presented when Kirk was still in the band was "Strike of the Beast," and Kirk wanted to change *that.* I'll blow my own horn because, as we know now, that riff is fucking perfect. You don't need to change "Strike of the Beast"; that riff is gold. So when I had time to process what Kirk's departure meant for Exodus, I was like, *I'm cool with it.* I inherited Exodus, and Kirk—by joining Metallica—got a fuck ton of money, fame, and everything else, and deservedly so. From there, along with Paul Baloff, I was able to form Exodus in the vision he and I had—more violent, gnarlier, heavier.

WHEN KIRK LEFT FOR METALLICA, WE WERE KIND OF AT A CROSSROADS ON a couple of fronts. There was no question that we would replace him in the band; that was a given. I liked being the chief riff writer, but I didn't want to be the only guitarist. I've always been a massive fan of two-guitar bands, whether it's Thin Lizzy or Iron Maiden or Judas Priest or the Scorpions. It's always about two guitars, two soloists, harmonies, and all that shit. Before we had that second guitar player, though, Tom and I just started writing songs. We finished "No Love" and "Strike of the Beast." Jeff Andrews, our bass player, didn't seem to be around much, and we just felt like we needed to make a change. Paul's roommate, Rob McKillop (always known to us as Robbie), was a guitar player, so we asked him if he wanted to play bass for us. Robbie was an animal, especially when he was drinking, so he was perfect for a band of animals. Unfortunately, we neglected to tell Jeff Andrews. One day when Robbie had come over to my parents' house to jam with me in the garage and go over the songs, Jeff showed up to grab something. There I was with another guy with a bass in his hands and I was teaching him Exodus songs. Jeff saw that he was being replaced, and that was kind of it right there. He grabbed his stuff and left. We never really said, "You're out"; we just kind of got caught auditioning a guy. To this day, I feel bad about that. But that's how it ended with Jeff. In hindsight, I probably should've gone somewhere else to audition Robbie.

Finding a new permanent bass player was the easy part, as it turned out. Replacing Kirk took some time, and there were a couple of false starts. The first guy we hired was Mike Maung. Mike was a great guy and a great musician, just not the perfect metal guitar player. Which is why he wasn't in the band that long. We only played one gig with him. He ended up being one of the founding members of another legendary Bay Area band—the Freaky Executives—but they were legendary for their funk. He used to say, "I played in the heaviest band in the world and in the funkiest band." Obviously, there were some fit problems when he was in Exodus. He was meant to be playing funky shit. Then we found this kid named Evan McCaskey, who was like a phenom. He was seventeen years old, and it was like this guy was going to go on to be the best guitar player ever, like a Marty Friedman–level shredder. He only played one show with Exodus, because in between joining the band and that show, his father found out he'd been faking notes to school and all this stuff and not going to class, and his father cut off all his hair. He'd had hair halfway to his waist. His dad also wrote *Liar* on his forehead in Sharpie and took his guitar and smashed it. So Evan did his one show with Exodus playing one of Robbie's guitars. Sadly, he ended up killing himself in 1989. It's a tragedy; he was such a great guitar player.

I hate to use terms like *blessing*, because I'm not a religious guy, but it was a blessing finding guitarist Rick Hunolt. I still count him as one of my two or three closest humans on this planet. It was actually our manager at the time, Adam Segen, who found Rick, who was from Berkeley. Rick came to my house one day to check out what we were doing, and I played a bunch of riffs for him. He had a Gallien-Krueger solid-state amp, and you couldn't hear it over my hundred-watt Marshall. Years later, Rick told me he thought I was from Alabama or something because I've always had that little bit of my father's Oklahoma twang. Rick was like, *Who's this motherfucker, this hillbilly from Alabama with his crazy riffs and his loud-ass Marshall?* Nonetheless, Rick wanted into the band. And after seeing what he was up against gear-wise, he did what any dedicated guitar player would: He sold his truck to our new bass player, Robbie, to buy his first Marshall amp. Clearly, his commitment was strong. We just knew he was the guy for the job. And just like that, the H-Team was formed—Holt and Hunolt.

What Rick may not have considered at the time was that he had joined a band with a rabid following. For his first gig, not long after he'd signed on, he got thrown in the deep end. We were opening for Japanese metal legends Loudness, who were playing their first US show, at Wolfgang's (formerly the Old Waldorf) on July 11, 1983. As much as he turned out to be a dynamo onstage, for his first gig, he was frozen with stage fright; he played half the show facing sideways to the crowd. He was scared. But it was a sold-out show and we were doing really well by then, so he was under a lot of pressure.

With the final piece of the revamped Exodus in place—Tom was now the only original member—Baloff and I started to shape the band in the way we envisioned it. In this post-Hammett era, he and I just wanted to write songs about killing people, so as we wrote, we started to weed out some of the lighter songs from the original Exodus era. This was even happening while Kirk was in the band. Some of the later stuff Kirk wrote before joining Metallica was getting really heavy and really thrashy, and we kept those in the set—"Dying by His Hand," "Hell's Breath," "Impaler"—but the older NWOBHM-influenced songs, where Kirk and Jeff wrote the lyrics, were getting kicked aside.

In our effort to write darker and more violent stuff, we, naturally, wrote a song about fish, "Piranha." We just loved piranhas; they're snappy little devils! Then there was "And Then There Were None," which was cowritten by Tom and me; that was the only song from that era that was political. Everybody had to have the obligatory song about nuclear war back then. Lyrically, the lyrics we were writing weren't quite split fifty-fifty between Baloff and me, but Baloff wrote quite a bit, and he wrote some of my favorite lyrics that ended up on *Bonded by Blood*. He wrote amazing lyrics. Sometimes I'd write faster than other members of the band, so if I wrote a song, I might have already had lyrics in mind as the riffs were being created. But it was pretty collaborative between Paul and myself. Our goal at that point was simple: we just wanted to play music that reflected our own behavior, which was pretty bad most of the time.

This all coincided with the Ruthie's era of Exodus that started in late 1983. Ruthie's Inn was a Berkeley club that catered to both the punk and metal crowds. Our first Ruthie's show, September 17, 1983, was when the audiences crossed over. That's when we started getting all the local punks coming to our shows, and we were no longer just "those filthy longhairs," and they were no longer "those dirty, Mohawk-havin'

losers." Our music appealed to them. They didn't care that we had guitar solos. They loved it. And we would go to all the punk shows, too,
whether it be Fang or GBH coming into town. That's also when things
got violent; that's when the *real* Exodus was born.

There were some other rock bands playing on the bill that night at
Ruthie's, as well. They'd sold tickets to their friends and family, and
those people were up at the front of the stage watching the band play
and rocking out with their drink glasses in their hands. They left the
glasses there sitting on the edge of the stage. We came on, and glass got
broken. Our fans were down there beating their arms on the stage, and
there was blood all over the stage. (The song "Bonded by Blood" was
born from that first Ruthie's Inn show, BTW . . . "There's blood upon
the stage.") A girl who came to see one of these rock bands must have
seen something she liked in our set, because she stayed up front and
was sitting there bobbing her head back and forth, rocking out. Baloff reached down, smeared his hand in the blood, and painted her face
with it. She screamed bloody murder and ran off. And I assume never
went to another Exodus show.

The Metallica house in El Cerrito, which James and Lars moved
into after leaving LA, was another scene of nonstop debauchery. The
parties at "Metallica Manor" were legendary, but most of them didn't
involve Metallica. Those guys were busy; they were on the road or
recording in Copenhagen with Flemming Rasmussen. Our friends
Connie Bryant and Pam Peters looked after their place, and we were
welcome there at all times. No one cared. We just threw ragers. That's
where all the after-parties ended up, since the house was about a
ten-minute drive from Ruthie's. Shit got wild. While Metallica were
off conquering the world, we were conquering their house. And when
they *were* in town, we always knew where the party was going to be.

One of those times happened to be September 2, 1983, when the
Kill 'Em All for One tour—Metallica and NWOBHM maniacs

Raven—played at the Keystone, and Exodus opened. We all ended up back at the Manor and it turned into total insanity. Raven drummer Rob "Wacko" Hunter broke his hand punching some dude—not a good idea to do while on tour. (That's why you always lead with your feet.) Some random stranger, not even someone from the show, got into an argument with one of the girls there who was close friends with everybody. And that turned into two girls arguing over whose boyfriend was tougher or some shit. Next thing you know, Rob Hunter punches the dude and breaks his hand, and everybody is just swarming around throwing kicks and just rat packing the dude. It was crazy times.

If I were a religious man, I'd pray for forgiveness. There was a guy named Dan Mora, who was a phenomenal bass player, but he was also kind of like our pincushion. (That's how he earned the nickname "Dartboard Dan.") At that same after-party at the Metallica house, we were throwing steak knives at Dan. We weren't *really* trying to hit him . . . but maybe we were. On the thanks list on *Bonded by Blood*, it says: "Thanks to Dartboard Dan & knives, forks, scissors & deadly hot pokers!" One day, I heated up a fireplace poker and gave it to Baloff, and Baloff had Dan cowering in the corner with a red-hot poker hovering above him. Finally, Baloff relents and says, "Ah, I'm not gonna burn ya," and when Dan relaxed, Paul scorched him on the arm. Another time, Baloff took his Motörhead pin off his vest and he was sticking Dan with it. We were fucking animals. We thanked him for it on the back of *Bonded*, though! We loved the guy, but as Paul said, "Some people are born to be victims."

CHAPTER 8

BONDED BY BLOOD

THE BIGGER EXODUS GOT IN THE BAY AREA, THE GREATER THE SWATH of destruction we left in our wake. Our shows had reached a new level of insanity. It may be hard to fully comprehend the vibe in the scene at the time if you weren't there, but the best way to describe the energy of the mix of punks and metalheads at these shows was rabid. We had a violent thrash metal gang of lunatic friends we dubbed the "Slay Team"—Andy "Airborne" Andersen, Alexis Olson, Lonnie Hunolt (Rick's bro), Toby Rage (RIP), and others—who were typically the primary instigators of mayhem. They were doing *severe* stage diving, like off the top of the PA, and also a little thing we called *head walking*. The Slay Team would be onstage drinking for most of the show doing security, but when it was time to join the fun, Toby would run off the stage and step on people's heads. I've seen him make it twenty or twenty-five feet. The guy was like six foot three or six foot four, with long, giant legs, and he'd be walking on heads like they were stepping stones. Or he'd leap off the balcony, doing these helicopter stage dives, his legs twirling like a top.

But the bad behavior wasn't limited to the Slay Team. Baloff, as our front man, put the fear of god into people in the scene, should they be a poser. If you look at old photos, you'll see he had these scraps of fabric tied around his wrists. We all did. Those were peoples' hair-band shirts. We all carried knives back then—I still carry a knife—and Paul would go up to someone, "Fuck Mötley Crüe! I'm gonna cut that shirt!" He'd pull out his knife, slice off a big shred, and tie it around his wrist. He had four inches of poser shirts around his wrist. He was also known to randomly shout: "All posers must die! Kill a poser!" and posers got nervous when Paul said that shit. That said, we had a couple of hair-band dudes on the Slay Team who were on our protected list, because they were every bit as obnoxious and horrible as we were.

We once again found kindred souls both musically and personally when Slayer made their way up from LA for their first Bay Area performances in January 1984. You could say that Exodus helped prime the pump for these guys to be welcomed with open arms. They'd just released their debut, *Show No Mercy*, the previous month, but the glammed-up LA scene didn't exactly appreciate the music they were playing. Thanks to the groundwork Exodus had laid by this point, though, Slayer, just like Metallica a year previous, found a very receptive audience for what they were doing.

They were in the Bay Area for two nights, and the first one, January 27, 1984, we weren't on the bill. We'd already heard some of their music, and Baloff and I loved 'em from the first listen, so we went to the show to meet them. Not surprisingly, we bonded immediately. It was a spontaneous Vulcan mind meld, and we were instant friends. Back then, that's the way it was if you liked this music. It was the same with Metallica. We were partying after the show from night one like we had been friends for years.

The funny thing is, in Slayer's early days, Kerry King didn't drink, but the rest of the band did. So I hung out with Jeff Hanneman more because he liked to fucking pound the beers and shit. That first night at the Keystone, Jeff gifted me the slide guitar upside-down cross that's in his photo on *Show No Mercy*. It was probably one of the single greatest pieces of Hanneman memorabilia, and it was in my possession until the '90s, when I somehow lost track of it. Maybe it got lost in a move or my divorce—I don't know. To this day, I'm super bummed about that.

After that first show, we ended up at their motel, the Cove Motel on University Avenue in Berkeley, and we proceeded to destroy the place. I mean, we reached a level of destruction that had to be admired. We tried creating—and were pretty much successful—a doorway from the wall into the bathroom. We spiked pizza to the ceilings with screwdrivers. Jeff pulled out a giant bag of popcorn the size of a beanbag chair, and before he could even get out the words *You guys want to destroy the room?* we were on it. Popcorn flying, television ruined. We wrecked the place. We even used the upside-down cross Jeff gave me to rip the mattresses up. At one point, someone said the cops were coming, and we said, *See you tomorrow, bye!*

Before we left, though, we gave them a piece of advice for the next night's show with us at Ruthie's: Lose the makeup. We told them, *With the Ruthie's in-crowd, it's gonna change their entire perspective of you if you're wearing eyeliner. You gotta get rid of that shit.* So they never wore it again. After the show, we went back to the Cove, pulled the pizza off the ceiling, and ate it.

THE NEXT TIME I SAW KERRY KING, A MONTH LATER AT RUTHIE'S, HE WAS playing guitar in Megadeth, Dave Mustaine's new post-Metallica band. I hung out a lot with Dave when Exodus played those early Metallica shows together, more than with James or Lars. We all did, but I kind of gravitated toward Dave more, and vice versa, because we were both evil as fuck. Kerry was temporarily—emphasis on *temporarily*—helping Megadeth out as they got on their feet; Slayer were still together. A headstrong guy like Kerry's not meant to be in a band like Megadeth with one guy (Dave) calling all the shots. That would've been a hard lineup to make work long term, I think. Their playing styles are also very different. Thank Satan for Kerry staying in Slayer!

But the Exodus crew all showed up to support two of our friends. We were fucking stoked to see Megadeth and were probably fucking hammered because Ruthie's fed us all the alcohol we could want for free. I thought Megadeth were killer and musically different from Metallica. Dave definitely went in a little different direction. It would've been real easy to just do "Hit the Lights Part 2" and songs like that, but he went a little more technical, and the rest is history. He's a legend, a good friend, and he's always been a big supporter of Exodus, which I suppose he has to be since we're blood brothers.

One night sitting around Baloff's house—drunk as fuck and probably snorting a little meth—Dave, Baloff, and I cut ourselves, shared blood, and became blood brothers. This is something we did back then—remember, we all had knives or a razor blade—blissfully unaware of hepatitis C, AIDS, and other blood-borne illnesses. Fortunately, the only thing I'm carrying around today are the scars and memories, but these incidents were yet another inspiration for the song "Bonded by Blood."

By early 1984, Metallica, Slayer, and Anthrax had all released their debut albums. We knew it was time for Exodus to do the same. We had the songs. By this point, most of the Kirk-era material was gone from our set. We'd play some of those older tracks—"Dying by His Hand" and "Impaler"—if we needed to lengthen our set, but we knew we weren't going to record them for our debut. Though this lineup of Exodus never made a proper demo, live recordings of our shows and rehearsals were circulated by tape traders around the world. As a result, we were a known commodity worldwide, even though we'd never played outside the Bay Area. It was this notoriety, as well as our reputation in the Bay Area, that led to a couple of Exodus fans in Scarsdale, New York, Todd Gordon and Ken Adams, starting their own indie label, Torrid Records, and offering to put out our debut. Though we could have checked in with the other indie metal labels of the day that our friends and bands we admired were on—Megaforce (Metallica), Combat (Venom), Metal Blade (Slayer)—we were super excited that these guys were launching their label to make an album for us. They were the ones who showed up, and we were just like, *Yeah, a record deal! Let's go!*

In late May 1984, about a month before we were to go into the studio to record our debut, we loaded our gear into Doug Piercy of Anvil Chorus's studio on Turk Street to record a preproduction demo. We laid down ten tracks in total but never really finished them, adding vocals to only three. There are aspects of my performance on this recording, however, that I prefer to what I did on our debut. There are some solos I like better because I was using my preferred guitar, my candy red Strat. We were poor kids back then, and by the time we recorded *Bonded by Blood* in July, that guitar wasn't working right. It had some structural issues, and it wasn't staying in tune; the intonation had gone to shit. So for *Bonded*, I used my black Fernandes Strat that had a Kahler whammy bar, and I just couldn't hit the high-pitched whammy bar dive bombs that, around the Bay Area, I was famous for. I hate Kahlers to this day. It's a beautifully designed whammy bar, but it just doesn't do what I want it to. There are some lead breaks on the Turk Street demo that are exactly what I wanted. It was a shame I couldn't have transferred them over to the album sessions.

The preproduction demo was a good warm-up, but when it came time to make the album, our manager/producer, Mark Whitaker, found us a studio, Prairie Sun, which was on a big ranch up in Cotati. It was perfect for us because it had multiple cabins on the property so we could live there while we were recording. It wasn't so good for studio owner Mark "Mooka" Rennick, because in typical Exodus fashion, we left a trail of destruction that was second to none, to quote Judas Priest. We spent about two weeks on the album, and we just *raged* at night. We had the full Slay Team entourage there with us. And since Cotati is about an hour and a half north of San Francisco, other friends would come up in the evenings, and we would commence to let loose. Our beer of choice was Schmidt's, this shitty, cheap beer that had fish on the packaging. We drank I don't know how many cases of Schmidt's and the cheapest vodka you could buy. And we smoked a lot of weed. We were partying and getting fucking hammered and breaking shit. Friends would get into fistfights with friends just over some bullshit. And then we'd wake up the next day and start tracking again.

It was probably the most fun recording session I've ever had. We were super well rehearsed. The songs were part of our DNA by then. All our parts were totally down. We just rocked it. Baloff killed it except for one line on the album that Paul could not get no matter how many times he tried. It was a line in "Deliver Us to Evil" where he sings, "By my lord, my god, my master, Lucifer." He couldn't get the phrasing; it just threw him off. Finally, John Volaitis, our engineer, ran out of the control room and into the vocal booth and said, "I'm gonna do it." He did his best Baloff impersonation on that one line, and it was perfect; it's on the album. It's the ultimate piece of *Bonded by Blood* trivia. Paul killed everything else really well. Another smaller bit of trivia is that we actually recorded one track that didn't end up on the album, "Death Row." We'd demoed it with Doug during preproduction but never ended up putting vocals on it at Prairie Sun (or at the Turk Street session). And since the *Bonded by Blood* master tapes are missing, that one is lost to the ages.

There was definitely some serendipity that helped make this session special, though. In addition to the fact that my main guitar wasn't working right and I had to use the Fernandes, my main Marshall amp was on the fritz. I ended up borrowing a Hiwatt amp from John Marshall, who's known in the thrash world for filling in on guitar for James Hetfield in Metallica after James broke his wrist skateboarding (in 1986) and had a pyro accident (in 1992). I used his Hiwatt amp, which isn't known as a thrash metal amp. But to get the sound I wanted, I ran two Boss Super Overdrive distortion pedals in front of it, both with the levels on ten and the drives off, just kicking the shit out of the front end. It was super crunchy and killer, and Mark captured it well. It ended up a defining part of the guitar sound on that album. (When I got my Marshall fixed, we found a cheap gold-plated chain that fell inside and shorted it out. Killed by fake jewelry!) Mark was an integral part of the making of *Bonded by Blood*, including knowing when to tempt me with a giant joint to nail a solo. I struggled with the ending solo on "No Love," and by take four or five, I just wasn't feeling it. Mark held up a huge joint, the size of a large cigarette. He said, "Get it right in the next take, and this is yours." He rolled the tape, I nailed the solo in one take, and ran into the studio and fired that fucker up!

I don't even remember how long we spent mixing it once the recording was done, but it was probably just a few days. Is there a little too much reverb on the vocals? Absolutely there's too much reverb, but everybody had too much reverb on everything back then. It's a moment in time. How can you improve it? Even the running order, in my mind, is perfect. There's nothing I'd change. "Strike of the Beast" closed the album, and it closes every show we play. That'll never change until the day I die.

As thrilled as we were with how the recording turned out, we had no idea what an ordeal it was going to be to release it on Torrid. Realistically, in an era when you could issue an album just a few months after finishing it, this should have been out before the end of 1984, and we would have been right in the mix with our peers, who were out there touring and starting to work on or were releasing their *second* albums. Metallica's *Ride the Lightning* literally came out the same month we recorded *Bonded by Blood*. Unfortunately, there were several issues that pushed the album release back.

First, there were problems with the artwork. The album was originally called *A Lesson in Violence*. We had an album cover done, which was like a silhouette of us with just piles of body parts and stuff. But the label got spooked, because they thought no one would carry it, because it was too violent. But any store that would have been put off by that kind of imagery wouldn't have been stocking Exodus (or Slayer or Anthrax) albums to begin with. So in my mind, that was kind of a nonissue. (Honestly, I'm not sure how the two silly babies we ended up with on the cover are any less offensive.) And then there was the matter of getting the distribution sorted out—the kind of growing pains a brand-new record label experiences. Keep in mind, the guys who started Torrid were our own age and were jumping into this endeavor blind. They had no experience running a label; it was totally learning on the job. While all these delays were happening, dubbed copies of *Bonded* were circulating like wildfire. It seemed like well before the album came out—eight months after we'd finished it—everybody had heard it. Fortunately, there were no digital files back then, so all the copies out there were like third-, fourth-, or fifth-generation dubs, so the quality was really crap. It would have been disastrous now if everybody in the tape-trading scene already had a perfect copy of the record. But because the dubs were poor, people still bought it anyway upon its release.

Thankfully, due to that tape-trading circuit, we already had quite a lot of notoriety, so there was plenty of excitement when the album finally came out in April 1985. Even the press treated us well (for the most part). English metal magazine *Kerrang!* bestowed a five-K rating (the highest rating). However, I still have a fanzine where some guy said that it was "totally forgettable, second-rate Metallica-clone shit that'll be forgotten in a year." And to that I say: *Fuck you, motherfucker. Suck on that, ya bastard!* I've been known to hold a grudge. Just a little bit. That dude was obviously proven wrong, because years later, *Rock Hard* readers voted it the greatest thrash metal album of all time.

The reality is that *Bonded by Blood* is a keystone of our discography, and to this day, it outsells our entire back catalog, even our later records that made the *Billboard* charts. We weren't trying to invent a new style of metal on *Bonded*, but we wanted to go fast. And we wanted the fast shit to make the mid-tempo stuff seem even heavier. We were young, with boundless energy—both natural and pharmaceutical—so playing fast was easy. Getting to sleep at night was the hard part.

CHAPTER 9

ULTIMATE REVENGE

E VERYBODY WAS TERRIFIED OF EXODUS. AND RIGHTLY SO, I SUPPOSE. WE were destroying everything in our path. We were also snorting it, drinking it, smoking it, whatever. Havin' a good old time, though, being out of control. As a result, we had quite a lot of notoriety. The stories got out there about the extracurricular activities and the shows and the violence in the crowd. It built hype, and it lent itself to the mystique of Exodus.

We'd never met the dudes in Anthrax when they rolled into town with Raven for their first gig in the Bay Area, in July 1984 at the Kabuki Theater. That was when Neil Turbin was fronting Anthrax, so there was a lot of chain mail onstage and a lot of shirtless guys with zebra-striped guitars. Guitarist Scott Ian later admitted to me that they were very intimidated to be crossing paths with the infamous Exodus. He'd probably heard stories from Metallica, who'd hung with Anthrax in NYC when they were preparing to make *Kill 'Em All*. Back then, we didn't have a lot of ego—we'd already sold out the Kabuki as headliners—so when we got a call asking if we wanted to open the show, we said sure. However, we had to call the dogs off, so to speak, with the Slay Team, because they were insulted that Anthrax were playing *after* Exodus. The Slay Team were fully prepared to make life a living hell for Anthrax, so I had to say, *No, don't do that. These guys are cool.*

Because the release of *Bonded by Blood* was delayed so much, there was little that we could do during this waiting period other than play shows. Despite the delay, we played some of our most iconic gigs of this era before the record was even out. In October 1984, Mercyful Fate were on their first US tour, and we opened their first California date ever (and second ever US date) at a club called Can't Tell in Sacramento. Playing this gig and meeting them was a huge moment for us as a band. Mercyful Fate were instrumental in the creation of Exodus. There were other factors and influences, but they were our favorites. That's when we first met vocalist King Diamond, who turned out to be a super nice guy.

This downtime also allowed us to play our first show outside the Bay Area in LA at the Country Club in Reseda on February 28, 1985. After years of thrashing SF, it was time to take our act on the road. And here's a little bit more Exodus trivia for you: seventeen-year-old drummer Gene Hoglan, who'd soon join LA thrashers Dark Angel (and later go on to play in a ton of other bands), did our lights at that gig. Gene knew the lighting board, and he told the house people at the club, *I know these songs. Let me do it.* As I said, even though our record wasn't *officially* out . . . it was out there.

Being as we were touring amateurs, that foray into LA was typically chaotic in that special Exodus way. None of us in the band who drove (I didn't) owned a vehicle up to the task of hauling both the band and our gear to the gig, so we hired some guy to drive our equipment in his truck. It was one of those U-Haul-type trucks where it had a doorway so you could go from the cab into the back. Slay Team member Andy

Andersen went with us, and the driver would jump out of his seat *before* anyone could grab the wheel, and he'd say, "Grab the wheel," and go in the back to do cocaine. He ended up hijacking our gear after the show because we didn't have money to pay him. My mom had to pay him off so we could get our equipment back.

We needed that gear for our upcoming first tour—again, before *Bonded* was even out—and some of the momentous gigs on the horizon: We'd been booked to play a series of US dates in April with our friends in Slayer and our English heroes Venom, starting in New York City on April 3, three weeks before the official release of *Bonded*. Don't even ask me how we got this tour. We were so clueless about how anything worked back then, so I have no idea how we landed it. We were just told by management we were doing it. We had a booking agent, but do I even know who that agent was? No. We were young and just wanted to party. Maybe that's the big difference between us and Metallica; those guys were paying much closer attention.

That first gig with Venom, at the notorious Studio 54 in Manhattan, was documented for posterity and released later in the year on VHS and Beta videotape as *Combat Tour Live: The Ultimate Revenge*. This was not only a career highlight for me but a personal one. Never mind we were going to be one of three bands featured on a nationally distributed live video, we were playing with Venom! Venom were all-time heroes of mine—they still are. Kerry King feels exactly the same way I do about Venom. That tour was just *rad*. I was hanging out with bassist/vocalist Cronos, who was bigger than life to me, and we were with our old friends in Slayer.

I may not have made it out of NYC were it not for my (now) old friend Bobby "Blitz" Ellsworth, lead singer for Overkill, who was at the Studio 54 gig. He and I met for the first time at this show. Overkill had signed to the label Metallica was on, Megaforce, and would eventually release their full-length debut, *Feel the Fire*, a few months after

Bonded was finally set to come out, April 25, 1985. After the Exodus set, he and I were way up in the upper deck of Studio 54, and I was incredibly high because somebody gave me a quaalude. I'd never done a quaalude before—that's a New York thing—and I was just teetering back and forth on the stairs. I started listing, like I was going to fall down the stairs, and Bobby reached out and grabbed me by my belt and saved my life. He's still a close friend to this day, and I love him to death. He's the reason I'm still playing music and not a paraplegic.

After the close call at Studio 54, the rest of this tour was less insane. We had a few shows in the Midwest and then ended on the West Coast. By the time we got to LA for our show at the Palladium, our tour van was in dire shape. It was spewing horrible black smoke like a vicious dragon. If you punched the gas pedal, it would belch out an acrid cloud. I don't think it would have made it another week, so we basically just limped into town. As we arrived in Hollywood, we spotted a bunch of people at a bus stop near our stoplight. We were like, *Get 'em! Choke 'em out!* We hit the gas hard when the light turned green and smoked out the entire bus stop.

This first tour with Slayer and Venom was just the warm-up for our summertime headlining stint across North America, which was about as insane as you'd imagine Exodus left to our own devices and turned loose on the road might be. Unfortunately, there wasn't a lot of structure to it as far as routing went. This was easily the most ridiculously inefficient and poorly planned tour we've ever done, and it provided us with way too much time to find/get into trouble along the way. But we didn't care. We were seeing the United States for the first time. I'd been on one family vacation in my life with my parents, when we all went to Crater Lake in Oregon. That was as far as I'd ever gone. So we had no idea what awaited us in Canada, the Northwest, the Bible Belt. Every day was a new adventure, and we were soaking it in and leaving casualties in our wake.

Our first leg took us to the Pacific Northwest, where we played three shows with our friends in Megadeth (now with Chris Poland replacing Kerry King) and Canadian thrashers Exciter: Portland, Seattle, and Vancouver, British Columbia. This wasn't part of *our* tour, exactly, so we had a full week to kill in Vancouver before we were to head east across Canada. We stayed in a live-work warehouse that a friend of our then manager, Toni Isabella, owned. Days were spent in typical Exodus fashion: wreaking havoc.

I used to pride myself on being an awesome caveman-style hunter, like, *Give me a rock and I'll feed the band if I have to.* So we were walking down an alley, and there was a seagull sitting two stories up on the edge of a building.

"Watch this," I told my bandmates as I picked up a rock and pointed at the seagull.

"Bullshit, you can't do that," Tom said.

"Watch me. I've been doing this shit since high school." I let fly and dropped the bird with a rock from two stories down. Don't worry, we didn't eat it. Sorry, PETA!

Canada is a big country, and it says a lot about our routing/booking that we played a total of three gigs in two weeks from Vancouver to Montreal. We traveled three thousand miles and did a show every thousand miles. It was crazy. Granted, one other show in Regina, Saskatchewan, got canceled because the guy didn't have money to pay for the PA. We got fucked on that. But he left his wallet in our van, so we threw everything away that was in it and took the cash. There was also a locust storm in Regina when we were there, and these things were literally everywhere, including on the walls of our hotel room. Paul took a buck knife and stuck the locust to the wall with it. That would have been the equivalent of a two-foot wide blade penetrating you or me, right? This is when I realized, we shouldn't fuck with insects. If they even double in size, we're done. Paul pulled the knife out the next day, and the thing crawled away. If that two-inch locust were four inches, a thousand of them would carry us away and eat us.

Toronto is where we learned an important tour lesson: Don't drink all night if you're the headliner. The day before the Toronto gig, Rick Hunolt and I had found an army surplus store that had these six-inch-long, .50-caliber bullets. They already had holes drilled in them, so naturally, we made bullet belts. I sewed mine really well, but Rick didn't. We were hammered onstage at two in the morning, and Rick's belt was dropping giant bullets all over the stage, which basically turned the stage into a roller rink. We were trying not to kill ourselves dodging these giant bullets. We'd been drinking right up until we went on at 2:00 a.m., and after that fiasco, our tour manager laid down the law about booze before shows.

In Montreal, we met up with Slayer, where we both played the Montreal Metal Fest on August 17, 1985, with Metal Church and Agent Steel. Most notable for me, personally, was the paper airplane long-distance record I (surely) set. No one was there to witness but my own bandmates, but I must have set a world record. I launched that thing from our hotel room on the thirteenth floor and it caught an air current and stayed thirteen stories high and kept going. You couldn't even see it anymore. It went miles!

From there, we went back into the States, where we had an extended stay in New York City. All this free time was, of course, spent enriching our minds and bodies in one of the great cultural meccas of the world, right? Not so much. But then, this was a different NYC—the old New York City when shit was sketchy. We stayed in the craziest hotel, in a giant room that slept about ten people, with beds everywhere. Back then, things were scary in downtown New York City. We got robbed when we were trying to buy some weed. Rick gave this guy who had a bag of weed some money, and the guy turned around and ran so fast that he was two blocks away before we even realized what happened.

Our first show was at L'Amour in Brooklyn on August 25, 1985, and it was not exactly a triumphant return after our Studio 54 gig in April. L'Amour was another venue where we'd go on super late, but people in New York always had cocaine to hand out to keep you on your feet until showtime. Unfortunately, Paul had gotten sick and couldn't perform at that gig, so we went on without him. We played the whole show with no vocalist, and I even attempted to sing a little, which was just terrible. The crowd, however, sang every word, much to our amazement. During the show, the club handed us a note saying that they'd booked us for the next weekend, so that gives you an idea of what kind of time we had on our hands. That rebooked gig turned out to be pretty special since they paired us with Carnivore, which included Peter Steele (RIP), who went on to be in Type O Negative. When Carnivore were setting up for their sound check, Pete asked if he could borrow my tuner. As I stood there, he hit a couple bowel-shaking notes on his bass.

"What are you tuned to?" I asked incredulously.

"C, I think," he replied.

Standard tuning is E, so he was two full steps down from that. It was crazy to me. Nobody tuned that low back then. But then again, those guys were crazy heavy, and I loved it.

Once we were done in New York, there was nothing really to do other than drive the nearly three thousand miles back to San Francisco, since we didn't have any more gigs. Much of this remaining time on the road was spent whiling away the days and torturing our road crew, at least the ones that remained. We ended up bringing out Doug Piercy from Anvil Chorus, who was totally one of us. You had to really be part of the clique, part of the gang, to survive, because we were merciless. We were hard to work with back then. We would burn through our road crew. We just abused tech guys. Baloff traveled with a pellet gun, and we called it the "Pelican." We found out that Nerds candy make excellent ammo. You didn't need to go to a sporting goods store to buy pellets; you just put a piece of that candy in there. I shot one of our guitar techs right in the ass as he was getting out of the shower and sank a piece of candy an inch deep in his butt cheek. He was screaming. We would just yell right back at him, didn't even say sorry: "Fuck you, it's biodegradable! You're fine! Don't be a fucking pussy!"

And when we weren't abusing our roadies, we were bored as shit. How bored were we, you ask? We were so bored, we'd pull into a truck stop and let flies into the van just so we could hunt and squash them with rolled-up maps. We were in that van so long, and all we could see were cows and cornfields. We actually had two vans, one with the gear and also a passenger van. Baloff would sleep across the top of the bench seat like Snoopy on top of his doghouse. I'd wake up from a nap and Paul would be pressed up against the window.

"What are you doing, Pavel?" I'd ask. He'd start singing a song he made up.

"Cows, cows, millions of cows. Some they go moo, some they go poo. Cows."

I'd look over later, and Paul would be lying on the floor of the van.

"Pavel, what are you doing?"

"Hiding from corn."

THE FINAL LEG OF OUR *BONDED BY BLOOD* TOUR BROUGHT US TO Europe—a first for all of us—for another run with Venom. Going to Europe for the first time...we'll never, ever replicate that feeling. In the UK, we traveled in a van, and our driver would stop wherever we wanted. We were just a bunch of young fucking lunatics, so if we saw a giant, grassy hill near a derelict castle, you'd better believe we'd stop and roll down the hill and explore the tunnels around the castle. And the next thing you know, we're playing the vaunted Hammersmith Odeon. Playing the Hammersmith Odeon with Venom was a dream come true.

We actually held the volume record there, or so we were told. We had that record for all of forty-five minutes, until Venom came on.

The gigs were insane. We were *crushing* Venom, which I'm loath to say, because they mean so much to me. But on that tour, we were the new "it" band. We were the Zooey Deschanel of thrash! The response was fantastic, and the shows were fucking nuts. We couldn't have asked for anything more. There was way more excitement over Exodus, since it was our first time over there, than there was for Venom, who'd toured Europe many times. Venom, for us, were godlike. We watched their set every night, in between drinking and raging and destroying shit and bleeding.

Every day was a new adventure once we crossed over to Europe. In Italy, we were dropped off right in front of the line of people going into the club. All of a sudden, the punters descended on us like insects. We'd never experienced anything like that in our lives. We literally had to grab some guitar picks and throw them to get the swarm to go the other way. We were thinking, *This is the raddest thing ever. This is what we want to do.* Italy is also where I met my good friend Matthias Prill, who was president of the Venom fan club at the time. We bonded immediately, and he ended up moving his bags into our tour bus and traveled with us the rest of the tour.

In Copenhagen, Denmark, we met up with King Diamond. When we were on the bus partying, King Diamond taught me how to open a bottle of beer using a lighter. Metallica were in Copenhagen recording *Master of Puppets*, so James and Lars were at the show. Messiah, the singer for Candlemass, was also on our tour bus, and when it was time for us to play, our road manager said, *Okay, everybody's gotta go*, and Messiah didn't move. We really didn't know who he was at the time, and Baloff attacked him and punched him, right in front of King Diamond. Someone told me that Paul broke Messiah's nose, but I never got confirmation. I did apologize to him a couple of years later. *Real sorry about that, bro. Love your band. You guys are great. But you didn't move fast enough, damn it. We told you to get off the bus and you didn't go.* He probably didn't understand a fucking word we were saying. I don't know.

That sense of wonder we had on our first European tour can't be replicated. Every day was a party. If we weren't cutting ourselves in blood rituals, drunk on vodka on the bus, we were dodging barbells. Upstairs in his bunk, Paul brought some barbells with him. There was about a ten-inch space under the bunks, and we put them in there, but when the bus moved back and forth, they'd come rolling out. We named them "Crusher" and "Mauler." You'd be sitting in the back lounge at the rear of the bus, not paying attention, and all of a sudden, there's a fifteen-pound dumbbell coming at you at twenty miles per hour.

And we got along great with Venom, as always. There were times when we were partying in Europe at a bar and Cronos would be watching me sing every word of a Madonna song that was playing, and he'd just be shaking his head like, *This guy is a fucking idiot.* I love Madonna, and I've been a big fan since day one. The Venom road crew also adored us. They thought we were funny and that we talked like absolute aliens as far as they were concerned—*hella, rad, what's up?* Before we'd play "Piranha," Paul would go into his rap about "This song ain't about no goldfish," and Venom's monitor engineer would say, "It ain't about no codfish," in our stage monitors! The last show of the European tour was in France on Halloween. We were all saying our goodbyes at the venue. The stage was a few feet high, and I was way out on the floor. Venom drummer Abaddon was going up the stairs at the rear of the stage, and he hocked a loogie that flew like a home run baseball, and I caught it right in my mouth and swallowed it. "Yoor a sick bastard!" he shouted.

That tour was a monumental moment in my career. I'll never, ever do another tour that means as much to me as that one. Not even the Ultimate Revenge tour in the US could match it. We soaked it all in and took a million photos. It was spectacular.

CHAPTER 10
DERANGED

WHILE METALLICA WERE OUT CONQUERING THE WORLD SUPPORTING their first two albums for two years, Exodus had been conquering the Bay Area with violence. Despite what people think of the Bay Area thrash scene as this tight-knit thing, there were sort of geographic pockets. Death Angel were in San Francisco, Legacy (which became Testament) were in Dublin, Possessed were from Pinole, and we fucking owned Berkeley. That was ours. That's where Exodus set our roots. These early years, the scene was like a brotherhood. Well, a brotherhood of guys who were brothers like a couple of nights a week, I guess you'd say. Because we didn't have each other's phone numbers, but we saw each other and hung out. Mostly we were bonded by this shared musical style we were playing, a style that Exodus and Metallica pioneered. Our two bands influenced everything that came after; it's that simple. There's no room for argument there. But look, we stood on the backs of the bands we loved, too, and then these younger bands—Death Angel, Possessed—came up a little bit behind us and saw our shows and said, *That's what I wanna do.* It's a big circle of metal, everybody giving to each other.

When Metallica returned to San Francisco after recording *Master of Puppets* in Copenhagen in late '85, we knew where to find them. Despite their growing success, they were still at the bar at Ruthie's every night when they were home. They, however, made the mistake of asking us to support them at their New Year's Eve show at the San Francisco Civic Auditorium. We were more than ready. Our own brief touring exploits had honed us to a razor sharpness, and we were, as always, super well rehearsed. For this gig, I borrowed every Marshall cab from every friend I had, so we had more stacks and we had a bigger riser than Metallica. Typically, as a supporting act, your shit's onstage, and then the other band's stuff is behind you looming larger. We obscured all of it.

And we fucking killed it that night. The crowd was violent as fuck, and we just raged. We destroyed Metallica, destroyed 'em. We made 'em look foolish. We just fucking flattened them. It wasn't even fair. It wasn't out of spite or anger; it was just, *We're gonna go out and fucking rage.* We had more amps and a bigger riser, and we took it to 'em.

Before the show, I'd painted my white Hondo Strat—the one I'm playing on the back of *Bonded*—primer gray and scratched a bunch of shit in it. At the end of our set, I smashed it to pieces. That's one of those moments in Exodus history I wish I'd never done, because I'd trade guitars twenty times its value to have it back. At the time, though, I swapped the smashed-up body to somebody for an eight ball of cocaine after the show. It was New Year's, and I was gonna party.

Afterward, while we were all partying and getting wasted, James kind of chuckled and (I thought) jokingly said, "That's the last time you'll play with Metallica." Turns out, maybe he wasn't joking, because it was, in fact, the last time we played with Metallica. They never had us on a show again—ever. They were terrified to play with Exodus after we crushed them. A lesson to you kids out there—don't crush people too hard; you might fucking regret it.

The high note we ended 1985 on carried over into 1986. Even after the delayed release of *Bonded*, we had a lot of momentum going and we were hungry for more. One way of doing that was to move on from Torrid to a more experienced label we could continue to grow with. Combat Records had been distributing *Bonded*, and they knew exactly how well it had been selling, so they approached us about signing directly with them. In wooing us, they flew Rick and me down to Los Angeles and put us up at the Le Mondrian Hotel (now just Mondrian Los Angeles). David Coverdale of Whitesnake was staying there at the time. Here I am, the biggest Whitesnake fan ever, but at that particular time, they were posers, right? Anyway, Coverdale was by the pool, and we were just relentlessly mocking him. We were such assholes. We also charged about $500 in drinks to our room. We charged watches from the gift shop to the room, all on Combat's dime because they wanted to sign us. And they let us do it.

Combat had worked with a lot of other bands we liked—Megadeth, Mercyful Fate, Venom—and the deal was really good, so we ended up signing with them. When the deal was done, the band and our manager and lawyer all went out to a five-star restaurant called Maxwell's Plum in San Francisco, where we proceeded to start a food fight. Would you expect anything different? That sent our lawyer packing, who said, "I don't want to take up criminal law, so I'm leaving." After that, we went and bought three or four bottles of Mad Dog 20/20, just total rotgut ghetto wine, and *really* celebrated.

In addition to our new deal with Combat, the band had started generating income from merchandise deals and publishing, so we bought a bunch of new gear: six Marshall stacks, a new Yamaha drum kit for Tom, a PA, and new bass gear. Unfortunately, we weren't the best businessmen back then. We were still behaving like kids. And we didn't closely look at the contracts we were signing. Any money we generated went into the band fund and paid for everybody's everything. As long as our bills were paid, as long as we had weed and liquor and amps, we fucking didn't ask questions. We had everything we thought we needed. We didn't need real money and savings. *Who needs savings accounts? I've got amps and weed!*

Paul, in particular, struggled with looking after his money. When he joined the band, he was living off a trust fund his deceased parents had left him. But that money ran out eventually, and he continued to live the life of a guy who had never-ending funds. There was an end in sight, but he never saw it. So he partied. We all did. He eventually lost his house and ended up living in our rehearsal room. This at least made it convenient for him to come to rehearsals when we started writing our follow-up to *Bonded by Blood* for Combat. We were heading into a— how do I put it?—more professional point in our career, so we decided to demo a few of the songs prior to going into a pro studio. Making a demo allowed us to have a better grasp on what we wanted to do when we did the real recording, at a lower price. I think also we wanted to hear how Paul would do on the new material. So we went in with Sylvia Massy, who's since gone on to engineer multiple-platinum records, and recorded "Pleasures of the Flesh," "Brain Dead," and "Seed of Hate," which Paul wrote all the lyrics for. We busted those three songs out in two days, and they turned out great. It took a lot of effort to get Paul's vocal performances, though; it wasn't easy. But in the end, the demo sounded really good, and the lyrics he wrote were fantastic.

Paul had frequently struggled with his timing when we would play live. It wasn't unusual for me to sometimes have to go up and kick Paul in the leg to try to get him back on time when we were playing, because he'd just come in early and wouldn't correct. So the verses were all fucking out of sync. It was like an overdubbed kung fu movie. But that's part of the beauty of Paul—you never knew what you were gonna get.

You didn't know what was going to happen, the thrill of the unknown at an Exodus show with Paul onstage. That said, we had a lot of people whispering in our ear at the time that the band would go further with someone else singing. Exodus have historically been too easily swayed by outside influence, because all we gave a fuck about was where the next bottle of vodka was coming from. So maybe we were being manipulated, I don't know, but Baloff's shit wasn't together—personally and professionally—and we decided to make a change before we made our second album. There wasn't any one specific incident, anything he did wrong. It was just a lack of timing and musical ability, and his current life situation was pretty bad. So we had a meeting and we told him he was no longer in the band.

Kicking him out was the hardest thing we ever did. It was a sad thing. Maybe the band's trajectory would've gone differently if we hadn't. Maybe we never would've achieved certain commercial successes if he were still in the band, but maybe we would've hung on to our underground credibility and the rabid fucking fan base. Who knows?

Word got out quickly that Baloff was out and a coveted position was open in the Bay Area thrash scene. Legacy vocalist Steve "Zetro" Souza was someone we had our sights on. Legacy played shows with Exodus at Ruthie's, so we knew Zetro from the club scene. But because Legacy were from Dublin, a different part of the Bay Area, I'd never hung out with him other than at a show. Rick and I were huge fans of Legacy's first demo, so we invited him to try out. That may seem like a lateral move today, considering the success Legacy later had as Testament, with Chuck Billy singing, but in 1986, the position fronting Exodus was a huge step up for Zetro. We were bigger. We were fucking Exodus, and Zetro wanted the gig.

Baloff was irreplaceable, but Zetro came in and sang with perfect, flawless timing. We started him off with "Bonded by Blood," and it was like, *Wow, that was fucking tight!* The decision was pretty much made right there. It was the first time he'd ever picked up the mic with us, and he just drilled it, knocked it out of the park. We went through other *Bonded* songs, and he sang that shit album-performance-tight, first time. He just sounded a lot better timing-wise than Paul did on the album, and we had worked really hard on Paul's timing on *Bonded*. But with Zetro, we heard what the songs sounded like when someone's on the beat, not constantly behind or early and never knowing it.

Two months later, July 17–18, 1986, we did our first two shows with Zetro at a place in San Francisco called the Farm. The first night was rough on him. The long-standing diehards—people who'd been there from the Hammett era on—were offended and so angry about Baloff's expulsion from the band that a couple of beer cans were thrown at him. Zetro actually caught one like he was playing center field. He was singing, and he just reached up and plucked it right out of the air. Great move, perfect hand-eye coordination.

For the second night, we knew that we needed a little icebreaker— something to tame the bad blood, so to speak—so we asked Baloff to come up and sing one of the new songs we'd been working on before he was fired, "Brain Dead," and that seemed to ease the tension. Other than a few disgruntled fans, the shows were killer. They were sold out, and the second night, we didn't really get the hate, although there were still divisions among some of the old-school heads. But Zetro brought along his fan base, who were also already Exodus fans, so they were super supportive of him being there. Eventually, people came around, but Zet has always (unfairly so) had to sort of live in the shadow of what Paul did on our debut. The fact is, Zetro's an amazing vocalist, and he's as much a part of the band's history as Paul. But the first album's always gonna be the first, and it's the one that helped start it all.

After Exodus, Paul formed Piranha, which he used as motivation— revenge, you might say. But they were never as heavy as Exodus, no matter how much Paul wanted them to be. On a personal level, there was definitely some tension between us, but eventually, the awkwardness went away. He would come out to Exodus shows when we played, and he'd still come up and sing something with us. And I'd see him at a Piranha show, or he'd come out to Ruthie's, and we'd fucking laugh and hang out. We still saw each other at the local parties and all that shit. So the awkwardness passed, and it became much cooler. However, I don't think he ever fully let the grudge go, especially between him and Zetro. You can't fault Zetro for taking a gig that he wanted. He didn't lobby to steal it while Paul was in the band. We called *him*.

At this point, we needed to continue the work we'd started with Paul on the new album, our first for Combat. In that era, we rehearsed like it was our day job, so in addition to the three tracks we'd demoed with Paul, I still had a lot of other material in the works. We just kept writing. I wrote a lot of the new songs; some of it I handed to Zetro to write lyrics. And Rick was writing some stuff, as well. Rick and I used to do a line of meth before a rehearsal, and we'd call that our "warm-up session." Like, *Let's get warmed up*; we'd do a line. We used it as a tool to work longer hours, like a lot of people do. There are people in all sorts of fields, even wearing suits and ties on Wall Street, doing meth. They're working longer hours, and it keeps them going. We did the same thing. We used meth as a tool. We used it to drink longer; we used it to play longer.

THE MAKING OF OUR SECOND ALBUM, *PLEASURES OF THE FLESH*, WAS one of the most difficult things we've ever had to do. It's the one album in our catalog that I wish I had a time machine for and could go back and restart the recording process—not change anything else in history, just the making of the album. We were still working with Mark Whitaker, our manager and producer on *Bonded by Blood*, but he walked in with predetermined ways of exactly how the album should be made. And they didn't work. The recording took place at Alpha & Omega, which was owned by longtime Blue Öyster Cult producer/lyricist Sandy Pearlman and was located right in the fucking Tenderloin in San Francisco—a shitty neighborhood, but a great studio. The best thing that came from this situation was meeting Marc Senasac, the house engineer there, whom we'd work with a lot later down the road.

Mark Whitaker had a lot of ideas about how he wanted to record *Pleasures*, and he wasn't willing to budge, even if they didn't work or make sense. To start with, he wanted to trigger the drums. He was so confident in the triggers, he didn't want to waste any time on actually making sure the natural drums sounded good at all. However, the triggering unit would not trigger Tom's manic drumming properly—it was just mis-triggering everywhere—and despite having mic'd the whole drum kit, the drum sound sucked. He also was forcing us to use these Mesa Boogie amps and record them the way he wanted the guitars to sound, because Metallica used them. So we weren't being allowed to get our own guitar sound. It was a problem. We had to try to save the record before it got any worse. Rick and I went to our manager Toni Isabella's house, because Mark no longer managed us at that point, and we said, *Look, this is just a nightmare. Something's gotta give.* We ended up firing Mark and continued on trying to fix the mess with Marc Senasac at the helm.

Tom had to replay every drum one at a time. Like if there was a drum fill that went from tom one to tom five, when he hit tom one, Tom had to sit there and go *thump* and get each one and replicate what he played, because the drum sound naturally was bad. To this day, Tom says some of the drum parts aren't right because he was having to play them one drum at a time. To this day, Tom hates *Pleasures* because it was such a bad vibe for him. I never liked the rhythm guitar sound at all on the record, but we weren't able to go back and rerecord that. My leads were done *after* the change in producer, and they sound killer because I was using my amps.

Even Zetro had his struggles. He came in perhaps a little overconfident, telling us, *I do all my stuff in one take.* I think he thought he was just going to sing it exactly how he wanted. But he didn't realize that there were other guys, including me, the guy who wrote most of the lyrics, who had a set way of thinking how the vocals should be. So after ten or twelve takes sometimes, he'd start getting mad, and he'd start cursing and throwing a fit. He's not the only musician in Exodus to throw a fit in the studio when shit's not easy. I mean, I've thrown a couple myself, I'm sure. But in the end, he fucking killed it. And his timing was always impeccable. It was all about just getting the performance that the whole band wanted. He'd be the first to tell you that after all those takes and struggle and stress, the end result was the right one.

For the second time in as many albums, we had trouble with the cover art. There was the concept we wanted (cannibals!), and then there was the cover the label wanted—us sitting at a bar lined with a row of skulls. This is why the title doesn't actually seem to connect to the cover art. Apart from the struggle that went into making and finishing it, I still love *Pleasures*. I think the songs are really good, but it's an album that we play very few of the songs from live. Maybe it's just because we burned out on it. There are plenty of Exodus fans who love that album, and I know drummers who say it's their favorite drum sound of any Exodus album. It was a big step forward for us, and when it was released in October 1987, it eventually made its way onto the *Billboard* chart. We were, however, still behind the curve in many ways, because Metallica had already released album number three, *Master of Puppets*, and were conquering the world in a big way, despite the death of bassist Cliff Burton in September 1986.

CHAPTER 11
THE TOXIC WALTZ

EVEN THOUGH CASTRO VALLEY, WHERE METALLICA BASSIST CLIFF BUR-
ton was from, is only about thirty miles south of Richmond, the first
time I ever went there was for Cliff's funeral in late 1986. At the time,
Castro Valley seemed like a million miles away. I didn't drive until I was
twenty-five, because I never had a driver's license, so Castro Valley might
as well have been in another state, because I wasn't going to walk there.

Cliff's death left a huge hole in Metallica and the whole Bay Area scene
in general. He was the warmest, most awesome individual. He would be
front row at shows or right on the side of the stage, furiously headbanging
when we'd play. His death in the bus accident in Sweden was a horrible,
tragic loss. There aren't a lot of guys in music who inspire you to spend a
lot of time imagining what their band would have been like if they were
still around. And with Metallica, you're talking about the biggest metal
band of all time. But you still go, *Wow, imagine what they would have done
if Cliff were still around.* He never would have cut his hair off during the
Load/Reload era, and put on mascara, I'll tell you that much! Fuck no!

And maybe the rest of the band wouldn't have done that either if Cliff had still been around. He taught James everything he knows about harmony and melody. That influence, which is still there today, is from Cliff.

Cliff's impact on Metallica was never more pronounced than on his final record, *Master of Puppets*. While Exodus were just being ourselves—fucking goofy and stupid—they were writing some masterpieces that you kind of, from a Bay Area insider, overlooked how amazing the songs were because we were all still a bunch of young, dirty thrash kids drinking vodka together. But they were secretly creating their epic masterpiece. I still think *Master of Puppets* is the best metal album ever made, a perfect record, back to front. Back then, we hadn't seen this thing thrash becoming some global phenomenon or anything like that, or Metallica becoming a global phenomenon. They were still Bay Area guys, a couple of transplants and a couple of lifers.

We never felt bummed or left behind when they started to take off. We cheered them on, but we had our sights set every bit as high. We always believed we were every bit as good. And I think Exodus's strength was the live show. We were a way more dangerous live band than the other guys. None of them were jumping over each other's heads off the top of drum risers. We could barely keep Rick Hunolt on the ground. Unfortunately, I don't think Exodus ever worked hard enough, as far as touring goes. Metallica, on top of making some of the greatest metal albums of all time, never stopped touring. I look back now, and I know Exodus should've toured a lot more. I was young; I was ready to do it. Fucking stupid. Everything Exodus did back then was backward. We should have been playing every fucking market that'd have us and playing maybe some really bad bars or something, but building an audience. We never played Boise, Idaho, and Billings, Montana, and shit like that back then. We played the major cities, and that was that. We should've worked harder. We would've built a bigger fan base that way.

But when Combat released *Pleasures of the Flesh*, we hit the road in a way more organized fashion than our *Bonded by Blood* touring days. The US leg of our Meat Party tour kicked off in California with a short run of co-headlining shows with Switzerland's Celtic Frost. We were happy to rotate support slots with them. There was no ego from our end, and those guys were super cool. Their front man, Tom G. Warrior, was a real quiet guy, a real artist. There are a lot of guys who are great musicians and great songwriters, but some of them cross that bridge over into art. I always considered Tom as one of those. Back then, he really, really loved aviation and NASA. It was one of his obsessions. He had a NASA jacket he wore all over the place on that tour. We were a bunch of space cadets in Exodus, so it was a perfect match. Exodus were already living on another planet.

We eventually connected with headliners Anthrax in the Midwest for the rest of the run. Those guys had gotten over their fear of us, and they became regular tour mates—and great friends—in the ensuing decades. This tour, to this day, ranks as one of my favorites. That's when the scene was really energetic and people were really into the thrash thing. We were playing theaters and really large clubs and selling them out. Even though people are really into thrash now again, it was a different vibe in its infancy. A perfect illustration of this fervor for thrash was a gig in Tampa, Florida, on December 17, 1987. We were opening that day, and early on in our set, the barricade in front of the stage collapsed, and a security guard got his leg pinned in between the broken barricade. It broke his leg badly—like a compound fracture—and we were onstage trying to get the crowd to back off so they could get the guy out. We played I think four songs and attempted to keep going. Celtic Frost came on after us that day, and the crowd wasn't as violent for their set. But then Anthrax came on, and they managed three songs or four songs and were done. It was just too dangerous.

As much as their music made crowds violent, the dudes in Anthrax were pretty chill, at least compared to Exodus. The band didn't even drink, except for maybe Joey Belladonna. Maybe they'd have a beer every now and then, but they didn't rage. They're supergood friends of ours to this day, but they were fucking boring (or at least we thought at the time!). Celtic Frost were pretty chilled-out guys, too. So we had to fly the freak flag for everybody on that tour. Anthrax's road crew, on the other hand, they were fucking dogs. They were like the worst—total animals. And thankfully, once we got outside the Bay Area, we didn't encounter any of the Baloff-versus-Zet bullshit. It was just the Exodus camp. And the crowds were totally fucking insane and sick and violent and thrashing.

In the new year, we did a month of headlining dates with M.O.D., a crossover band fronted by Billy Milano. Billy was friends with the Anthrax dudes, because he'd played in Stormtroopers of Death (a.k.a. S.O.D.) with Scott Ian, Charlie Benante, and original Anthrax bassist Dan Lilker. This was post-S.O.D., and Billy was a fucking riot to be on tour with, making you laugh all day, every day. This tour's most notable for an incident in the Midwest. Zetro was riding in our gear truck, which was being driven by our friend Walter Morgan. Back then, we didn't pull a gear trailer behind a tour bus; we just had like a Ryder truck. If someone in the band decided to hop in the cab of the truck, which we would all do from time to time, it just meant we were doing drugs and hanging out and cranking metal. Well, Walter was pulling in for a sleep stop at a motel, the Jesse James Motel, somewhere in the Midwest, and the truck was higher than the awning. Not noticing this, he drove forward and wrecked the entire front end of the motel, exposing a couple of the rooms, just took the whole thing out. It dumped bricks all over the manager's new Camaro and pretty much destroyed it. Fortunately, Walter's father was a lawyer.

Another highlight was our headlining show at the Warfield in San Francisco, February 26, 1988. That was the last show that the Warfield had seats, because the crowd tore them all out. The *San Francisco Chronicle* writer who covered the show wrote more about the audience than the band. We were barely mentioned. What was mentioned was someone jumped off the balcony, then his girlfriend jumped off behind him, and of course, the writer had to mention that all the seats had been torn out and were flying everywhere.

The insanity of the Meat Party tour continued in Europe in the spring when we brought our buddies in Làáz Rockit over to Europe with us for a double bill of Bay Area mayhem. Zet had gone to school with their bassist Willy Lange (RIP), so we figured it would be fun to tour with our friends, who were having their own moment with their third album, *Know Your Enemy*. It's one thing to play in your hometown with a band you know, but a whole other deal to tour with them. We always knew that the Làáz Rockit guys were maniacs, but we had no idea what kind of trouble they were capable of causing when on the road together. Paul went to school with most of them, so we'd known them as long as we'd known Baloff. On our other tours, we were usually the animals, and everybody else was a little more restrained. Not this time. One of the last dates of the tour was in England, at the Hummingbird in Birmingham. The Hummingbird was a really nice venue, and we were treated super well. A lot of alcohol was consumed and probably some blow. Who knows? Cocaine wasn't always around in Europe, but vodka definitely was. We drank a lot, but if someone had some blow, we were going to fucking snort it all. At the Hummingbird, the Làáz Rockit guys, along with Zetro, started going nuts. They had one of those big steel tubs the club had put their beer in in their dressing room. So they moved it under the sink, turned on the water, and let the sink overflow into the tub and then, *Ha ha, let's fucking flood this dressing room.* Rick and I, sensing a catastrophe about to happen, retired to the bus. We said, *We're fucking out of here. This is getting out of hand.* Well, it flooded and drained down to the lower level, all over the club's expensive monitor board. Unbeknownst to us, the club was run and owned by Triad gangsters. I got called back into the venue along with our manager, Toni, who was in town with us at the time. We were sitting in the club manager's office, and he pulls out a gun and puts it on the fucking table and basically says, *Damages have happened, and we need to sort this out right now.* It was fucking scary, sitting in the office with a guy who puts a revolver on the desk in front of you. Message received!

So we took our lumps and paid our damages that night and went back to the hotel. I remember looking outside the hotel window, and it was surrounded by cars full of Triads, ready for the word to come in and fucking kill us all. Lääz Rockit, on the other hand, bounced out of town. They ran, but they didn't escape it. When we got to the final gig of the tour in London, the Triads were waiting for them. Lääz Rockit were forced to make their amends and settle up. That whole thing was not my favorite moment. My thought at the time was: *Let's not fuck with Triads, let's* play *triads.*

WE ARRIVED BACK IN THE BAY AREA TO FIND THAT THE SEEDS THAT WE'D sown in the early '80s had blossomed into quite the vibrant thrash scene. There was a whole new generation of bands who'd cut their teeth on the first-wave bands—Exodus, Metallica, Slayer, Megadeth, Anthrax— that were making their own noise. Zetro's old band was now called Testament, and they were signed to Atlantic Records (via Megaforce), and bands like Vio-lence and Forbidden were drawing crowds, as well. The cool thing was, though, that the camaraderie remained. The old-school bands were comingling with the upstarts. It was an exciting time for thrash metal. It felt like, thanks to the growing success of the first-wave bands, thrash metal had been legitimized as something more than just heavy metal's redheaded stepchild, some ugly offshoot. It was a movement that now reached way beyond the Bay Area, to all corners of the US, to Europe, and to Asia.

It was in this vibrant, exciting atmosphere that we were poised to make our third album, our second for Combat. A lot of things had stabilized in the band when we replaced Baloff with Zetro. The constantly living-on-the-edge presence of Paul was replaced by a dude who always hit his marks and ultimately made us a better band in many regards. So we went into writing and recording with a confidence and ease we'd never really experienced before. There were fewer uncertainties, especially since we had the good sense to enlist Marc Senasac as our engineer for the recording sessions.

We worked really hard rehearsing for the album. We knew the songs were savage, and we knew it was going to sound the way we wanted it. Everything worked exactly how *Pleasures* should have worked. I walked in with *my rig*, and Rick and I plugged in and got the shit crushing. We got the drums sounding sick before we ever hit Record. Two or three days were spent tuning and mic-ing and trying different mics, instead of relying on technology. It was the polar opposite of *Pleasures*. Zetro had obviously been part of the band longer by this time, so we weren't new to each other anymore. He knew what our expectations were going to be and how we generally operated in the studio. The vibe was always great with Marc, and we loved Alpha & Omega. We didn't have to record from 10:00 p.m. to 6:00 a.m. anymore. We recorded in the day. We'd go late if we wanted to, but we were able to live and work around normal hours.

This was the first album where Rick and I shared producing credit with Marc as the H-Team. He and I were just guiding the process. Having written a lot of the lyrics, it falls more on me to work one-on-one with Zetro while he's tracking. Exodus is a guitar-based band, and Rick and I knew what we wanted and how to make it heavy. That said, Marc's opinion was every bit as important and valid as our own. There was really no singular producer entity on the record. Everybody in the band had their say, but Rick and I were the ones who were there every day, so that made us and Marc the producers.

We loved working with Marc. So many funny things came about because of him and the people he knew. Dov Christopher, the guy who did the narration for the intro to "The Last Act of Defiance," was a *big* six-foot-four African American who made half of his money hustling people playing golf. He was a golf hustler. He also played the harmonica on "Cajun Hell." When he was in front of the mike, he had a little flask of scotch or whatever was in it and a little grinder of cocaine. He'd be out there in front of the mic, taking a couple of pulls and doing a couple of bumps. *All right, let's do it.* We still quote the album intro as "The prison system, *snort, glug, glug*"!

And, hell yeah, we recorded a cover of War's killer funk song "Low Rider." While Metallica were doing NWOBHM covers on their *Garage Days Re-Revisited* EP, we were going back to our literal roots. I grew up surrounded by lowrider culture. I remember hearing that tune on the radio one day and thought, *That's a heavy riff.* I learned the riff, and Rick and I learned the horn melody. We tried it at rehearsal and thought it was killer. Marc brought in some percussionists to do the stuff in the intro. We were always down for doing unique creative things like that, and Exodus fans love that song. I get requests to play it all the time. It's just one riff, but it's driving and it's cool as fuck . . . and we did it before Gary Hoey did it!

Fabulous Disaster, whose title we took from the movie *Sid and Nancy* (Nancy Spungen calls her boyfriend, Sex Pistols bassist Sid Vicious, a "fabulous disaster"), was going to be a pivotal record for us. We knew we were releasing something we were really proud of at a time when people were excited about thrash metal. There was so much opportunity for success, for us to take the next step up. The album debuted at number 82 on the *Billboard* charts, buoyed by the first single, "The Toxic Waltz," which confirmed our confidence in the album. This was in the MTV era, when Music Television had a huge impact on the success (or lack thereof) of a band. So naturally, we made our first video for the cable channel for "The Toxic Waltz."

Our manager at the time, Toni Isabella, was part of the Bill Graham Presents team, so we had access to Bill Graham's iconic venue, the Fillmore, for a couple of days to make the video. The first day, we filmed without the crowd, with just some staging and extra lights. Day two, we brought in people, who went fucking berserk. We were just lip-synching the song over and over, but I think two people left on stretchers during the filming. Toby Rage, of Slay Team fame, was the star of the whole thing, as he was doing his helicopter stage dives and just destroying people. Too bad we didn't have GoPros back then that we could have strapped to his head; it would have been amazing! All our friends in the Bay Area were there, along with Billy Milano (S.O.D./M.O.D.) and members of Anthrax. It was hella fun, and the song, thanks to this video, went on to become an iconic ode to the mosh pit, in all of its cheesy lyrical glory. Bands like Exodus didn't get played much on MTV's *Headbangers Ball* show. It mostly featured the likes of Mötley Crüe, Poison, Guns N' Roses, and Skid Row, who didn't really need the extra exposure. But in the last hour of the show, they'd throw in the more extreme bands, and we actually got to see ourselves on TV, which was fucking rad. You dream about that shit.

Coincidentally, the making of this video coincided with the start of the MTV Headbangers Ball Tour that we were asked to do with Anthrax and the German band Helloween, who would rotate with us as direct support to Anthrax. To be honest, we weren't thrilled with that situation at the time. Helloween now are bigger than we are, but back then, they weren't. But they were managed by Rod Smallwood, who managed Iron Maiden, and he had a lot of industry clout. From my perspective, I couldn't understand why in the world they'd want to play between Anthrax and Exodus on a tour like this. They were getting crushed. They're super nice guys, and I'm a huge fan, but going on between our "Last Act of Defiance" and Anthrax's "Among the Living," it was kind of like a brutal sandwich.

The tour was fun, but most of the members of Anthrax and Helloween were super teetotalers. I don't think I saw anyone in Anthrax drink, other than Joey. He would come and hang out with us and partake, then run back before he was missed. So once again, we were the fucking animals. We ran the ship into the rocks; it was good times. We never turned down a party. We drank it, smoked it, and snorted it, and had a good ol' time. We also picked up our old competition with Anthrax to see which band could destroy the most barricades. The first show of the tour was in Seattle, and the barricade didn't last but a few songs into our set. I'd look over at Anthrax bassist Frank Bello and say, "Gotcha!" Then they'd bring down a barricade and would throw it right back at us. We were playing good-size arenas and theaters on this tour, and it gave us the opportunity to walk the stages of some iconic places. A big one for me was Cobo Arena, which was where Kiss recorded some of *Alive!* We also played the Felt Forum in New York City at Madison Square Garden, and the Henry J. Kaiser Convention Center in Oakland, where I grew up seeing tons of hard rock shows—everybody from Judas Priest to AC/DC—and we sold the place out.

This tour, however, was not fun for Tom, who had to be hospitalized after our gig in Salt Lake City. We didn't really know what was going on with him at the time; I was just told that he had to go to the hospital. I was tripping balls on a horse-drawn carriage ride around downtown with our stage manager when it happened, so I wasn't there at the time. What we didn't know then but that we all know now is that he'd had a panic attack. These can be crippling. They come out of nowhere, and nobody can tell you whatever you're feeling isn't real, because to you it's fucking real as fuck. We did a few more shows with him, and we even flew his girlfriend out to make him more comfortable. He did well for a couple of shows, and then he really went backward and just couldn't do it. He said he needed to go home. It was pretty scary for a bunch of guys who were still pretty fucking young to find themselves in the middle of a tour without a drummer. Nowadays, I could go on YouTube and find a guy who already knows all the songs in the city we're playing. But back then, with no cell phones, it was like, *What are we gonna fucking do?* We were on the biggest tour we'd ever done in the United States. Luckily, on very short notice, we were able to call in Perry Strickland from Vio-lence and only had to skip one show. The day Perry arrived, we rehearsed in a room at a music store and then went onstage that same day. After that, we just went on with the tour, with the intent of finishing it and getting home and figuring out what was going on with Tom.

When we were all back home and the dust had settled after the tour, we had a band meeting to find out Tom's situation. Would he be able to go on tour with us again? We were making major steps forward, and we knew that touring was going to be essential to our ability to earn a living and make the band bigger. We asked him point-blank if he was able to keep touring, and he couldn't tell us he could. We felt we couldn't risk the same scenario happening again, so we parted ways with the only remaining original member of Exodus. Hindsight's everything, just like with the Baloff situation. Exodus has a long history of maybe not standing by our guys like we should. I look at Def Leppard; they stood by a guy losing a fucking arm, and we didn't stand by a drummer who had fucking anxiety attacks. It makes me feel like fucking shit—guilt again, just like with Baloff. Guilt being a recurring theme in my life. In retrospect, we should have definitely stuck by Tom. We could have used an interim guy, but I guess at the time we felt like we maybe needed to make the change because we didn't know if we could rely on it not to happen again.

CHAPTER 12

WITHIN THE WALLS OF CHAOS

For the first time in our ten-year existence, Exodus needed a new drummer. How do you replace a founding member? Kirk's tenure in Exodus had only been four years, and he never played on any Exodus albums, but Tom Hunting was an essential part of Exodus's sound, as we would soon discover. Rather than open up finding his replacement to a long series of auditions, we reached out to someone we knew and could easily vet further: John Tempesta, who was Charlie Benante of Anthrax's drum tech on the Headbangers Ball Tour. Though we didn't really know John before the tour, we watched him play Charlie's kit at sound check and thought, *Wow, that guy's fucking great!* As the tour went on, we found he was a cool dude and we vibed. So we asked him to come out and jam and join the band, and we found that he fit right in. His drum set, not so much.

Johnny owned a Pearl drum kit with two gigantic twenty-six-inch kick drums. They looked killer, but for thrash metal, you need something smaller and tighter, with a quicker response. And even though

Johnny was from New York, which is how he knew the Anthrax crew, he lived in Hollywood, which meant we had to fly him up for rehearsals and such. At first, we'd get him a hotel, and then he'd stay with me. He was already fully immersed in the California lifestyle, but he wasn't as immersed in the Exodus lifestyle. To be fair, he'd *seen* it firsthand on the Headbangers Ball Tour, when we were like bulls in a china shop, just fucking drinking and snorting and wrecking everything. And yet he still wanted in. If you're witness to that kind of stuff up close and you still want to be a part of it, I guess you're not afraid of it.

With the release of *Fabulous Disaster*, we had completed our studio album obligations to Combat Records and were free to look elsewhere. Capitol Records had actually been trying to sign Exodus since we inked our deal with Combat in the mid-'80s. Our manager's best friend, Rachel Matthews, was an A&R rep at Capitol, and she wanted to sign Exodus. She had convinced everybody at the label to sign us and had them trying to buy out the rights to our Combat contract, much in the same way that Elektra Records bought Metallica's Megaforce contract. We were hoping at the time that we'd get the same sort of deal. But Combat wasn't playing along; they were asking for too much money. A million dollars, if I remember correctly. So Capitol waited out our Combat contract. This all played out while we were touring for *Fabulous*, so it was kind of strange supporting an album for a label that we would soon be leaving. But ultimately, we were finally headed where we needed to be, and we were fucking stoked. We were now a major-label band. Everything was supposed to be great, and we were supposed to become super famous. But first we had to make our major-label debut.

Writing new material without Tom playing drums was an adjustment for me. I don't know if it changed the songwriting, per se, but I didn't realize until playing with Johnny that nobody can play Tom Hunting's parts right, nobody—left-handed drummers like Tom are totally unorthodox. Other people will play Tom's stuff and it sounds *almost* right, but it's not. Gene Hoglan has said to this day that it'd be terrifying to have to play all of Tom's stuff because it's fucking totally different and people can't do it right. They'll do a good impersonation of it. The rhythm is there, but the hits are wrong and different. So there was a lot of that with Johnny, adjusting to a different sound from a guy I'd played in a band with since I was seventeen. Even the positioning of the drums—left-hand drum kits go in one direction, so I'm used to hearing some drums better, whereas with a right-handed drummer who drums on the other side of the riser, I don't hear it as much. Johnny is an amazing drummer, but there was a lot I had to get used to.

We wrote and rehearsed obsessively for our fourth album and major-label debut. We knew we had to be prepared, because the stakes had gotten that much higher. For recording the drum tracks, Rick, John, and I decamped to the Music Grinder on Melrose in Hollywood. Normally, I would be the only one to record scratch tracks for the drummer to play along to, but this time, Rick and I both tracked because we wanted Johnny to have two guitars to vibe off. We wanted the full Exodus energy to be there. While we were down in Hollywood, Rick and I spent tons of stupid money on stupid crap at Melrose shops, because that's what Rick and I used to do. We'd go buy fucking stupid shit, like *Look at these Nike Air Pressure shoes we bought that come in a fucking, like, a cooler.* At that time they were like three hundred bucks, which, today, would be more than seven hundred! They looked like fucking moon boots! We were the kings of buying dumb shit.

Once we finished the drums and had our fun in Hollywood, the whole band convened at a studio, Record Two, way up in Mendocino with our engineer, Csaba Petocz, who's Australian. Rick and I loved Csaba, because he'd worked with Prince, and we're both *huge* Prince fans. Csaba was also a taskmaster, and we loved that about him. He would work us really hard. The band stayed in a big vacation home overlooking the Albion River on the property, while Csaba stayed at the studio because they had accommodations there. He realized after the first couple of days we were fucking animals, and he wasn't going to get any sleep anywhere in our vicinity.

Though the accommodations and setting were great—it was like recording summer camp—all was not copacetic in the band. The material we'd assembled for the album—more brutal and more epic than anything we'd done previously—challenged Robbie's skills as a bassist. When it came time to record his parts, he'd pick a song to start with and work on it for hours. To be fair, the songs were really difficult; *Impact Is Imminent* is a tough album to play, and I wanted him to play the guitar riffs exactly like I did. If I was making the same record now, I'd have the bass find its groove with the drums. So he'd be like, *I'm not feeling this one. Let's go to another song.* He was struggling to put down his tracks. Robbie's an amazing bass player, but he always had a bit of studio fright. After trying four songs in two days, he hadn't completed one of them. Finally, he said to me, "Maybe you should play them, Gary." So I recorded all the bass tracks for the album, and I did them in two days. Not long after the album was done, Robbie decided to retire. He never played in another band. Exodus was his first and his last.

Most of the first-wave thrash bands we came up with had signed major-label deals earlier than we had and were already a couple of albums into that whole world by the time we found our way to Capitol. They had experience bringing extreme music to the masses, not necessarily by compromising but maybe by refining their sound in certain ways—production, songwriting, performance. They were making, arguably, some of their best records and were seeing the results in growing sales. Thrash metal was becoming big business, in spite of the fact that we were all still being relegated to the last-hour ghetto of MTV's *Headbangers Ball* show. Thrash, as it turned out, didn't really need to rely on having hit videos or airplay; making good records and touring constantly was the way to build our audience. Metal fans were loyal, and they appreciated that we weren't pandering to the mainstream. So in this climate of mass acceptance of the genre we helped create, we delivered a *bludgeoning* record: *Impact Is Imminent*. It's an album that I admit to this day has flaws, but it also has some of my favorite riffs I've ever written on it, like the opening riff of the title track. That intro is string-skipping madness; it's so fucking heavy! We didn't deliver "Toxic Waltz Part II" on *Impact*, we delivered the start of Exodus's foray into longer epics and super brutal shit, with scattershot vocal melodies. It's fucking bludgeoning and ugly and not all that catchy. The timing of this was made all the worse by the fact that when it was completed at the end of January 1990, everybody who'd been part of the journey to get us signed to Capitol was gone: our A&R rep (and good friend) Rachel Matthews, the head of A&R, and the president. All gone. They were replaced by people who had no attachment to Exodus whatsoever, musically or emotionally. The new people at Capitol were now like, *Who's this band?* Not a good start for our major-label career.

Without crucial label support, all we could do is go out and tour once the album was released. Before that, though, we needed to replace Robbie. For the first time ever, we did real auditions. Rick and I each had guys we were grooming for the position. Mine was my best friend Jimmy Lapin, whom I'd known since we attended Helms Junior High and Richmond High together. He was there through the whole backyard party thing, and had even played guitar in a band called Führer with Exodus's original bassist, Carlton Melson. I really wanted him to get the gig, but Rick really wanted *his* guy to get the gig, and we ultimately decided that we would hire neither because we didn't want them to be "my guy" or "Rick's guy," were one of them to join Exodus. We wanted someone who maybe didn't have a specific allegiance one way or another. Sadly, Jimmy passed away a few years later—and I was a pallbearer at his funeral—one of many friends I'd lose to drugs over the years.

We didn't have the same kind of cattle call Metallica had when they replaced Cliff Burton and ultimately chose Flotsam and Jetsam bassist

Jason Newsted, but we did have a like-minded goal in a way. We had been joking that we were looking for what Rick and I called the "Newsted chin." Jason had that granite chin that just stuck out, and he had that fucking intense look. In walked Mike Butler, and Rick looked right at me and went, *It's the chin! It's the chin!* Right off, Mike had that granite chin that we wanted in our bass player. Mike later told me that he fucking got totally self-conscious when we said this and thought we hated his chin. Actually, it was the chin that got us interested. Then he put on his bass, and it was hanging right down at his knees. We thought, *All right, this guy's punk rock as fuck*—which he was. He used to be in a band called Stevie Stiletto and the Switchblades. And he was killing it in the audition. He came in and just had the look, had the chin, had the low bass. His bass sound was great, and he was a great guy. Perfect fit.

By early 1990, Exodus was a substantially different band from just a few years previous. We now had a new bassist to accompany our new drummer. One evening in February, when Johnny was in town from LA, he and I went to see McAuley Schenker Group at the Warfield in San Francisco. Because Exodus were managed by Bill Graham Presents and they owned the Warfield, I'd walk in and be handed a three-foot-long strip of drink tickets. I'd be carrying the strip over my shoulder like a fucking jump rope: *Who wants a drink?* Needless to say, Johnny and I got hammered. Afterward, we heard that longtime local hard rock favorites Y&T were playing at the Stone in San Francisco, so we decided to hit that as well. There was a show at the Stone, but Y&T wasn't playing; it was a hair band called Christine. I went there thinking I was gonna watch guitarist Dave Meniketti of Y&T just shred, and it's just all fucking big hair and cowboy boots. And this is, of all places, where I met my first wife—at a hair metal show. She was there to look at pretty guys in cowboy boots and big hair, and in walk two super drunk dudes, hoping to catch Y&T. It was just one of those chance encounters. At the time, she knew nothing about Exodus. She was into LA Guns and shit like that, although I think she learned to like Exodus. Within a year, we were married.

As part of the *Impact Is Imminent* sessions, we recorded a couple of covers for B-sides. I always thought that Exodus, at least in the early days, had bad album covers, but we did great cover songs. For this session, we did "Free for All" by Ted Nugent and "Good Morning" by Blackfoot, two tracks that paid homage to my hard rock roots and influences. One morning, I was in my apartment during an era when I probably slept until 11:00 a.m. or noon. I got a call at six in the morning, so I picked up.

"Hello," I answered with a definite edge to my voice. Who the fuck was calling so early? I figured it must be a wrong number.

"Wake and bake, it's your old buddy Rickey Medlocke of Blackfoot!"

"No, you're not," I mumbled. "Fuck you." But it really was Rickey. Apparently, at the time, he was living in Michigan, and while driving in his car listening to Z Rock, a nationally syndicated radio network, he heard our cover of "Good Morning."

"When I heard that come on, I was so taken aback I had to pull over to the side of the road and listen. It was awesome!" he gushed.

"Did we play it right? Were there any wrong notes anywhere?" I asked.

"No, I loved it!" He gave me his number and said to keep in touch. I think at that time, in the early '90s, Blackfoot really weren't on anybody's radar. And since it was the start of our major-label era, it appeared we were on the rise. So for him hearing a young band cover one of his songs when he didn't even know if this next generation of bands was into his music, it kind of blew him away. I also later heard from a journalist friend of mine who used to write for *Guitar World* that he played our cover of "Free for All" for Ted Nugent and Ted loved it. He said Ted didn't like the guitar tones (not surprisingly, since thrash wasn't his thing), but he apparently said we played it with "balls and attitude like the song demands."

When *Impact Is Imminent* was released in June 1990, it didn't fare as well chart-wise as our previous two albums, which was surprising since we now had the backing of a major label and some of our peers were doing good business. I suppose it wasn't helped by the fact that the cover was another confusing one, insofar as how it related to the title and the music itself. We had a long history of having some questionable art and questionable concepts, usually because they were concepts born of marijuana. When we were high as fuck, the idea sounded great: us in a car and a giant pinball's about to roll us over. After some fucking bong hits, it made sense, at least to us. Now, not so much. And once again, we hit the road, but definitely not for as long as we should have. Some of that was our doing, some was the label's. We had a good run with Suicidal Tendencies and Pantera in the US in the late summer, and then a short headlining US stint in winter. For our European run, we were offered a slot on Judas Priest's two-month tour supporting their return-to-form album *Painkiller*. Unfortunately, because of the diminishing lack of support from our record label, we had to turn it down. Capitol refused to give us the necessary tour support, back in the days when bands relied on it. Pantera ended up taking our spot, and I fucking shed a tear over that one. Priest are like my fucking heroes. I would've given a kidney to do it if I had more than one (more on that later).

CHAPTER 13

'TIL DEATH DO US PART

T HOUGH I WASN'T OFF TOURING EUROPE WITH JUDAS PRIEST, THERE
was still cause for celebration in early 1991, when I got married in
February. Exodus also took this unexpected free time—we didn't
play a meaningful gig in 1991—to start working on our second album
for Capitol, whose interest in us seemed to be fluctuating by the day.
For this album, we decided to record preproduction demos of the whole
album. Capitol didn't ask us to do that. We just knew we needed to run
the new material by them, so the new people at the label could hear it,
because they were kind of terrified by *Impact Is Imminent*. By then, our
A&R person was William Howell, another lifelong friend, so we had
one ally at the label. But he still had to convince the higher-ups that we
were viable.

We demoed almost all the songs that would end up on *Force of Habit*
in two different sessions. Rather than use Marc Senasac, we did some
at Prairie Sun in Cotati, and we did some with Damien Rasmussen,
brother of Thaen Rasmussen from Anvil Chorus, at his small studio.

When Rick and I were driving together in his late '70s 2002 series BMW to Prairie Sun, we would be cranking Metallica's just-released fifth album, *Metallica* (a.k.a. *The Black Album*). I loved it from the moment it came out. It was never like, *Oh, what, they sold out!* "Enter Sandman" is a song that a lot of people are sick of because it was such a giant hit. But when I first heard it, I wasn't like, *What, they're not going all fast?* I was like, *This is fucking* great! Rick Hunolt and I were listening to "Sad but True," and we almost went off the road, because we were like, *This is so fucking heavy! Whoa, dude!* Rick had a tendency to almost kill you if he was really into a song playing when he was driving. But I'm not gonna lie, after hearing that album, I felt like we needed to aim for what Metallica were doing a little bit more.

The demos turned out great, and we proceeded to spend *a lot* of Capitol's money recording *Force of Habit* in England with producer Chris Tsangarides (RIP). We knew Chris's work from the albums he'd made with Thin Lizzy, Tygers of Pan Tang, Concrete Blonde, and Judas Priest's latest, *Painkiller*. Working with Chris was an honor, but he had been abroad recently producing a lot of albums, so he wasn't working the kind of hours that we were accustomed to. We'd show up around noon, and he was ready to quit and go home for dinner at five while we were ready to go until we fucking couldn't go anymore. So we worked a pretty easy schedule, and because of that, we fucking drank a lot. We spent a lot of time pounding pints and playing quarters at this nearby pub, O'Henry's, that embraced us like regulars. We probably partied more hours than we worked.

Guitar-wise, Chris was monumentally important to Rick's and my performances. I think this album has some of our best guitar work, but I think Zetro's performances were better on the demos. That's partially my fault because I let him and Chris do a lot of the vocal takes without me. We'd already demoed everything and we knew what we wanted, but sometimes you still have to push a guy as hard as you did on the demos. Just because he'd tracked it once before didn't mean he was gonna track it as good. Looking back, there were a lot of positives about the album, but there was more energy in the demos. We worked hard on those, and they're a little rawer and a little more furious, I think. The relaxed schedule we worked on the album made it sound a little relaxed. Zetro's vocals are better on the demos because we pushed harder. We weren't going, *I'm gonna go see Big Ben. You just track by yourself.* My advice to bands is: Don't do demos. Because you might put all your fucking energy into those, and then you're just kind of repeating what you did already, without the fire.

Another possible misstep was including two covers on *Force*, "Bitch" by the Rolling Stones (complete with the Tower of Power horn section!) and "Pump It Up" by Elvis Costello. Maybe one of the covers would've been cool, but we didn't need both. We could have saved them for B-sides, because we left two original songs off, "Crawl Before You Walk" and "Telepathetic," and the latter was really heavy. That one should've been on the album. Once again, Exodus, not exactly known for making the wisest decisions. Still, there's a lot of good shit on *Force of Habit*. People have been critical of it, saying we slowed down and that it was our response to Metallica's *Black Album*, but the album has tons of high-speed thrash on it. It didn't *open* with a fast song, so maybe that's why it's seen as a slower album, because that's the only album we've ever done that didn't start fast. It has its flaws; it has its great points. Capitol had invested a quarter of a million dollars in it by the time we were done—including a mixing session with hot producers du jour, Steve Thompson and Michael Barbiero (Guns N' Roses, Metallica, etc.)—so the pressure was on to deliver.

And obviously after spending all that money, we were eager to preview the album for Capitol. A big meeting was set up in LA to play the new songs for them, and it was a *really* uncomfortable situation. We were in a big listening room with a lot of label people we didn't really know. We played the new songs—us nervously looking around for any hint of a reaction—and when it was over, they stood up and fucking applauded, like it was the best thing ever. They gave us a standing O. That awkward show of approval turned out to be about the extent of their support for it.

THERE'S AN AXIOM ABOUT "NEVER MEET YOUR HEROES," BUT WHEN ONE OF your heroes is Ronnie James Dio (RIP), there's no chance for disappointment. For our first significant tour in support of *Force of Habit*, we scored a support slot on Black Sabbath's *Dehumanizer* tour, which featured Dio back in the band again after a ten-year absence. In the '70s, Ronnie had been in Rainbow with my all-time guitar hero, Ritchie Blackmore. So the idea of touring with Sabbath fronted by Dio was unreal to me. Just a couple of weeks before the tour was to start, I was in LA at the Foundations Forum, the big metal convention they used to have, and I saw Ronnie and his assistant waiting for a car to pick them up. I went up and introduced myself: *My name's Gary, and I play guitar for Exodus, and I'm a huge fan, and we're also your support act on your upcoming* Dehumanizer *tour, and we're thrilled to death. This is a watershed moment for us as fans, and this is gonna be the baddest thing ever, blah blah blah, and thank you!* He was so polite and so nice as I gushed.

Two weeks later at the start of the tour, I see him walk into the backstage area, and I wave hello. He goes, "How you doing, Gary?" I was shocked he fucking remembered my name from a five-minute conversation! The whole tour was just phenomenal. We hung out with Ronnie all the time. Tony Iommi and Geezer Butler were super nice to us, too, but they had their own dressing room, and Ronnie and drummer Vinny Appice had their own. Ronnie was looking to hang out. So we hung out, and we fucking partied together. We shot pool together. He was superhuman in his drinking abilities. He'd pour these drinks, almost like a piña colada, made with Malibu rum; he called it "a drink of the islands." He'd just pound those things down and smoke hella weed. We tried to keep up and we couldn't even walk, and he'd be perfectly fine. We'd be shooting pool, nearly ripping the felt, and he'd sink like ten balls in a row. I don't know how he did it. He was half my size, and he could hold more liquor than I could at a time when I drank *a lot* of fucking liquor. He even let me pick his brain about Ritchie Blackmore for hours, which was fucking amazing because I know they didn't have the world's greatest relationship, even though they made some of the world's greatest music. He sat there and answered all my questions about him.

I should mention that my then wife was pregnant with our first child, who was due during the last week of this tour, which was scheduled to end in California. As much fun as I was having with Dio and Sabbath, this was never far from my mind. I was hoping that my firstborn would be a little late in arriving and I could be there for the birth. But Chelsea had her own plans and was born on her exact due date, as we were on our way to play the third-to-last show of the tour in Phoenix. I found out on a pay phone in Burger King, with Whitney Houston's "Greatest Love of All" playing in the background. To this day, I have a soft spot for that song, "children are the future" and all that shit. Perfect fucking way to find out you're a dad. So I flew home from Arizona to see Chelsea and my wife, then flew back to play the Arizona show. Our final dates were in the Bay Area—Sacramento and Oakland—and I had a fistful of those shitty "It's a Girl" cigars I was handing out at the Oakland show. Nobody would really smoke them, but I spotted Ronnie at the back of the stage during Vinnie's drum solo, and I handed one to him. He said congratulations, and he lit it up and smoked it right there. I still have my daughter's Black Sabbath tour laminate; it has a picture of her from the hospital when she was just five minutes old. What a life-changing ending to an amazing tour. I was now a father.

ON THAT TOUR, WE WERE ALL GETTING ALONG FINE, BUT THERE WAS DEFI-
nitely a division developing between us and Zetro. I don't think it was
entirely his fault. We're East Bay guys, and even though we were only
separated by forty minutes of fucking geography, it's a different world,
from his hometown of Dublin to Richmond and Berkeley. And he's a
singer, and I'm a guitar player. I think he'd be the first to say he suffered
from a bit of "lead singer disease." But all lead singers do. You have to, to
be a fucking singer. I get to hide behind a guitar. He has to stand there
with his hand in front of his face holding a microphone—you have to be
wired differently. Sometimes that wiring can short-circuit.

A lot of shit started short-circuiting during our winter tour opening for Ice-T's Body Count. I had less than a month at home with my
wife and baby before we were back on the road. This tour was a stark
contrast to what we'd just experienced with Sabbath. Money was tight,
budgets were tight, and while everybody was still getting their salary
and stuff, Capitol was clearly not as enthusiastic about Exodus as when
we got the standing ovation in the boardroom. And maybe because of
all this, attitudes weren't as fucking awesome as they should've been.
There was definitely tension between me and Rick with Zetro, the three
guys who'd been doing this the longest. It probably wasn't a really comfortable situation for the new guys, Mike and Johnny.

In the last week of the tour, I found out from someone back home
that Johnny was planning to bail on Exodus to join Testament. He, of
course, hadn't told me or anyone else in Exodus. When I heard this,
I was so fucking pissed off at him. I love the guy like a brother, but I
was so mad. We played a show in Boulder, Colorado, and I got really
wasted backstage with some of the Body Count guys who were drinking Oil Slicks (Jägermeister and Rumple Minze). Jello Biafra of the
Dead Kennedys—who grew up in Boulder—was there that night,
too, because he's friends with Ice T. I went onstage fucking hammered; I was just blackout drunk. I ripped my fingernail and was all

bloody, and I was flipping Johnny off between songs—not my greatest moment. But the news that he was leaving hurt on a lot of levels. The fact is, we took pretty fucking good care of Johnny, made him a full member immediately upon joining the band. I know that things weren't great in Exodus at that particular moment, but sometimes you've got to ride that shit out. If he had left us and made that next move up to, say, Rob Zombie (which he did years later), I'd have completely understood. But leaving to go play with Testament, that was a fucking slap. This guy, who's my brother, is leaving for the fucking competition across the bay? Not cool. But Testament gave him an offer of, I guess, temporary financial stability, and he took it. He did what he felt he had to do. I've got mad love for Johnny—we're still the best of friends—but I was pretty fucking angry at the time. So Johnny left at the end of the Body Count tour in early 1993, which put us in an awkward position because we had some huge international dates looming not far off in the spring.

To add insult to injury, Capitol Records (not surprisingly, all things considered) declined to pick up the option on our next record. We were effectively dropped from the label. We no doubt could've signed a deal overnight with one of the metal labels, where we probably should've stayed, but that seemed like a significant step backward, so that wasn't an option for me. I just wasn't having fun anymore. But we had obligations to play our first gigs in South America, as well as some dates in Japan, which would at least put some money in our pockets, despite the overall lack of camaraderie in the band at that point. But first we needed to get a drummer in place.

Our first ask was Chris Kontos (of Attitude Adjustment and Verbal Abuse), who'd been one of my friends since the beginning of Exodus and was a legendary Bay Area drummer. We played a warm-up gig in the Bay Area a week before our Argentina shows, where he pulled off the classics, which was the stuff he grew up on, but he wasn't yet as familiar with the newer stuff. We knew, though, that by the time we got down to South America, he'd be good to go.

Part of the appeal of these two shows in Buenos Aires was that we'd be opening for Motörhead, whom we all loved. We'd met Motörhead front man Lemmy on previous occasions (he thought we were a punk band) and were eager to see him again. The first thing we discovered when we arrived at our hotel was a huge mass of people hanging out there. *Wow*, I thought, *who knew we were so big in Argentina?!* Well, it turns out Exodus *isn't*, but Ricky Martin, who was staying at the same hotel, *is*. The crowd was just waiting for the dude from Menudo. The second thing we discovered was that cocaine was fucking ten dollars a gram, and we fucking did a lot of cocaine. And speed, thanks to Lemmy. Lemmy seemed to have a soft spot for us. He wouldn't even share it with his band members, but he gave me, Zet, and Rick some fucking crank, which was awesome. I also came to discover that he was like the Confucius of rock and roll, a man of many gifts.

I was sitting backstage, and Lemmy was eating this cheese that was super runny, like you'd tip the plate and it fucking oozed.

"Eeeww, what is that, Lemmy? That cheese looks nasty as fuck," I said.

"You haven't tried it?" he asked.

"No." The "of course not" was implied.

"How do you know you don't like it?"

Fair enough, right? How *did* I know I didn't like it? It might've been the best fucking thing in the world. So I tried it, and it was the *worst* thing in the world. I reached for the nearest thing I could to wash the taste away, and it was his Jack Daniel's with a splash of Coke.

"Now you *know* you don't like it," he announced. "You're a real cheese marine!"

I've been a cheese marine ever since, and now I'm a fucking sergeant in the Cheese Marine Corps. But you know, I couldn't argue with him.

How did I know I didn't like it? It just looked gross. It was gross; it was fucking horrible. One of the worst things I've ever eaten in my life.

The Argentina shows turned out to be amazing. After whatever angst we might have had regarding Chris Kontos's familiarity with the newer songs, he nailed it, and the band was in really good spirits. I think Chris realized how high the stakes were for these gigs, and he fucking buckled down and destroyed it. However, because we weren't sure how it would all work out and whether he'd be available to do more shows, we arranged for another drummer, Gannon Hall of Mordred, to go to Japan with us a month later. Unfortunately, a different drummer wouldn't erase the ongoing issues in the core of the band.

As opposed to South America, the vibe within the band in Japan was totally different; it was horrible. It was really an uncomfortable situation to be around. The band didn't have any money; we were broke. We felt defeated. It felt like it was over. We'd been dropped by the label, it felt like the end of my career, and Zetro was kind of miserable to work with at that time. Everybody had different priorities. I was a father; Zetro was a father; Rick was super heavy into the rave scene at the time. And the minute everybody's not on the same team, the team can't win. You're gonna lose, you're gonna get crushed. I felt like the industry was crushing me a little bit. People don't understand, it's fucking work, especially if you don't enjoy it. When you really are not enjoying it, you want to be anywhere else but there. You wanna run and flee somewhere else and hide.

So sitting in a press conference with the Japanese media, I unilaterally announced that this was the end of Exodus. I just said, *These are our last shows. I'm done.* The band's run was done, and it was time to move on. I always said the minute it became like a fucking day job that I didn't like, I'm out of there because it's not worth it. When you're uncomfortable in your own band and there are two totally different camps, to me, it was a no-brainer to break up. Quitting the way I did was a spur-of-the-moment decision that I probably should have thought on a little harder. Maybe if I'd waited until I got home, I might've reacted differently. But at that point, it was like, *I just wanna go home and be with my wife and baby.* Strangely, nobody in the band fought for it. I wish I had, but everything happens for a fucking reason. If we fought for it, we might never have come back around to making the kind of albums we do now. We might have extended it a couple of years and fell apart then, who knows? We might fucking hate each other if we didn't have that time apart. But as far as I was concerned at the time, that was the end of Exodus.

PART II
SELF-IMMOLATION
1993—2002

CHAPTER 14
RIFFING IN '83, ROOFING IN '93

N THE EARLY '90S, A LOT OF METAL BANDS, EVEN SOME OF OUR PEERS, were quick to blame grunge for their fading fortunes and getting dropped by their labels. When I quit Exodus in early 1993, the rock charts were being dominated by Nirvana, Soundgarden, Pearl Jam, Alice in Chains, Smashing Pumpkins, et al. But the fact was that we were dropped by our record label because we weren't making our best music anymore, and we were expensive. If a major label signs a band to a big record deal and the band isn't generating the sales, that's what it comes down to: Are you worth the investment? We were no longer worth the investment.

Pantera blew up at the same time flannel sales skyrocketed, so that tells you everything you need to know. Those guys were making records full of guitar solos and shredding and crushing riffs, and they succeeded because they managed to resonate. And I think all of us, with the exception of them and Metallica, weren't making our best albums anymore. Maybe we were running out of ideas, although I think *Force of Habit* has a lot of great material, which most definitely needed some editing. But everybody wanted to blame it on someone else and not look in the mirror. I don't care if it's fucking Exodus or Testament or fucking Kreator or fucking anybody. We weren't making great albums in that period. It all fell apart. I was fucking completely out of music, with *no* prospects. I was a fucking bum. I went from playing Cobo Hall in Detroit to doing nothing. Talk about a fall from grace.

It was something of a scary position to be in, considering I had a young family to support and no real means to do so, nor any savings whatsoever. Exodus had been horrible with our money over the years. We had to have our money budgeted by our management, because if they ever gave us a big lump sum, we would fucking spend it on stupid shit. Like, *Fuck rent! Look at this watch I bought!* I didn't even own a home. My wife and I had been renting prior to Exodus's breakup. And unfortunately, I hadn't worked any kind of day job since my Kenco Paints stint, which was pretty short-lived. At that point, the "Experience" part of my résumé consisted of "warehouse worker" and "thrash metal guitarist," which doesn't get you too far in the real world. I'd never even fucking done a job interview in my life. I felt no shame in working a day job, though, like my father did for decades to support his family. Some musicians are quick to say, *Oh, everything fell apart, and I was forced to work some lowly job.* Well, fucking so does *everybody*. Join the fucking club. You had to work, boo-hoo, cry me a river. A fancy guitar player had to go out and work and take orders from someone above him. It happens. And it happened to me. I was perfectly fine with it. What was a hard pill to swallow was the fact that I had to move my family into my parents' house while I got on my feet.

I was obviously not alone in needing to get a job. When Tom left Exodus, he went back to his gig as a repairman at an RV dealer. Zetro transitioned back to the work world quickly, before I did. He learned a real trade (and a earned a union wage) working as a foreman at a roofing company called Cypress Roofing. Rick and I both interviewed for jobs there, but they initially didn't want me. I just didn't sell myself that well, because I didn't know how. I'm a fucking guitar player. But I ended up getting hired after all and lasted a lot longer than Rick, who showed up for a week or two before he took off for lunch one day and never came back. I had no skills outside of playing music, so everything I learned working for Cypress I learned on the job. I was lucky they hired me. I needed work, needed to pay bills. That's why Zetro started working, why anybody did, not because we wanted to. I just didn't wanna be homeless.

Zetro helped a lot of us out during this time. At one point, Rick and I were working with Phil Demmel and Sean Killian of Vio-lence— thrash metal roofing! Word of my new employment must have gotten out to UK metal magazine *Kerrang!*, which wrote a where-are-they-now piece about Exodus with the headline "Riffing in '83, Roofing in '93." It was funny, but brutal. I remember when someone told me about it, I was like, *Ah, that hurts!* Because at the time, it was being broadcast that, yeah, I was doing nothing. I didn't play anymore. I get all this respect as a guitar player now, as one of the creators of a genre of music, but people don't remember that I was a completely forgotten footnote in thrash metal for a while. Like, *What's that guy doing?* I was doing what I had to do. I had to feed my family.

The job at least paid well, and so we only had to live at my parents' place for about three months before we were able to move into our own house again. And Zet was a great boss, at least for me. He gave me all the good jobs everybody else wanted, which was cool. He took care of me like that. He'd pull me off a roof and have me go seal a deck while everybody else was on a ladder hauling felt paper rolls in ninety-degree heat. Working for Zet had its perks! I worked at the roofing job for a good six months, and then the jobs we were working on ended. Cypress

Roofing offered to take me on permanently, but I said, *No, I'm done with this shit.*

Job aside, the adjustment to family life was initially challenging. When I first got married (and was still in Exodus), having kids wasn't that important to me, because I was young and selfish and probably freaked out about the prospect of fatherhood. I was like, *Oh, what about my career? What about tours? It's summer. I'm supposed to be on the road.* But when Chelsea came along, I fully embraced it, and I was fucking thrilled from the first moment I held her in my arms. Being able to be part of my new daughter's life was definitely a factor in my leaving music behind at the time. I was a different person, a different man now that I had a family.

That first year after leaving Exodus, I really didn't even think about music. I'd occasionally go see other bands' shows, and I'd get really fucking discouraged and disgusted, because I watched dudes with zero talent doing quite well, and it pissed me off. I'd end up walking out of the show early, just like, *These guys can barely fucking play, and I'm sitting at home doing nothing. What the fuck's wrong with me?* Or if the band was killer, I'd be angry that I wasn't doing it, too. No doubt sensing my frustration, my wife told me I needed to play guitar again, which was awesome. We didn't agree on a lot, but I had her support on that. Sadly, one of my best friends in the world, Jimmy Lapin, would never see the next chapter of my musical career. He died of an overdose in 1993, just as I was about to return to playing guitar again. I was a meth snorter at that point. I'd go to a party, drink beer, and do a line. When I was at home, I didn't use at all. I didn't realize that Jimmy had turned to shooting speedballs—heroin and meth combined. He basically stuck a needle in, got too large a dose, and died. He had a heart attack, or whatever, and had to be put on life support. He never regained consciousness. It was a devastating loss to me, something I'd have to deal with many more times in the future.

I can't say that this gave me any pause regarding my own meth use. Probably because I wasn't that deep into it like Jimmy apparently was. During the initial part of my marriage, when I was still touring, I was hiding the road party or the occasional bump, but it wasn't a day-to-day thing, like I had a bag of drugs hidden somewhere in my car at all times that I didn't want to bring into the house. I wasn't sober, but I also wasn't strung out. I was a weekend warrior, so to speak. When I decided to start playing music again, my "drug use" meant a *small* amount of drugs. My wife's family was from Sacramento, and she would take Chelsea and spend the weekend there to visit her sister. I'd stay home alone so I could riff out and play guitar. But sometimes, those riffing sessions required a little writing fuel. I'd go and get less than a quarter gram, a little ten-dollar bag, for the weekend. By the time she and Chelsea came home, life was back to normal.

CHAPTER 15

THROWING DOWN

O NCE I WAS READY TO START PLAYING MUSIC AGAIN, THE FIRST PERSON I reached out to was Tom. I didn't want to re-form Exodus—that was a done deal, as far as I was concerned—but he was by far the best drummer I knew, and we understood each other on both a personal and musical level. Since we were just planning on jamming—no pressure to tour or whatever—he was eager to reconnect, and his previous issues with panic attacks weren't a concern. The music Tom and I were working on was heavy and a little bit Pantera-influenced; I think a part of me subconsciously was trying to not be thrash in any way. For this music, I didn't think we needed a second guitarist, which was a first for me. When it came time to find a bass player, I reached out to Exodus's last bassist, Mike Butler, but he already had a bunch of projects going and was living in San Francisco. We wanted someone on our side of the bay, so we held auditions for both bassists and vocalists. Our new band was going to be called Wardance.

Oddly enough, we found our bassist when we were auditioning a vocalist, Sean Smithson, who'd been in a local band called Grinch with Chris Kontos. We'd liked Sean's voice on the Grinch demo he'd given us in advance of the audition, but he showed up and didn't sound like he did on the demo. So it ultimately didn't work out. But he brought along his bass-playing friend, Jack Gibson, whom we didn't know, to the audition. Jack saw a bass rig in the rehearsal room, and he was like, *I play bass.* Next thing you know, Jack's in the band.

The songs we had then were very one-dimensional, one-riff basic shit, but Jack just had amazing tone, he played great, and his bass meshed so well with my guitar. His tone blended perfectly. It kind of reminded me of how, in Anthrax, Frank Bello's bass tone always made Scott Ian's guitar sound bigger than it was. Scott's guitar sounds big on its own, but when Frank's below it, it just fills in all those frequencies and makes everything huge. Jack did the same for me and the material we were playing. It sounded perfect right from the get-go, and personality-wise, he was something special. Jack used to make his own moonshine. I never tasted it, not once. That shit looked like gasoline. But back when Jack drank—he's been sober for a long time now—he fucking bootlegged his own 'shine. He was big into hiking and playing Dungeons & Dragons and making hooch. He was like this moonshine-bootlegging, nerdy, bass-playing, awesome god—and a great guy to hang out with.

Finding and holding on to a singer proved to be the bigger challenge. We eventually settled on a guy named John Miller, who was an unproven commodity in the scene, but he definitely was a good fit for what we were doing. He could sing the occasional Priest cover we'd throw in ("Rapid Fire") and wasn't afraid to give the odd *Bonded by Blood* tune a go ("A Lesson in Violence"). As for the originals, I think we suffered from a little bit of an identity crisis. It was heavy, but very groove-based. At the time, I thought being the only guitarist in the band would be liberating, but looking back, it seems empty, like there was something missing. A lot of the songs were very basic and simplistic. We had some moments that were good, but sometimes it was just like one riff recycled far too many times.

We did manage to record a demo that came out sounding sick; there was potential there. It was just done at a home studio, someplace in Berkeley—I can't even remember the guy's name—but he had a really cool setup, and he was really a good dude to work with as far as creative input. We tried some different things production-wise that worked well for certain parts of the songs. By my recollection, we only recorded three songs, and they were never released. We also didn't play many live shows during our short time together, maybe just a handful. Our first one was a packed show at Berkeley Square (now defunct), which was sold out. Chris Kontos had a cane at the time, and he was beating people on the head with it when we were playing "A Lesson in Violence"! We definitely had some fun around the Bay Area, but it was going nowhere. John Miller was a phenomenal singer, but a little unreliable, to say the least. The band eventually broke up because John kind of vanished. No one could find him or get in touch with him. *What do we do?* It was just frustrating. That pretty much spelled the end of Wardance.

Because I wasn't playing music anymore, I needed to go back to work again. Finances were getting tight at home. Zetro wasn't there with a roofing job offer and the good pay that came along with it, though. This time, I was bailed out by another Exodus member. Tom had been working for years at an RV dealer in San Pablo called Camperland doing repair work, so he offered to get me a job there as well. I had none of Tom's repair expertise, so I was pretty much starting at the bottom. And when I tell you it was a shitty job—a total low for someone who'd performed at England's Hammersmith Odeon—it doesn't get much shittier. I was basically what you'd call the "lot boy" at Camperland, making seven dollars an hour. It was a shit job, working for a fucking asshole boss who used to demean me and talk down to me and walk around like he was king of San Pablo. If you grew up where I lived in San Pablo, proclaiming yourself a big shot in that town is fucking nothing. It's fucking San Pablo, dude. (Years later, I heard that prick was arrested in Mexico for running some kind of scam and I could not have been happier!) I was the low man on the totem pole and treated as such. Tom got plenty of respect, probably because he'd been there longer and was indispensable to the company. RVs would come in busted up from a crash, and he'd fixed them right up. Me, I got all the worst tasks: I washed RVs, I dumped the shitters, I cleaned up the dog shit around the lot. I had to clean one trailer that'd been infested with mice so badly that I'm surprised I didn't die from the hantavirus. I was in there fucking steam cleaning years of mouse piss out of the carpet and shop-vacuuming up fucking ten pounds of mice turds. It was horrible! It was the worst job I've ever had, except for the fact that I worked around Tom. But I guess that was just part of my journey, and I think it all has something to do with the person I am today, going from thrash metal originator to mice piss steam cleaner and back again. It was humbling. I'd felt a little bad when *Kerrang!* roasted me for working as a roofer, but this was a whole new low.

To maybe further distance myself from my thrash days, I completely changed the way I looked. While other dudes were growing their hair back out, after cutting it in the early '90s, I did the opposite. I also did stupid shit like dyeing it black and wearing clothes that were twenty sizes too big for me. I was super hip-hoppy-looking. I pull out old pictures of myself now, and I just want to kick my own ass. Like, *What the fuck were you thinking, dude?* But part of me was trying to feel like I was doing something different. And maybe trying to fit in. It was this version of Gary Holt who decided to join the Parent-Teacher Association at my daughter's elementary school. The first time I walked into a PTA meeting, I had big chrome-plated Diesel brand glasses on, I was wearing big, baggy, stupid pants, and my black hair was all spiked up. I stepped through the door and people looked like they thought they were about to get robbed or something! They probably all started clutching their purses, like, *What is this guy doing?* Yeah, that was an entrance. But as part of the group, I ended up going to all the functions. We'd take the little kindergarteners bowling, just me and a bunch of moms. It was fun; we had a good time. They quickly accepted me. I regret it not one bit; I enjoyed being the black sheep of the PTA and spending time with Chelsea and her classmates.

Even as I was trying to distance myself from my past, I had a lot of people whispering in my ear about returning to it. Andy Andersen—one of the original Slay Team guys—just kept saying, *You need to get Baloff back, get the band back together.* At first I was just like, *Ha ha, yeah, sure, right!* But then I started thinking, *You know, that sounds like a pretty fucking good idea, actually.* I was fucking doing absolutely nothing, so why not at least give it a go? I started with Rick, who'd been hitting the rave scene for the last few years but hadn't been playing in any bands. Tom was easy, because we were already working together at Camperland and had been playing music in Wardance. We wanted to get Robbie McKillop, so we could have the complete *Bonded* lineup back, but I suspected he wouldn't do it. If he had said yes, Robbie would have been our guy with no complaints and no second thoughts. But he said, *Man, I haven't played this kind of music since I left the band, and I don't think I can do it.* He was working day jobs and jamming Hendrix songs with his friends. To be honest, Jack Gibson, my Wardance bassist, was our preferred choice, but for the sake of legitimacy, we had to at least ask all the original guys. So Jack was the guy, making it four-fifths of the *BBB* lineup. But it worked out well, because Jack was able to nail everything, and he was super hungry for the gig. That just left Baloff, and I couldn't track him down. I'd heard he was living in Monterey, building sandcastles for tourists, but I didn't have a phone number. I put the word out about what we were doing in hopes that someone would be able to let him know, but I had no solid leads. Without Baloff, I couldn't see relaunching Exodus. It was Baloff or bust.

Out of the blue, he actually called. Hearing his voice, I immediately launched into my spiel.

"Dude, we're gonna get the *Bonded by Blood* lineup back together! Rick's in and all," I rambled, assuming he already knew what I was talking about. But he seemed really weird about it, like he didn't have a lot to say, so we got off the phone. He immediately called back.

"Are you serious?" he asked.

"Yeah, I'm serious," I practically shouted. "Isn't that the reason you called me? I've been trying to track you down."

"No, I was just calling to see what's up."

"Well, okay, let's start over: I wanna get the band back together, the *Bonded by Blood* lineup. Tom's in, Rick's in, Robbie's not. Are you in?"

"Fuck yeah!"

CHAPTER 16

GOOD FRIENDLY VIOLENT FUN

I N THE DECADE-PLUS SINCE ITS RELEASE, *BONDED BY BLOOD*'S LEGEND HAD only grown. There was a new generation of metalheads who'd never seen the band with Baloff fronting it, but knew every song on that album by heart. *Bonded* had taken on a mythical aura and was considered one of the key releases—like Slayer's *Reign in Blood* and Metallica's *Master of Puppets*—in the thrash metal canon. I was proud of everything Exodus had done up to that point, but fans had a lasting, unshakable affection for our debut. So if we were all willing to give it a go again, why deny them? Realistically, the *Bonded* lineup hadn't exactly played to too many US markets outside the Bay Area on our first go-round. We'd toured—and the Venom tours were rad—but those first efforts were poorly organized and mostly involved a lot of driving and not a lot of playing. Reuniting with Baloff at least gave us the opportunity to correct that. And it just seemed like everything lined up to make it happen.

What I may have overlooked, though, were the challenges of having Paul back in the band. For him to rejoin Exodus, he had to relocate from Monterey to the East Bay. He'd been living in a trailer, which he put up for sale and promptly sold to two different people! How those people figured it out when they both showed up to claim it, I have no idea, but that should have been a clue that we were inviting serious mayhem back into our lives. Paul was still doing hella drugs and still drinking hella tons of vodka, but the rest of us couldn't really throw stones, because we weren't much better. We were all snorting meth—except Jack—and Rick and Paul were especially heavy into it. So we weren't exactly starting off on a good foot as far as functionality goes. And honestly, Paul had kind of gone to seed in the intervening years. Let's just say he wasn't the most fashionable guy in the world. He literally had speaker wire for laces in his shoes! Whatever keeps your shoe on your foot, right? Fucking genius. Although now, with the price of copper, you're better off getting some fucking shoelaces. So when he rejoined, I took him shopping at JCPenney and bought him some new clothes and shoes.

Unsurprisingly, there was a lot of enthusiasm in the metal world for our reunion with Baloff and the nearly complete *Bonded* lineup. It felt special. Initially, the whole thing was geared toward a big reunion show at the Trocadero in San Francisco, which we'd planned to record for a live album. This became the most talked-about Bay Area gig in years, and it gave us something to work toward, to get us back in shape, so to speak. We rehearsed quite a lot, and we came in fucking ready to go. Before that, though, we had to reacquire gear for Rick, who'd sold all his stuff after we'd broken up in '93. He bought an amp and some cabs; it was like starting over in a lot of ways for him. I still had all my shit.

Prior to the gig, we secured a deal with Century Media Records to release this momentous event as a live album, and we even started setting up tours to support its release. We had the opportunity to make the most of the buzz surrounding the reunion. The Trocadero show, March 8, 1997, which we recorded with a mobile unit, was magical. It was special. Everyone in the Bay Area scene showed up, and we had a blast. But in classic Exodus fashion, we were wildly underpaid and we kind of got taken. That was always Exodus's lot in life, to not get our just rewards for things. We'd sell out a place and then barely get paid anything. Except for some technical snafus, our performance was fantastic. The concert was like the Paul Baloff comedy hour; his between-song banter was so good, and it was all just right off the top of his head. And the vocals were just full-on raging. He was in peak form; he was at the top of his game. He was the star.

The gig was also videotaped for potential release, but some equipment glitches rendered it useless because there were gaps in the audio recording for the live album that we had to patch up in the studio. Most bands do that on live albums; there's always a bit of touch-ups necessary after the fact. That wouldn't have been a big deal, if we'd all made an effort to replicate what we'd played live as best we could when we were putting the live album together. Tom's tracks were kept as is, and Baloff fixed some stuff, but when Rick was doing his touch-ups, he didn't play the same solos, so when the final audio tracks for the album were completed, Rick's hands in the video weren't matching what he'd rerecorded for the live album. It looked like an overdubbed kung fu movie! Also, because my amp rig failed on a couple of songs—something was cutting out—those would have been unusable, as well. Another opportunity missed, because that video never saw the light of day.

Before the live album, titled *Another Lesson in Violence*, was released by Century Media in July '97, we went over to Europe to play the Dynamo Festival in Eindhoven, along with some headlining gigs and a short Summer Metal Meeting festival run with Kreator, Sodom, Dave Lombardo of Slayer's new band, Grip Inc., In Flames, Samael, and a few other bands. This should have been our triumphant return to Europe—the first time a Baloff-fronted Exodus had been there since the Venom tour in 1985. It was anything but. The whole thing was mismanaged from the start, and it should have been a huge thing, a windfall for the band. We didn't have a booking agent, so we left it to the label, which didn't exactly sell the reunited lineup with much gusto. It was only the Dynamo Festival where we had a spot on the bill where we should've been, and that was largely because we had a connection with the long-time promoter André Verhuysen. The other headlining gigs in between were just random club shows booked by Century Media, not by an agent. It was like someone at the record label calling a club: *Hey, will you give these guys five hundred fucking euros?* There was zero advertisement and all that.

On the Summer Metal Meeting tour, we were originally supposed to be at the top of the fucking bill. That package should've been one of the biggest tours in fucking thrash metal that Europe had ever seen. But by the time the tour happened, we were moved down one band too low to have our own drum kit. So every night, a right-handed kit had to be turned around for Tom Hunting, who's a lefty. It was a fucking nightmare. We outsold everybody like a fucking thousand to one on merch—not literally, but yeah, we dominated. We destroyed everybody. Kreator were headlining, and we fucking wiped the floor with them. *We* should've been headlining things, should've been making twenty times as much money. We didn't. Exodus's way of doing things was wrong so many times. Why were we opening under any of these bands? We shouldn't have been, that's for fucking damn sure.

Because the entire European tour was horribly mismanaged, we had to resort to our thieving ghetto-kid ways. Instead of selling our merch inside the venues and giving up a cut to the promoters, we'd steal merch from ourselves and hock the shit outside for a cheaper price. There'd be five thousand punters a night at some of the festivals, and we'd be cruising around in the parking lots selling long-sleeved *Bonded by Blood* shirts. We were just a bunch of fucking tweakers trying to make a dollar, so we sold whatever we could. *Another Lesson in*

Violence wasn't even out yet, but our reunion was off to a rocky start, at least financially.

Back in the States, things didn't start off much better for the scheduled three-month US tour with our friends in Skinlab. They were signed to Century Media Records at the time, as well, and Century Media had promised to give them tour support, so they could hit the road with us and share our bus. Well, the night before the tour was to start, Century Media withdrew their support, so Exodus had to foot the bill for Skinlab's tour expenses. They were our close friends, but that's not how this business works. Any other headlining band would've kicked them off the tour and said, *Sorry, we can't pay your way.* But we couldn't say no, so we kept them on.

And what a tour it was. It was fucking crazy. We were doing like twenty-something shows in a row. In three months—in a scorching hot summer—we had eleven days off. It was just brutal. Other than the major cities, we were playing for nobody. It was horribly put together, and we weren't making any money. We were pretty disenchanted, to say the least. And there was no shortage of drama along the way. Anytime you're with the same small group of dudes, crammed in a bus for days on end, nerves get frayed. Tom and I got in a big fight while we were helping to load the gear trailers. It was 100 percent humidity, 1:00 in the morning, a hundred degrees. We were at each other's throats: *You're doing it all wrong, motherfucker! Put that case in first, asshole!* Five minutes later, we're all hugs and *Ah, man, I'm sorry. I love you. Let's go have a drink.*

In Boston, Baloff was jumping off the front of the stage, well after the show was over, and there was a hidden step. Upon landing, he twisted his ankle horribly bad, probably tore some ligaments. Totally fucked himself up. But the tour went on, despite the fact that we were at near-meltdown stage. When we rolled into Orlando a couple of weeks later, we had a rare day off. Debbie Abono, our manager, sent us all to

Disney World, and it saved the tour. Fuck Ron DeSantis, Disney World saved the Exodus tour. Because we were literally about to just go home.

We headed into the park, and Baloff's ankle was so fucked up that he had to be pushed in a wheelchair. He couldn't even walk. Nobody in the band wanted to push him around Disney World—that is, until we found out that we got to go to the front of the line with a guy in a wheelchair! So, of course, we immediately fought over who got to push Baloff, because we could just fucking ride Space Mountain ten times in a row. Baloff would even pretend to be mentally disabled in the wheelchair, shouting, "I wanna ride Space Mountain!" over and over! We'd hear grown-ups go, "That poor man. That poor, poor, dirty, filthy-looking man. Life has dealt him such bad cards; it's so heartwarming to see him having so much fun."

When we got back to the hotel that night, we all fucking felt rejuvenated. There's nothing like rides and roller coasters and funnel cakes to save a tour. It was fucking great. The Mouse saved Exodus. That night, we were smiling from ear to ear. Paul and I watched the movie *Anaconda*, and we never laughed so hard in our lives as when the snake barfed up Jon Voight. What an awesome day. We were ready to do another month and a half! But we needed some more meth. Our brilliant solution to the problem was to have a friend of ours ship us drugs via FedEx. But we kept missing the fucking pickup, so we'd reroute it to the next place, just trying to catch up with this fucking box that had some hidden crank in it. We chased that thing for probably five days before we finally caught up with our dope. We coined the term *FedExodus* for our quest, and to this day, once in a blue moon, we'll rerelease a limited run of FedExodus shirts. The back of the shirt said DELIVERING YOU TO EVIL or something like that, but delivering meth to the band is what it really was.

Another time, Tom's drum tech, Josh Frizzell (RIP), and I got so desperate to get wired that we got into Baloff's asthma medicine, theophylline, because we'd heard that Baloff snorted it when no one was looking. We figured there must be something to it. If Paul did it, so could we, so we stole some of his meds, ground one up, chopped out a line, and snorted it. It was by far the worst thing I'd ever put in my nose in my life, and I've put a lot of shit in my nose. I immediately blew it out.

"Ah, that's awful!" I said, gagging. The second it hit my nostril, it caused a huge sinus blockage.

Josh looked at me and said, "Maybe we did it wrong. Let's try it again."

"What do you mean we did it wrong?" I said. "We fucking crushed it and snorted it, and it was awful. How is the outcome gonna be any different if we do it again?"

So, of course, we did it again, and it wasn't any different. It was fucking awful. I blew it out of my nose and never did it again. For real. It was fucking terrible. We were fucking nuts. We would snort asthma medicine because someone said Paul did, so it must work. It must do something if Paul was doing it. Not smart!

The tour reached its final crescendo of insanity, however, in the home stretch. At a show in Colorado Springs, there was a washer and dryer backstage. We were filthy, rotten, smelly men by this point, so we all did our laundry. Before Baloff could get his clean clothes into the dryer, it broke down. So he stuffed all his wet clothes into a giant garbage bag and took it with him. We had a few days off before the final shows, which were in Washington, Oregon, and British Columbia, so we headed back to the Bay Area. By the time we got home, Paul's wet clothes were mildewing and smelling really fucking awful. He lived at this infamous Oakland warehouse where a lot of people lived and a lot of bands rehearsed. So he climbed up on the roof of the warehouse to hang his mildewed clothes to dry out—rather than rewash them— and he lost his balance and fell through the building's skylight, and he landed on the floor. Remarkably, he only needed some stitches and had a slight crack in his sternum. But when we left a day or two later to do the final shows of the tour, we realized Paul was pretty fucked up. The first show, he did really well, but he was massively abusing the pain meds that he was given for his injuries. He took them all in the first few days, of course! The second show, he managed to sing half the set. By the time we got to Sacramento, the last show, he couldn't go on at all. He was out of pain meds and in tremendous pain. He just couldn't do it. So we had no Baloff for the last show. Because Baloff couldn't go on, Rick assumed the show was canceled, so he went home. That left three of us to play to a crowd who were expecting a reunited Baloff-era Exodus. We started inviting people in the audience up to play guitar. A guy from the band El Dopa sang a couple of songs. It was a fucking disaster, and it put an exclamation point on what was a train wreck of a tour, a tour that barely paid my rent for the three months I was gone. Fucking Exodus knew how to crash a train, that's for sure. Impact is fucking imminent. Stay away from the tracks when we're fucking piloting it. We will run you down.

CHAPTER 17

CRIME OF THE CENTURY

AFTER THE TRIUMPH OF THE REUNION SHOW AND LIVE ALBUM IN '97, things just never materialized into anything positive, other than the fact that we were back together again. *That* will forever be a positive to me, to be reconnected with the guys, but everything surrounding our reunion was done wrong. And realistically, I don't know if we could've done it right. To do it right would've meant that all four of us would've had to be cleaner than we were in the early days, not twenty times worse. That was a recipe for fucking disaster. And disaster seemed to follow us wherever we went.

After months spent touring the US and Europe with little to show for it in 1997, our efforts were focused on South America in 1998, a continent where we'd played just a couple of shows in the past, but where people actually wanted to see us, instead of playing for fucking nobody in Boise or fucking Lawrence, Kansas. The South America shows were booked by my good friend Matthias Prill, whom we first met back in 1985 on the European Venom tour, so at least we felt confident that someone had our backs. Which was good, because we weren't exactly keeping our eyes on the prize ourselves. When we weren't doing drugs, if drugs weren't around, alcohol was always available in abundance. Usually, the two went hand in hand, and when we were in South America, we fucking drank so much alcohol. We just fucking partied; there was a party fucking every day. In some places, cocaine was easy to find. It wasn't our preferred drug, our usual drug of choice, but we always had alcohol, and if someone had some cocaine, we'd do that, too. Fuck it. This was our first exposure to South American audiences as headliners, and they were fucking crazy. They still are. There's always someone in the crowd with a road flare.

After a week spent doing shows in Brazil in March, we returned to the Bay Area so that I could be home for the birth of my second daughter, Sophie. It was amazing being there and seeing her born, since I'd missed out on Chelsea's birth, because I was on tour with Black Sabbath in 1992. In one regard, I was better equipped for Sophie's birth, having been a father for six years (and proud PTA member), but I don't know that I was the best parent or husband at that point. Just being there wasn't enough. My drug use in the '90s had become super heavy, but it was still kind of a hidden thing, as far as my family knew. My ex probably would never know the extent of it unless she reads this book. It was sneaky drug use. But I guess it's good that it was sneaky, because if it were out in the open, it would've been a thousand times worse, at least around the homestead. More of the guilt that I carry like a cross to this day.

The *Bonded* lineup of Exodus had been reunited for more than a year; we'd played shows in Europe, America, Mexico, and South America; so the next logical step would be to write new music and record an album, right? We talked about doing this, but through the course of us reuniting, we reunited with and amplified every bit of drug use we had back in the old days on a whole other level. When we'd first reunited in

A school picture from my Dover Elementary days. I was eight.
(photo courtesy of author)

Photo with all my siblings from around 1975 or '76. Back row, left to right: Donald Earnest, Steven Earnest, John Earnest. Front row, left to right: Charles Holt, Kathi Earnest (now Elvira), and me.
(photo courtesy of author)

A family wedding in my hella pimp tan suit. That's cousin Marlene second from left, Aunt Judy third from left, and my lifelong friend, James Maxwell, second from right.
(photo courtesy of author)

Early Exodus shot—me and Jeff Andrews—playing Jame Maxwell's eighteenth birthda party in San Pablo, Californi *(photo courtesy of author)*

Raging on stage at Wolfgang's in San Francisco in 1983. *(photo by Brian Lew)*

Exodus with Slayer's Tom Araya backstage at Wolfgang's in 1984. *(photo by Brian Lew)*

With Paul Baloff and his girlfriend Lizzy Green at Prairie Sun studios while we were recording *Bonded by Blood*. This was the rare calm amongst the storm of destruction and partying. *(photo courtesy of author)*

On a *real* good tweak in San Pablo at Tom Hunting's house. That's Robbie McKillop, me, and Jimmy Lapin (RIP). *(photo courtesy of author)*

Paul Baloff, covered in blood and raging, with me on the tour bus in Europe during the Venom tour! *(photo by Matthias Prill)*

Tracking guitars for *Pleasures of the Flesh* at Alpha Omega studios in San Francisco, with my H-Team partner, Rick Hunolt, circa 1986. *(photo courtesy of author)*

With my parents, June Holt and Bill Holt, and oldest brother, John Earnest, at the Henry J. Kaiser Auditorium while I was on the Headbanger's Ball Tour in 1989. *(photo courtesy of author)*

Dennis Hopper showed up at a date on Exodus's tour with Body Count in 1992 (he knew Ice-T). Dude was nice but intense; he rolled through a sold-out club and people moved out of his way. *(photo courtesy of author)*

With Sophie and Chelsea . . . and my shitty haircut. *(photo courtesy of author)*

Day drinking with Rick Hunolt and Tom Hunting on Saco da Velha Beach, Paraty, Brazil, in 1998. *(photo by Matthias Prill)*

With Rick Hunolt and John Tempesta, circa 1994. (*photo courtesy of author*)

Enjoying the aroma of a shit ton of weed—courtesy of Bill "Kill" Harrell—which was a necessary ingredient in making *Tempo of the Damned*, circa 2003. (*photo courtesy of author*)

With all three of my daughters—Chelsea, Frances, and Sophie. *(photo courtesy of author)*

My wife, Lisa, and I exchanging purity vows at the NAMM (National Association of Music Merchants) trade show in Anaheim. *(photo courtesy of author)*

Having drinks with Kerry King, Matthias Prill, Steve "Zetro" Souza, and Jack Gibson. *(photo by Matthias Prill)*

The Rob Dukes–era lineup—Tom Hunting, Lee Altus, me, Jack Gibson, and Rob—with Matthias Prill (second from left) in South America. *(photo by Matthias Prill)*

Tom Araya and I meeting one of my heroes, Brian May, at the Sweden Rock Festival in 2016. Nicest man on Earth, extremely gracious. He asked if he could watch Slayer onstage; I told him he could have my wallet if he wanted. *(photo courtesy of author)*

Tom Hunting and I having a backyard party days reunion with Kirk Hammett in Paris. *(photo courtesy of author)*

Rare photo of all five Earnest and Holt brothers, along with other friends and family, in my parents' driveway in San Pablo. Left to right: John Earnest, Randolph Mangrum (RIP), myself, Jim "Moose" Mangrum, Steve Earnest, Donald Earnest, Matt Farrel (front), Ryan Earnest, and Charles Holt. *(photo courtesy of author)*

Jason Momoa reenacting a scene from *Game of Thrones*. Daenerys really looks like shit. *(photo courtesy of author)*

One of my favorite photos of Lisa and me, taken by Randy Blythe in Europe in 2019. *(photo by D. Randall Blythe)*

Find a wife who looks at you while you're flipping someone off like Lisa Holt looks at me. *(photo by D. Randall Blythe)*

At home holding my first granddaughter, Freyja, in 2017. *(photo by Lisa Holt)*

Freyja celebrating grandpa's birthday. She's clearly been raised well. *(photo courtesy of author)*

My first grandson, James, circa 2020. Even though I finally have a boy around the house to hang out with, I'm still a proud girl dad. *(photo courtesy of author)*

Grandpa Holt and his third grandchild, and second granddaughter, Layla, in 2023. *(photo courtesy of author)*

Onstage with guitar tech Warren Lee while on tour with Slayer. Warren was my right-hand man for nearly ten years. *(photo by D. Randall Blythe)*

After walking onstage with Freyja and James at Aftershock. They loved watching their grandfather crush, they rocked out big-time from start to finish—one of my career highlights, them getting to see me playing with Slayer. They still talk about walking onstage! *(photo by Lisa Holt)*

late 1996, Rick's meth addiction had progressed to where he was now smoking it. As a fellow tweaker, I wasn't going to be judgmental about it. Who was I to cast aspersions? I was just snorting (as was the rest of the band, except Jack), but one time when I was over at his place in Berkeley and he was smoking it, I said, "Let me try that." He handed me his pipe, I hit it, and after exhaling, I said, "I could get used to this!" Famous last words: *I can get used to smoking methamphetamine.* And get used to it I eventually fucking did. I got real used to smoking it, though I didn't immediately switch to smoking it exclusively. But it started me down a very slippery slope. My own doom loop.

So there were a lot of serious discussions about writing a new album, because that's what tweakers do: We talk about doing shit. I'm a-gonna. I'm a-gonna write an album. I'm a-gonna fucking get a new record deal. And it never happens. You go from being a musician who dabbles in drugs to being a drug addict who dabbles in music. They call it *projecting*, because you're always working on a project and never finishing it. And Exodus became the world's biggest project, never got shit done.

I'd show up to our rehearsal room—which was in the same warehouse where Baloff lived—and we'd spend hella time, like tweakers do, hanging our PA up all badass from the ceiling, so it looked killer. But did we actually sing into that PA? No. But we spent hours making it look rad. We even set up a drum riser. But did we actually go through our set? No. I'd play a couple of riffs and get high. That's just the way it worked. We never wrote anything, a couple of riffs here and there, then back to getting high. So it was doomed from the start. When four-fifths of your band are just wanting to get wired, you're really not gonna get shit done. Creativity's stifled, it's dead, it's dormant. We talked about writing new material, but we couldn't get out of our own way. Me, Rick, Baloff, and Tom were super spun; only Jack wasn't. Making a new album just wasn't gonna happen until the drugs were removed from the equation.

We didn't know it at the time, but the short run of South American dates in November '98 would be the last live dates we'd play as a band for years. But, hey, we went out with a bang. The first show was in Chile, where sadly a fan got hit by a bus in front of the venue and killed. Kind of an ominous (and tragic) beginning, but kind of on point for the mayhem that seemed to follow us. Prior to the show, we were cruising through the Mercado Central—where there's a seafood place, Donde Augusto, that I still go to when I'm down there (best seafood ever!)—and we found a butcher with a skinned goat's head for sale. So of course we had to buy it, and we named it Brutus. We carried Brutus around with us, and the next day, we brought it to the show. Our gear had gotten lost by the airline, so we had to play the show on borrowed equipment from a Chilean band called Criminal. The show was kind of run by some mobsters. As we sat in our hotel, we learned that the guy running the show didn't want to pay us. Matthias was talking to the guy, and pointing at us like, *Look, these guys are drinking. They're not gonna be in any shape to play pretty soon. You'd better come up with the fucking money.* A higher mobster basically got on the phone and made the guy pay us.

So we showed up and played the show. We were on someone else's gear, and I was fucking swinging the guitar by its whammy bar. The poor guy who loaned it to me was probably looking at his hard-earned investment about to snap in half. There was some drunk chick sitting on Rick's cabinets onstage; we didn't even know who she was. Security was loose, if not nonexistent. She just walked up and sat there all hammered. Baloff named her "Half Stack." He went, *Look at you go, Half Stack, you're raging!* At that point, Baloff kicked Brutus, the goat head that had been sitting unrefrigerated for twenty-four hours, into the crowd. The tallest guy in the venue—of course, it's got to be the guy who's like six foot four—got that thing, and he was running around in the pit with this goat head. It was fucking awesome. We were partying, having a good time. We weren't making any money. We just wanted to play shows and get wasted. We didn't really care about anything else.

IN 1999, EXODUS EFFECTIVELY DISAPPEARED AGAIN. WE DIDN'T BREAK UP, we didn't go on a hiatus, we just stopped functioning. We were less of a band than a collection of meth addicts. As much as we liked playing live, we liked getting high better. A lot of people in our little tweaker circle were smokers by this point. There were very few people who still snorted it. Everybody was smoking it. So people would pull out their pipe (we called them *bubblers*) to smoke, and I'd think, *All right, I did like that.* The next thing you know, I'd be asking them to hand me their pipe so I could put some of my meth in it. Then it was me filling up *my own* pipe to smoke it. After that, it was the only way I did it. At that point, if I were still snorting it, it was because I couldn't find a pipe or I couldn't find a light bulb.

Yeah, meth smokers can get pretty creative when necessary. Rick and I made a pipe out of a light bulb backstage at a gig in LA. We took a bulb out of the dressing room vanity, scored off and removed the metal part and all the electronics, and we took a coat hanger and made a pedestal. We then used the bulb as a fucking cauldron to smoke our meth. Bare minimum, all I needed was a piece of tinfoil and a Bic pen. I'd pull out the guts of the pen and turn it into a plastic tube, and inhale smoke from the meth heated on the foil that way. Whatever. I'd have to run out of a lot of options before I'd put it in my nose.

My escalating meth use, not surprisingly, did no favors to my already precarious marriage. It was easier to hide when I was just snorting a little here and there, maybe when my wife was out of town. I'd get a little ten-dollar bag; it was like nothing. But I was on my way to pretty good full-tilt drug addiction. It just fucking gets you, grabs you by the neck, and won't let go. But even when I was smoking it, I'd do my best to keep it a secret. At night, I'd pretend I was going to sleep—like I fell asleep on the couch—but I wasn't really asleep. I was wide-awake until I heard someone getting up, and then I'd lie down like I was asleep. It was deceptive, it was fucking dishonest, and it sucked. There was that guilt rising up again like bile.

I did my best to at least maintain a veneer of normalcy for the sake of my family. We moved out of our rental house in El Sobrante and bought our first house in Sacramento. A family friend owned it and basically let us do a rent-to-own deal. And since I wasn't playing any gigs, I got a job working for a construction company, making fifteen dollars an hour. Day-to-day, my addiction required constant attention, but my "sneaky" smoking didn't really get me high so much as maintain a level of stasis. I didn't even feel that spun, and I didn't look that spun. I was smoking just to kind of maintain normalcy. I was in the office every single day, and they didn't know. Meth became like my fucking coffee after a while. I had friends who were completely spun, and they slept every fucking night. They'd wake up and hit the pipe and go about their day and work a day job, and then they'd go to sleep. It can become kind of normal.

But as much as I may have thought at the time that I was covering my tracks, my marriage was suffering. There had been infidelity on my part, and as a drug addict, I wasn't really the best father or husband I could be. I, in essence, broke up my family. When we split, she got the house, and I, at age thirty-six, moved back in with my parents.

Welcome back to San Pablo.

CHAPTER 18
IN FLAMES

FIRE CAN OFFER DESTRUCTION, AND IT CAN OFFER RENEWAL. IT'S BEEN A bearer of both in my life. When you're staring at a torch flame inches from your face as it slowly turns the meth rock in your glass pipe into a vapor you can inhale, there's no renewal, only destruction. Repeated destruction. This fire ultimately brings only bad things. But it's not the sort of destruction that ends with a relatively quick and immediate finality—your house burns down, for instance. This is a slow and measured destruction that over months and years takes not only you down but everyone in your proximity. Your marriage, your band, your health, your sanity, your family. Your everything.

This fire isn't caused by an act of nature—a lightning strike that hits a tree. It's not accidental—a faulty rat-chewed wire that overheats and ignites insulation. This fire is self-inflicted. There were choices I made along the way that led to my meth addiction. Though I couldn't see them at the time, there were probably many off-ramps I could have taken, but my choices led me from razors—cutting up lines on a mirror to be snorted—to fire. Like every kid, I got the standard warning from my parents not to play with fire. But when you're putting a torch to a meth pipe, you're doing exactly that—literally and figuratively—playing with fire in a way that rarely has a happy ending.

The split from my wife effectively allowed me to take my meth addiction to a whole other level. I'd gone pro. There was no need to sneak around in the same way. At this point, I was surrounded by meth heads, including my own siblings. I'm one of five boys and one girl, and all five of us boys were spun out at one point. And we were all jointly spun out; we hung out and smoked meth together. My sister's never done a drug in her fucking life. I'd be surprised if she confided that she'd smoked a joint once. My parents raised us perfectly. We had every advantage, and why we all fell into it, I have no idea.

My brothers and I are super close now, and I think a little bit of our closeness is because we probably spent more time together while spun than we ever did before—and because we all survived. Before that, I was out touring and they were working day jobs. Everybody kind of had their shit together, and we didn't see each other much. And then when I was no longer actively touring, and we were all spun, yeah, I'd bounce from one brother's house to the next, hang out all night. I think it's part of why we're as close as we are today.

Even though I was living with my parents, I don't know if they ever knew I was spun out. They obviously knew some of my brothers were— one of my brothers temporarily experienced homelessness, living under an overpass. But my parents were in denial when it came to their boys. They didn't want to accept that their children were fucked up, especially since it was not how they were raised. My mom's always just denied what sometimes was right in front of her. She would take it personally, like she did something wrong as a parent, and she did nothing wrong. She was and is the greatest mother ever. I had every advantage for a blue-collar, working-class kid in the barrio. I was lucky to have the parents I have.

To feed my addiction, unfortunately, I resorted to some desperate measures. In the early days, the '80s, we'd get a half gram, cut it up on a mirror, and it would fuel our drinking: the whole band, the whole night, one little baggie. Once I started smoking it, though, it got to the point where I'd smoke a half gram myself in half an hour, no problem. There were times when I sold shit, especially CDs, back when they were worth money. I had the entire Frank Zappa catalog. I no longer have the entire Frank Zappa catalog, unfortunately. And like a lot of smart tweakers, I sold enough meth to finance my own drug use. I'd get an eight ball and sell enough to pay off the eight ball to buy the next one, and the rest was mine. As a result, I was now hanging out with some really down-and-out addicts. Though I may have felt some sort of superiority, I can't say I was much better off. Baloff and I would rip on some of these people, like, *Ah, here comes fucking Tenner*, someone who only ever had ten dollars and wanted a ten-dollar bag. We'd pick on him, and Baloff would sell him the world's tiniest ten-dollar bag, and he'd make him smoke it with us and chop out lines for Paul, because Paul never smoked. So Tenner came in and paid ten dollars, got seven dollars' worth, and we smoked and snorted it. No glamour involved at all, it's fucking horrible. I'd smoke with some pretty fucking scuzzy tweakers from the warehouse where Exodus practiced, people who I wouldn't share a bottle or *anything* with now. But who was I to look down on someone else just because I had a decent-looking car that I hadn't been making payments on and was hiding from the repo man? I'd grab their pipe, and if they weren't looking, I might wipe it on my shirt a little bit. But I didn't give a fuck; there were drugs in that pipe. They filled it up. *Awesome, thank you very much. Next.*

When smoking meth, I started learning the joys of staying awake for three days—total sleep deprivation and fucking psychosis. We would start making shit up, crazy shit—changing band names or people's names to be drug related, for instance—and it would fucking go on for hours. Tom and I would do that shit for hours, and we thought it was funny as fuck. But that's what happens when you haven't slept. Something's really funny to you, and it's funny to the other people there, but maybe not so funny to someone else. But it sure was fucking hilarious to us. Next thing you know, we're changing all band names and song titles into Islamic themes because that was the time. So we had Van Halen, "Islamic Punk," and Tom would sing it as Michael McDonald singing "Islamic Punk," and it was fucking hilarious. We were just fucking out of our minds. And sometimes it was fun. Insanity can be fun. It was also very dark, of course, but there were moments, those brief moments, where we were laughing so fucking hard we couldn't breathe and were pissing our pants. We *still* laugh at some of the shit we came up with to this day.

Pornography is also a huge part of being a tweaker. Watching porn is like watching an episode of *The Ellen DeGeneres Show*—it's nothing. You show up to someone's house and there's hard-core porn on the TV, and no one cares. No one's even watching it as if it's hot or a turn-on. It's just *on*. I remember Tom and I watched an episode of *The Montel Williams Show* about meth, and one of the guests was talking about their porn addiction, as well as their meth addiction. Montel goes, "Where there's meth, there's porn." Tom and I looked at each other and went, *That motherfucker's a tweaker!*

In the summer of 2001—three years after Exodus had last played an actual gig together—a longtime friend of the band, Walter Morgan, reached out to me to ask if we would play a benefit concert, Thrash of the Titans, for Testament singer Chuck Billy, who'd been diagnosed with cancer. I was like, *Yeah, sure, I'm down to help a friend. I just need to talk to the other guys.* Though Exodus had never officially broken up, people assumed we were "reuniting" for Chuck's thing. The actual reality was we weren't broken up; we were just strung out on meth. But at least we were still in contact with each other, so I called everybody and asked if they were into it. They were, of course, totally down for it, but we were a mess, and we became messier through the rehearsals for the August 2001 gig. I think over the course of about two weeks, we managed to play our whole set once, and I mean once. We'd play three songs and then stop and get high. Or we'd just get distracted, like tweakers do. We weren't very committed to playing music at that time.

We showed up to the gig, and it was cool seeing a lot of old friends and stuff. There was a big common area where everyone was hanging out, but we kind of hung out in one little room—hiding away from all the other bands—smoking fucking crank in our own little world. We were broke skids at that point. Tom had a Thrash of the Titans tank top, and he sold it to someone to put gas in his car to get home. It was like that. As for our performance that night, we didn't totally suck, I guess. It was a monumental event, and it raised a lot of money for Chuck, but we didn't take it all that seriously, as far as our performance was concerned. We were there to help out, but our heads weren't right. We were obviously more concerned about his health than our own. Thankfully, Chuck survived (and is cancer-free today) but, tragically, one of our own wouldn't.

In early 2002, I got a call that nearly destroyed me. It was Leda, Paul Baloff's girlfriend.

"Gary, you gotta come fast," she said through tears. "Paul's in the hospital. Something really horrible happened."

I got in my car and went to Highland Hospital in Oakland to discover that Paul had had a massive stroke. He'd had a huge brain aneurysm, and the initial assessment seemed dire. They did a CAT scan and looked at it and realized he'd previously had several small strokes. Paul, from the very first time I met him until the end, talked a thousand miles per hour. But later in life, it got to the point where he was very slurry and I could hardly understand him sometimes. He'd say something to me and I'd just nod, *Okay, Pavel,* and I'd had no idea what he'd said. It was easier to do that than to have him repeat it a bunch of times.

Here he was now, silent, with tubes and a ventilator keeping him alive. Because his parents had already passed away and his next of kin was Dorothy, a sister whom he was estranged from, we—Tom, Rick, Leda, Toby Rage, and I—were the only "family" by his side at the hospital. Dorothy was eventually tracked down by our manager (and the thrash scene's mother figure), Debbie Abono, and Dorothy ultimately gave us control over Paul's well-being.

"You guys are his family," Dorothy said. "I haven't spoken to him in many years, so I leave it to you."

The doctors attending to Paul inevitably broke the news that there was no way Paul was going to recover. Tasked with the most painful decision a person can make, we requested that the doctors take him off life support. And because Paul's love of Iron Maiden ran deep, we scheduled for them to "pull the plug" at two minutes to midnight (a reference to Maiden's "2 Minutes to Midnight" song from *Powerslave*). We all went home with the plan to meet back at the hospital at 11:00 p.m. and prepare for the gut-wrenching event. But Paul, like he was always prone to do, destroyed our best-laid plans and didn't make it until then.

His death also destroyed me. I loved that man. In my grief, I released this statement that truly showed the depths of my despair:

Words cannot describe the pain I am feeling, at the sudden and premature loss of Paul. As I sit here at the water's end of San Francisco Bay, I feel as if someone or something has torn my heart out of my body and smashed it on the rocks. Paul was my brother, my spirit, my soul, and he is gone. I wonder how I will ever recover, ever learn what it is to feel alive without him, and for this question, I have no answers. Paul loved Exodus, was Exodus, and we loved him for it and in spite of it. His flame burned bright, so bright, in fact, that in hindsight it was all but impossible to have burned forever. Still, it burns in us and we must never let that flame burn out, lest Paul's legacy and his contributions be forgotten.

During my impending divorce, my pain has been constant, but so has Paul's support. When my depression would occasionally reach its apex, Paul was always there. No words necessary, just Paul taking action. He'd offer a broken stereo receiver and an invite to launch it down the stairs, or a double-bladed axe and something to cleave in half. Therapy through vandalism, I called it! He knew how to bring me back. Yet, I have no way to do the same for him. I love Paul, always have and always will. There is a bond that even his untimely death cannot break, but right now my spirit is broken. The flame in me has died, my spirit torn asunder. I will fight through this. Paul was the ultimate fighter, he fought till the end, and to fight with anything less than his tenacity would be to do his memory an incredible injustice. I miss him, I love him and will keep his memory alive. I only ask that all of you to do the same.

To each and every one of you, from the bottom of my heart I say THANK YOU; Exodus thanks you, and Paul thanks you.

Paul was a genius at mythmaking. We found out after he died that his father *was* Russian, but Paul was born in Highland Hospital in Oakland, and his mother was Dutch. I'm sure neither emigrated out of Russia on horseback. And Paul had never been to Russia in his life. We found all these lies he told that people took for gospel truth. Even us; we thought he was born in Russia. We called him Pavel; we never called him Paul. His birth name was Paul Nicholas Baloff, not Pavel Nikolayevich Balakirshicoff—I have his birth certificate and his death certificate.

Was Paul ever meant to be anything other than the raging— mythmaking—Baloff we all knew and loved? I don't know. It sounds horrible to think it, but maybe some guys aren't meant to become sixty-five years old. Maybe they're meant to go out in a blaze of glory. I'd like to think that if Paul were still around and he had gotten clean, he could still be the Paul that we all knew and loved. But I'm not sure. I don't think he would've ever gotten clean. It was too much, at that point, a part of who he was, a fucking rager. Sober Paul without drugs and alcohol, I don't know what would've happened. Maybe he would've become ten times his former self. It's a big hypothetical.

In the aftermath of his death, we still had to figure out how to handle his remains and the burial. I was a fucking raging, drug-addicted mess and was having to find a way to bury one of my best friends. That was about as depressed as I've ever been in my life. I was completely at a loss how to get anything done. Thankfully, one of our closest friends, Pam Peters-Behrhorst (formerly Pam Peters), was instrumental in helping us take care of all that. We set up a fundraiser at the DNA Lounge and held an auction. A lot of people from the scene contributed items, like Johnny Tempesta and Chuck Billy, and we were able to raise the money to put Paul at rest. A friend of ours worked in a funeral home, and they took care of the cremation. And we buried him. It was hard times. He died February 2, 2002, and I continued to spin myself out. Nothing changed. I didn't wise up. I had crawled into a glass pipe. I'd buried more friends before I was forty than just about anyone I've ever known. And none of it straightened me out. I was still smoking as much meth as ever.

CHAPTER 19

DEATHAMPHETAMINE

FTER PLAYING THE BENEFIT FOR CHUCK BILLY IN AUGUST 2001, Exodus had actually started booking a few gigs, including some that
were scheduled not long after Paul passed in early February 2002.
We were supposed to play two nights at the Shack in Anaheim—
like we were actually in any position to do a multi-night stand anywhere—
but we had the shows booked, and we didn't want to cancel them. I spoke
to Zetro, and because the shows were in Anaheim, and it just so happened
he was going to Anaheim with his family to go to Disneyland that weekend, he agreed to play the gigs with us. He went and did the family thing
during the day, and when he left the park, he came to the club and sang.
At that point, Zetro was working a day job, was a family man and all
that. We, on the other hand, were blowing pipeful after pipeful of crank.
The shows were emotional so soon after Paul's death, but it felt good to
play with Zetro again. To say the shows in Anaheim went really well is
taking some definite artistic liberties. We probably had 100–150 people
at the Shack, but Zetro stepped right in with zero rehearsal, which he's

always able to do. He remembered everything and sang every part like he'd been singing it for ages, even though his last gig with Exodus had been in 1993. But it felt good, and we decided to keep doing it.

When we were in Anaheim, we met Paul's sister, Dorothy, for the first time, who lived in Southern California. She gave us some childhood photos of Paul from elementary school, including one where he's in a little cowboy outfit, really cute stuff. It was like, *Baloff was a baby? We didn't know that!* There was a whole other side to him that we never knew about. Paul found out later in life, not long before he died, that he had two, much older half brothers from his father's first marriage. One half brother, who died in 2013, ended up in the upper echelon of the scientific community . . . and Paul Baloff sang on *Bonded by Blood*. Talk about the apple falling far from the tree. His brother's name was Nicholas Baloff. He graduated from UC Berkeley with a master's degree; he went to MIT, all this shit. I'll take the Paul Baloff vocals any day over accolades and money. Dorothy also told us that their mother and father had died of a heart attack and a stroke, so Paul had a predisposition for it—things we didn't know.

The year went by, and I was just spun and spun and spun. None of us changed our ways in the wake of Paul's death. If anything, it probably increased the depths of my addiction. With Zetro back in the fold, though, we did have the opportunity to play a couple of summer festivals, including Wacken in Germany, and book a European tour for late in the year. For Wacken, we just flew in for the one show in August. The gig was pretty rough, though. We weren't very well rehearsed, to say the least. At least during the Baloff reunion in '97, when we played Dynamo, we were fucking tight. We were playing songs that were second nature to us, *Bonded by Blood* stuff. At Wacken, we opened up with "The Last Act of Defiance," which is a feat of right-hand strength to play on your best day. We went out, and we tried to give it our best, but it wasn't our finest performance. It wasn't a train wreck, just wasn't great. We didn't make an impression one way or another. We didn't leave people going, *God, they stunk*, but no one was walking away going, *Exodus stole the show, that's for damn sure.*

For the European tour in December, since we were smoking a significant amount of meth at this point and scoring it in Europe wasn't a realistic option, we decided to smuggle a huge bag of it in Rick's guitar pedalboard. Euro crank was shit anyway; we were "shard" snobs, the killer stuff that looks like pieces of broken glass. We arrived in England and had a free day in our hotel. In one day, we smoked the whole fucking bag. I was sitting in my hotel room scalloping the fretboard on my ESP Flying V guitar with a wood file—a big pile of sawdust all around me—tweaking out of my mind, grinding my teeth. Literally doing woodwork on a hotel bed! Just like that, the drugs were gone before the tour even started.

Our first show was in Thessaloniki, and since we were completely out of meth, we all became completely dope-sick. Withdrawing from meth fucking sucks. It's not like heroin or alcohol where you're having this shaking craving, it's just that your brain won't turn on. Your body won't get up. You're used to this turbocharged jolt. We'd get up and smoke a bowl of meth instead of having a cup of joe. So there we were, splayed out in the dressing room, sleeping on top of our luggage, and just a disaster, barely able to get up to perform. We played Thessaloniki and then traveled to Athens, via bus, with our tour mates in the Haunted. One of the members of the Haunted, Patrik Jensen, had a female friend with him, and she ended up sitting in a window seat next to Tom. Tom was dope-sick as hell, all six foot three of him passed out and leaning on her. She was wide-awake the whole trip, pushed against the window and too polite to say, *Get the fuck off me, dude.* Tom and I still laugh about this one.

After the Greece dates, we flew to the UK to start our Christmas festival tour. I was sleeping constantly and could barely function, but every day, I felt a little bit better. *Human*, even. I got to the point where I wasn't sleeping all day, I was kind of up . . . on my own, with no stimulants. I started feeling really good. I managed to get through the shows, and then they got better and better as the tour went on. I felt like a new man. Everyone had their own different level of recovery, though. I think Rick struggled more. We all were clean on that tour only due to lack of availability. Don't get me wrong—we *tried* to get meth. At one point, someone gave us a bit of bad Euro crank and I tried to smoke it on some foil, but it wouldn't burn. It just turned black. It was awful. So I did attempt to destroy my sobriety once on that tour, to no avail. Failure finally wins.

Returning home, though, would be the ultimate test. The one bit of meth that I didn't smuggle over to Europe was a rock a friend of mine had given me that was bigger than a golf ball. Okay, so it was more than a "bit." Anyway, this was what we used to refer to as our "get-back," when you leave some dope for when you get home, so you have something waiting for you when you get back. I left it in one of my road cases in our rehearsal room before we went on tour. A friend picked me up at the airport, because I no longer had a car, and brought me to the warehouse where we rehearsed. Before we went on tour, I'd called the repo company that had been trying to track me down and told them where they could find my car. It was the only new car I'd ever owned, and I hadn't been able to make payments for months. I couldn't afford it anymore, it had no insurance, and I was on unemployment and wasn't making any money on tour. I had to climb over a mountain of equipment to get to where I hid my get-back rock so no fucking tweakers who had access to our space would find it. I held it in my hand but knew I wasn't going to smoke it. I was a month clean, and I felt great.

I went to one of the people who lived at the warehouse who had a car and his own bad habits, and I said, *Give me a ride home for this?* I was trading him a huge fucking amount of drugs for about five dollars in gas. And he was like, *Fuck yeah!* That was the last time I held meth in my hand. I got a ride home and never fucking looked back. The biggest benefit I ever got from meth was a ride home. I got home and I didn't do it again—I never did another line, never smoked another bowl.

It took me most of a year to realize that I didn't want to follow in Paul's footsteps. I had been digging myself in a hole before he died, and then that hole got really dark with his death. The hole got deeper. I was digging down to the earth's mantle. I always told myself I didn't want to be a forty-year-old tweaker. I had a friend back in the high school backyard party days whose grandfather sold meth. I remember going to his grandfather's house, and his grandfather, who probably wasn't a whole lot older than I am now, would smoke meth. We'd be howling, like, *Look at that old guy hit that pipe, damn! That's funny as fuck!* Under no circumstances did I want to be the old guy with a pipe.

And when I eventually climbed out of my deep, dark hole, an amazing thing happened: I found my creativity.

I started writing riffs again. And a lot of them.

It was like, *Wow, I'm not lost here. I can do this again.*

I'd extinguished one flame—the crank pipe—and reignited another, Exodus.

PART III

REDEMPTION
2003—PRESENT

CHAPTER 20
FORWARD MARCH

Quitting meth didn't make all my problems disappear. I was going through a very unpleasant divorce (mostly of my own making), I had no car, no job, and no money, and I was trying to figure out how I was going to navigate playing in a band with meth users. I was also having to come to grips with the damage my addiction (and past behavior) had done. I made a lot of mistakes. I broke up my family.

If I'm being completely honest, a lot of my worst behavior in the past wasn't during or due to my meth addiction. I just got caught up in the clichéd rock and roll lifestyle, which probably boiled down to a total lack of self-confidence. I was trying to boost myself up by living that lifestyle and was needing people to praise me and tell me I was awesome and good-looking and a killer guitar player, and that I was special in every fucking possible way when I really didn't feel very special at all at times. Sometimes I'd look in the mirror and didn't like what was looking back.

Some people make changes and quit drugs because they have to. I did it because I wanted to. I learned from my mistakes and felt fucking humiliated by some of the things I did and the things I did to other people. I looked back on it with real regret and felt genuine sadness. It was enough to make me never want to do that shit again. Yeah, I made a lot of mistakes, and I owned up to them, and I committed my life to never being that guy again.

My ex-wife, on the other hand, made a completely different commitment after our divorce, one that didn't exactly sit well with me: She became a born-again Christian. She had always been a believer, but she became super dedicated to Christ, and while I respected *her* choice, I didn't like the sudden addition of God and Jesus into the family dynamic. As a nonbeliever, I wanted my children to have a choice. If they decided at some point they wanted to go to church and dedicate themselves to Jesus, that was fine. I just wanted *them* to choose, not someone else. It's all about choice for me. I support people's choice to believe; I just ask they support mine *not* to. My mom believes, and that's okay. I get the appeal of Christianity. People have questions in life, and sometimes it's easier to find one big blanket answer to all your mysteries: God did it; it's God's will.

I avoided any "higher power" discussions in my recovery from meth addiction by eschewing Narcotics Anonymous or any other twelve-step programs. That wasn't for me. Looking back, I'm shocked that I recovered as well as I did. But it took work, and it took willpower. Even after the debacle of (almost) the entire band being dope-sick and going through withdrawal on our last European tour, *I* felt creatively invigorated, and there was no question that we were going to keep moving forward. After writing very little new material over the previous decade—except for what I did briefly with Wardance—years of unrealized riffs came pouring out, some of the best shit I've ever written. The volcano erupted, blew off that outer crust layer. Out came the lava, the pyroclastic flow, wiping out everything. A thrash metal Vesuvius!

Since I no longer owned a car, everything in my life was a lot more challenging, especially seeing my kids, who still lived most of the time in Sacramento with their mom. Just to have a day and a half with them, I'd have to ride the bus to a BART station and then take a train. Then I'd call my dad to pick me up from the station, and I'd drive *him* home. I'd take his truck to get the girls and then do it all in reverse at the end of the weekend. And even though the riffs were overflowing, getting to rehearsal with Exodus to turn them into songs was an equally tricky task that required biking and BART rides, all with my guitar strapped to my back, which was not easy. Then I'd have to walk into what was basically a meth den, the same warehouse where I used to smoke with people who I wouldn't share a soda with. There'd be dudes hanging out in the hallways smoking meth, but I'd put blinders on and go to my rehearsal room and jam. My own band members—Rick and Tom—were still high, but they respected me enough to not do it in front of me. After rehearsal, I'd get the fuck out and go home. Riffs got me through it. As I realized I could write riffs—really good riffs—again, I enjoyed it, and I didn't want to jeopardize that. I clung to my sobriety. I felt like I had a second chance, third and fourth chance, however fucking many times, and I wasn't gonna lose it. I felt good fucking not being spun out. And I now liked the guy I saw in the mirror.

In 2003, there were no labels—major, indie, whatever—lining up to give Exodus a record deal. We'd been mostly dormant for the better part of a decade, and for the brief period we reunited with Baloff in the '90s, all we managed to put out was a live album. Plus, thrash metal was mostly kind of seen as passé in the metal world in the new millennium. Hard to imagine, right? In this climate, we figured that we were going to have to claw and scratch our way back on our own. We were confident in the material we were writing; the first seven came easily, and I felt like songs like "Scar Spangled Banner" were some of the best I'd ever written. Fortunately, there were people around us who still believed in us and were willing to help us make a new album. The drum tracks would be recorded at Prairie Sun—paid for by our good friend "Hippie Rob" Schatzer—and everything else was recorded for no money up front at our friend Shad Gibson's Tsunami Recordings in Moss Beach. Andy Sneap, who'd worked on our live album, even flew out on his own with his gear to record it. He'd only heard some cassette recordings of the new material, but he knew I was clean, and he knew it was going to be a special record. (We also sold our *Impact Is Imminent* stage backdrop to help finance the album. Someone gave us like $1,000 for this forty-foot, hand-painted backdrop, which I'm sure I could get more than that for it now.)

The only catch was, to get the studio time, we needed to get in there and do it before we had a full album's worth of material written and arranged. So to further flesh it out, we included two Wardance songs—"Sealed with a Fist" and "Throwing Down"—as well as a fresh version of "Impaler," from the Kirk Hammett days. With a little more time, I could've written three more songs, but we figured, *Let's fucking do it*, and we went with what we had. It was the first time we'd recorded anything from that era since the original demo. The recording process went surprisingly smoothly. Tom and I started off by laying down his tracks at Prairie Sun. Owner Mark "Mooka" Rennick was nervous to have us back after our outrageous partying during the making of *Bonded by Blood*, but we assured him we were not those guys anymore. He said during the *Bonded* sessions that we left a trail of destruction so great that it had to be admired! This time, we left the place cleaner than when we got there. That didn't mean that we didn't have some fun, it was just good clean fun—sometimes at Andy Sneap's expense. Since he was staying with us at Prairie Sun, when he'd fall asleep at night, we'd slowly roll a fully fucking plugged-in Mesa Boogie half stack into his bedroom, and I'd bust into "Riff Raff" by AC/DC at full volume and jump on his bed. Our version of getting "punked" was "You've been Riff Raffed!"

For the rest of the recording, we all lived at Tsunami. Moss Beach is south of San Francisco (by Half Moon Bay) and about thirty miles from Oakland, so we were close to home, but also just far enough to focus on making a really good record. At every step of the way, we were helped by the kindness of others. Our friend Bill Harrell, who had a warehouse space next to Shad's studio, would sometimes make us meals and let us shower at his place. He also was generous with his weed! Another key benefactor in this process was my longtime guitar tech in the '90s, Tom Montano, who loaned us his little Volkswagen Jetta, a piece of shit we called the Silver Bullet. Neither our manager, Steve Warner (who was as out of his mind as any of us) nor I owned a car at the time, so when we were getting ready to do the guitar tracking and realized my number one modded Marshall amp needed to be repaired, Tom set us up with the Silver Bullet. This amp was just so fucking killer—modded by the late, great Todd Langner—but it was shorting out a little bit. If I whacked it on the top, it would correct itself, but we decided that we needed to get it properly fixed to make the album because it was too unreliable. So we crammed the thing into the Silver Bullet and headed to a place in San Francisco called Magic Music Machines to get it fixed. The tech at Magic Music did a real rush job for us, and while he was doing that, we went to an ATM to get some cash. By the time we got back to the car with the amp, it'd been towed! The Silver Bullet was gone, and we were standing there on the street holding my Marshall, with no idea where the car had been taken. We finally figured out which impound lot it was being held at, and our only option to get it was to hop in a taxi with this heavy-as-fuck amp and get the piece-of-shit Silver Bullet, which we drove back down to Tsunami. It wouldn't be an Exodus record without a little bit (or a lot) of drama.

Tom and Rick were still using meth during the making of the new album, but Tom killed it on his drumming, and Rick killed it on his solos until he ran out of a little bit of steam toward the end of the recording process. But I did all the heavy lifting for him, and I didn't complain. One thing I always maintained through the time period when I was clean and Rick and Tom were not, was patience. You can't go from being a pipe-hitting meth addict and then all of a sudden start passing judgment on others. I always tried to counsel whenever possible, but I never passed judgment or wagged a finger at either of them because I was right there not long before. Someone's got to lead. If you lead musically, you can also lead with your sobriety.

Now, when I mention "sobriety," I should clarify that: I was off meth. But the entire band hadn't exactly slowed down on our alcohol intake and other proclivities. Once in a blue moon, I'd do cocaine if it was offered to me. There was never any chance it would become a habit, because, to be honest, I hated it. I might do it when I was drunk, and even then it didn't work so well. If I did it when I was sober, it sucked; I'd just sit there grinding my teeth.

The pranks continued, of course, because Andy needed to get his revenge. We'd all be in our sleeping bags in the studio, sleeping in front of the drums, and fucking all of a sudden, I'd hear this hum happening, and it was Andy turning the amps on, *brauuuugh!!!!* We had a good time. For Andy, working with Exodus was like being in a living cartoon, for sure. Because it was fucking lunacy, but in a good way, not like in the old days, when it was more about destruction. We were fucking hilarious. And we were fucking cracking jokes on each other, just a really, really ridiculously silly bunch of fucking people.

After many years away from the studio, it was nice to have this camaraderie of working and playing together while creating new music again.

We had a good time—pranks and all—and we were thrilled with how the album came out; it's remarkable how killer it is considering how it was made. I was thrilled to be back making meaningful metal again after what, up to that point, appeared to be a career of missed opportunities and wasted chances. I didn't want to be a footnote: that guy who was one of the pioneers—he and his band—of thrash metal. I had firmly been in the where-are-they-now category, and where I had been was not good: tweaking in a warehouse somewhere. Fucking awful, right? Terrible. Who wants to be remembered like that? I was going to make damn sure that wasn't my legacy.

We took the album we'd named *Tempo of the Damned*—recorded, mixed, and ready to go—and set out to find a label to release it. We figured it would be an easier sell going in with a finished record, since a label wouldn't have to advance any recording money. We approached German label Nuclear Blast, and thankfully, they listened without any judgment regarding our past behavior and performance. There was none of this "Exodus has a history of being a bunch of fuckups and drug addicts, and should we give them a deal?" We handed them the record, and they listened to it and were like, *Fucking holy shit! That's one of the best things we've ever heard!* They had gathered in their conference room in Donzdorf, cranked it, and were just crushed. They couldn't believe what they were hearing. It was fucking amazing, and it was the beginning of our partnership with the label that lasted two decades.

It definitely helped morale to get back in the game with a label that had so much (genuine) enthusiasm for what we'd created. There was none of this standing-ovation-in-a-boardroom bullshit. They were fully into it, all the way from Markus Staiger, the president and founder of Nuclear Blast, to Jaap Waagemaker and Andy Siry and everybody. They were headbangers. They loved *Tempo* and put the wheels in motion to promote the hell out of it. Leading to the release of the album in early 2004, their publicity team had me doing interviews nonstop. I don't think I've ever done as many interviews as I did promoting *Tempo*. They flew Tom and me out to Europe to do a whole press tour—Europe had always been our bread and butter—and we went to England and to Italy and bounced around. Nuclear Blast really pumped it. It made me wonder why Century Media couldn't have done the same sort of thing seven years prior for Baloff's return.

CHAPTER 21
TOURING FOR PENNIES

RUTH BE TOLD, 2004 WASN'T A GREAT TIME TO RESURRECT A LEGACY thrash band. As stoked as our label and we were about *Tempo of the Damned*, I can assure you we weren't hopping back on some bandwagon that was suddenly taking off again. Our timing, in typical Exodus fashion, wasn't great. A lot of our peers in Metallica, Megadeth, Slayer, Anthrax, and Testament had gone through some shit—some personal, some personnel—around the turn of the century and were finding their feet again in various ways. There was a lot of shake-up going on: new members, new sound, new record labels. We were hopeful that there was still a receptive market out there for what we were doing, but there was no obvious evidence that was the case. Musical trends come and go, and maybe our thrash return was a little premature. We really didn't know, but we were about to find out.

Positive record reviews and plaudits from metal journalists are great, but the real gauge for a band's success is what kind of business you do on the road. The first show of our spring headlining tour,

April 10, 2004, at 32 Bleu in Colorado Springs, wasn't encouraging. The venue had a capacity of about 750, and there were a total of 18 paid attendees. The people who *were* there were appreciative. They were no doubt thrilled they got to see "Deliver Us to Evil" up close and personal with no fear of stage divers landing on them. But we finished the set, I handed my guitar to my tech, bolted off the front of the stage—right through all 18 people—and headed straight to the bar. I ordered a double schnapps and a beer and fucking just tried to wash the memory away of the hour and a half I'd just spent playing what amounted to a sound check. It sucked, but I never gave up, because it was the only thing I knew how to do, and I was doing it again, and I was doing it without meth. We may have still drank like fucking madmen, but I was drug-free. Tom did his last bump of meth on this tour, but Rick was still using on the down-low, though everyone always performed really well.

There were some good shows and some not-so-good ones. In bigger cities, like Chicago, we'd get a solid turnout. Then we'd go to like Omaha and play a place we'd packed in years past, like Ranch Bowl, a place we always loved playing because if we got there the night before, we could go bowling for free. Back in the late '80s and early '90s, they'd let us go in the cooler and just help ourselves to beer. When we played there in 2004, it was worse than Colorado Springs. I think there might've been about ten people there, so we just started jamming Sabbath riffs. Ever since then, our whole joke has been, if we don't think a show is going to be good, we're like, *All right, I've got the set list: two songs, Sabbath jam, and out.* When there are ten fucking people at a show, the venue wants you gone sooner rather than later because they're not making any money, and the quicker they can send their staff home, the better. *Can you cut some songs?* they'd ask. *Can you play only like an hour tonight, because we want to let everybody go. We pay these guys by the hour.*

Fans would come up to me on this tour and say they were thrilled with the album. They're like, *This is one of the best thrash albums ever made.* And they'd say, *How does it feel to be at the forefront of this thrash metal renaissance?* But I had just played for 10 paid people the previous night, so it was like, *What renaissance? I'll tell you when I see it.* It was fucking awful. We were playing for nobody. A good show was 150 people, maybe 200. That would be a crowd. We were making no money. Well, most of us weren't. To get Zetro back in the band, we'd made a deal with him regarding his salary. Since he was leaving behind a proper day job and now had a family, he had to be paid what he made at work to tour with us. So *he* was making good money, and we were making no money. But that was the agreement we had. He couldn't just leave his job and go back to starving with the rest of us. Post-Exodus, he had gone on to create a nine-to-five life. So he had bills that had to be paid, and we understood it. But at the same time, it was hard not to have a little resentment when I was making nothing. My bills at the time were nothing, so I guess it somehow balanced out.

No matter how discouraging this tour might have been—our first in years—I wasn't going to be deterred. I knew nothing was going to be handed to us. We played really well on the tour, and I was proud of that. I felt reborn; I was killing it. I had a clear head and knew I just had to keep going, never stop. The alternative was to go back to working whatever fucking menial job I could find, because I didn't have any job skills. So I wasn't done, far from it. I still had metal to offer.

As much as I had cleaned up from meth, I still had the residual psyche of an addict, which I wasn't really conscious of until I was pulling out onto a busy street in front of where we rehearsed in Oakland and narrowly avoided what could have been a catastrophic collision. I was driving the used van I'd managed to buy with some of the advance money from Nuclear Blast, and as I was pulling out to turn left, a speeding car came flying around a curve. By some miracle, it only managed to leave a slash of paint on my bumper as they skinned me. Another half a second and it would have been a horrific accident. I panicked. I didn't even see if they pulled over, I just hung a turn and fled. I was taking as many side streets as I could, in a full panic to get out of there. I don't even think they saw what I was driving. I got home to my place in Oakland on Hillmont Drive and took a Scotch pad and scrubbed their yellow paint off my silver bumper. It didn't dent my van; it just took the slightest kiss of paint.

I could have just pulled over when it happened, but didn't, even though I had insurance and I was clean then. A tweaker would run, and I hadn't been clean for very long, so I still had that flight response. It was a "panic and run" residue of the methamphetamines; it told me to get out of there. It was that flight instinct that I had from being a meth addict for so many years. I was so used to running from the chance of being busted for anything, I didn't even stop to think if I was even at fault. I was super broke at the time, and some of the panic may have been related to whether an accident—even a small one—would hurt my ability to pay my insurance if the rates went up. Maybe it would have made me uninsurable and I'd lose my ability to drive. It was the paranoia of my former tweaker mind. So I ran.

It was around this time I learned another hard lesson—that not everyone's situation and investment in the band was like mine. We were no longer a bunch of twenty-two-year-olds—when some of us were still living at home—raising hell, with no significant bills, commitments, or relationships to attend to. We were in our forties now. There were kids and wives and ex-wives and mortgages and rent and all kinds of serious things. Our lives were more complicated, and we made decisions regarding the band that were influenced in a greater degree by things *outside* the band. But those things were important, too. I understand that now. It was hard to grasp, though, when Zetro bowed out of our planned Mexico and South America dates right before we were set to leave for Mexico. At the time, we were fucking furious when this went down. These were going to be very profitable gigs for all of us, but Zetro's home situation had changed, and he was trying to stay married. He was given ultimatums, and he chose not to go.

A lot of nasty stuff was said at the time that I'm not proud of. I aired a lot of dirty laundry in a public way because of my frustration. Just when I felt like Exodus were making progress—we'd done a great European tour with HateSphere in the summer—this happened at a very inopportune time. So Zetro was out. *Now* I understand the decision he made back then. I would have maybe understood more, at the time, if he'd said, *I'm doing these shows, and then I'm done.* It was only a couple of weeks.

Cue a mad scramble to find someone to cover for him, because we *weren't* going to cancel these gigs. On extremely short notice, we got Matt Harvey, of Exhumed, to fill in in Mexico City on Saturday, September 11, 2004, but we had to reschedule the South America shows we were supposed to play later that week for late October, just before we were set to do a US tour with Megadeth. Matt did a great job in Mexico City, all things considered, but we tapped our friend Steev Esquivel (of Skinlab) to go to Brazil with us.

What was supposed to be a triumphant and lucrative return to South America, playing upper-echelon venues, was anything but. The proposed Argentina gig couldn't be rescheduled, and in São Paulo, Brazil, instead of playing the (now-closed) Via Funchal, which was fucking insane, we ended up playing some giant warehouse, going on at 3:00 in the morning. In lieu of flying from city to city, we were in vans wherever we went in Brazil. Only the first show in Rio de Janeiro offered a little light relief, at least for some of us. Steev was still learning all the lyrics, so he had cheat sheets printed real big and had them laminated so they could be reused over and over. During the first song, Rick

Hunolt grabbed 'em and threw 'em into the crowd. Steev was like, *Oh no, my fucking entire set just went in the crowd! Rick, what are you doing, dude?* We were laughing so hard, and everybody was laughing except for Steev. He didn't think it was very funny.

The last show in Brazil was in Recife, which should never have been booked, because the very next night was going to be our first show on the Megadeth tour in LA. It was a no-win situation. We did not have time to play the fucking show. No way. We had flights to catch. We started playing before the venue opened the doors, and the crowd was still outside. We got through five songs and then told the people who'd managed to get in that we had to leave for the airport. I felt terrible, because our fans had paid their hard-earned money. As we were leaving, people were throwing beer cans at our van. We were fucking being booed. They were, like, *Fuck you, motherfuckers, fuck you!* We were sitting in the van, our heads in our hands. What could we do?

That was a fucking low moment in Exodus's history. The sad reality was that our flight to LA ended up being delayed for hours, so we could have finished our set and made it to the airport in plenty of time. But hindsight is always twenty-twenty, and amid all the chaos and turmoil that was happening in the band, we knew we couldn't miss the kickoff of the Megadeth tour.

DAVE MUSTAINE, BEING AN OLD FRIEND AND A BLOOD BROTHER, WAS always that one guy who would take Exodus out on tour, even with the reputation that we had. He would fucking extend his hand to help the band. Coincidentally, this was sort of Megadeth's return to the fray, as well. Dave was coming back from the nerve damage to his arm he sustained in 2002 that (temporarily) caused him to disband Megadeth. But he was back with a new album, *The System Has Failed*, and a new lineup. So he was kind of rebuilding his audience, too.

Steev Esquivel agreed to do the US tour with us, even though it was just temporary. It wasn't meant to be a long-term fit, because Skinlab were doing really well at the time, especially in Europe. Since Exodus were still rebuilding our own audience after a long absence, probably half the crowd didn't know he hadn't been in the band for years. And honestly, he did a great job. He's a killer vocalist, different from anything you've heard in Exodus, but it worked for me, and he was a good friend. And more importantly, him stepping in allowed to us to keep going and moving forward.

The Megadeth/Exodus pairing was a perfect bill for reestablishing both bands as thrash titans once again. Unfortunately, there was a third band on the bill, Earshot—kind of a Tool-sounding band—who did not fit the vibe at all, neither musically nor personality-wise. They were fucking egomaniac fucks, because they had one radio fucking hit. And they were dicks, too. We were the nicest guys in the world to them, and we heard them talking shit about us. We could hear them in the dressing room one night just mocking us, "Anybody could play that jugga jugga jugga jugga shit." They, on the other hand, did the drum solo from Led Zeppelin's "Moby Dick" as part of their set. Super original. And the singer had his James Brown / Elvis moment where he had his rug out on the stage, and he'd be pouring water on himself. During the drum solo, one of the crew guys would come up and drape a fucking towel over him. So lame. Even their crew guys were bad clichés. One of the guitar techs was one of those rock star techs with a big cowboy hat, and he had every laminate from every tour he's ever been on on his waist. It's like his "résumé"; that's what we call that, when a guy's got every laminate. Thankfully, partway through the tour, Earshot bailed. They went home—our driver saw them take a left when the route to the next city was to the right—because they were getting stomped, like stomped into the ground. We were all happy to see them go. Fuck those dudes. I wonder where they work now.

As the reigning kings of misadventure, this tour wouldn't have been complete without the kind of calamity that seems too far-fetched to believe. The day before we played the Warfield in San Francisco, Steev hilariously (at least for us, not so much for him) had a bad hair gel mishap. Some of that fucking hair gel's got a lot of alcohol and shit in it; it's not meant to be used before you go onstage and get all sweaty. It got in his eyes, and it burned his fucking eyes. He had to have them flushed with tubes, and he had to wear bandages. Perfect timing, just before our hometown gig. Since we weren't on good terms with Zetro, we asked Testament vocalist Chuck Billy to fill in at the last minute. Chuck came out and did the best he could on like a day's notice, and because he wasn't going to sit on the sidelines entirely, Steev sang some of the songs, as well.

The next night, we were set to play the Palladium in LA, and I felt like we needed to make a change. Not with Steev, though; I needed a new guitar tech. The one I had I'd never worked with in my life, didn't know his name, and it was not working out. So because we were still in California and he was a Northern California dude, I was like, *We've got to get rid of this guy; we can get him home easy from here. Let's just rip the Band-Aid off now.* A longtime friend of the band, Jeff Hickey, who was living in LA at the time, said he knew a guy named Rob Dukes that he'd recommend. Rob came out, pink Mohawk and all, and was ready to get on the bus right away, so he got the job. He ended up being the guitar tech for the entire band.

We did the whole Megadeth tour with him, and we fucking hit it off right away. At the end of the tour, when it came time for us to look for a singer, Rob threw his name in the hat. He'd already hopped onstage with us on the final night of the tour in Portland, Oregon, and sang "Deranged," so we had a pretty good idea of what he was capable of. Rob will tell you he got the job because he was the first guy who showed up, but he showed up and was killer. And just as importantly, we already loved the guy. I've always been one to want to look within my group of friends when it comes to adding people to the band—whether it's temporary, like Matt Harvey or Steev Esquivel, or permanent. Unfortunately, this was something I'd need to do more of as I struggled to keep the band together and maintain whatever small amount of momentum we had.

CHAPTER 22
GOING, GOING, GONE

For the second time in Exodus's career, Tom needed to exit the band. The anxiety issues that led to him leaving in 1989 had reared their head again on the Megadeth tour. He felt like he was no longer able to handle the anxiety and tour at the pace that I wanted Exodus to do. I always wanted to tour; it was the only thing I knew how to do. It wasn't going to work for Tom, though, so for the second time, I had to wish him well and find a new drummer. Tom and I had played together since I was seventeen years old, so we are completely simpatico with each other musically. Other drummers have different ideas, and quite often they work, but with Tom, he'd play *exactly* what I heard in my head when I wrote a riff in the first place because I'd be writing riffs to his drumming.

Before he left, Tom had recorded a five-song demo with us for Nuclear Blast, so they could hear Rob Dukes's vocals before they gave us the advance to make our next album, which would be called *Shovel Headed Kill Machine*. They originally signed a re-formed Exodus with

Zetro fronting the band, so it was understandable that they'd want to hear this totally unknown newcomer that we had brought in. Once they listened to the demo, though, they gave us the go-ahead to proceed. Tom stepped aside at that point so that the new record could be made with a drummer who'd be touring with us.

To find Tom's replacement, I once again looked locally to drummers we knew or already had a relationship or friendship with. Former Forbidden and Slayer drummer Paul Bostaph had been touring with Testament in 2004, but since that band was re-forming its "classic" lineup to do a European tour, he was the odd man out. I'd known Bostaph forever from the Bay Area scene, and Forbidden had supported Exodus on a tour in '89. We knew that he was a free agent when we were getting ready to record *Shovel Headed*, so we asked if he wanted to join, and he accepted. It was good timing for once on Exodus's part, because our timing's always been horrible. Paul brought a different type of drumming to Exodus—a lot of rapid-fire, sick double bass. There's always been *some* of that kind of drumming on Exodus's records going back to *Bonded by Blood*, but it was usually to build a key part. It was never like, *I'm gonna play double kick over this fast part for the entire verse*. We worked on the new material with Bostaph for two weeks, but Rick stopped showing up for rehearsals.

I can't say I was surprised. Sad, yes, but Rick was still working on himself, and he had some family obligations to attend to. Even when we were recording the demo with Rob for Nuclear Blast, he wasn't around much and only contributed solos; I recorded all the rhythm tracks. So I didn't freak out when, while we were in Trident Studios with engineer Juan Urteaga, Rick said he was leaving the band. I wasn't in a position to freak out. I had to fucking keep going. What was I gonna do, scrap the record? I had no choice but to just figure it out. And that was how it was with all of it. With vocals, just figure it out. I had to do it. I never wanted a bunch of lineup changes. Exodus's lineup history reads like a football team, or at least a basketball team with a deep bench. It's a lot of guys. I was now the last remaining member from the *Bonded by Blood* lineup. And three of the musicians who would play on *Shovel Headed* were brand-new to the band. It was a trying time, just fucking one domino falling after another.

It was also weird not having Rick there shredding in the studio with me, because other than the time we broke up, he was my six-string partner in crime through it all—we were the H-Team. We found a replacement, though, who fit in seamlessly. We didn't need to audition Lee Altus, who'd played in Bay Area thrashers Heathen and was a lifelong Exodus fan and a friend from the early days. I just called him and asked if he wanted to join the band and come in and play some solos. I've known Lee longer than I've known Rick Hunolt because he and I go back to the Kirk Hammett era of Exodus. Adding Lee was a no-brainer. All the songs were written, the basic tracks were recorded; Lee recorded his solos like a pro. He's been a solid, reliable, and super talented addition ever since.

Rob Dukes was the wild card of the new additions. As an inexperienced front man, he actually had to learn how to be a metal singer, because he blew out his voice the first day he was recording his vocals. That was kind of unsettling because I was like, *Fuck, I just hired this guy, and I'm in the studio for this new record, and the guy can't talk.* As it turned out, though, working with Rob was easy. If I told Rob, *Give me more Baloff,* he'd give me more Baloff. He wouldn't be offended by that. Now, if I wanted some Zetro-isms, I would use different wording. With a guitar player, if you say something like, *Give me a little Mike Amott bend right there*, I'd be like, *All right, I'll try.* I wouldn't be offended. But with a singer, if you start throwing out other singers' names, sometimes they get a little bit tender. Singers are sensitive souls.

Exodus did not have a good track record with matching our album titles to the cover art in a way that worked both conceptually for us and for the label's marketing purposes. We were either too brutal or too obtuse. We finally found the sweet spot on *Shovel Headed Kill Machine,* because the artwork's fucking great. The title came from our former manager, Steve Warner, who'd visited our friend Fozzy (RIP) in Holland. Fozzy owned some pit bulls that were friendly dogs, but one of them had this fucking head the size of an alligator. And Steve's words to describe Fozzy's dog were "It's just a fucking shovel headed kill machine." Exodus always grabbed little humorous bits or whatever from any conversation to use for titles. And that's where the title came from—Fozzy's dog. We had the good sense not to try to picture that literally, so we came up with the concept that appears on the cover—it's super detailed and fucking vicious. I think musically we sounded like that fucking tank.

One benefit we had to this new, untested lineup of Exodus was that everyone was fully available, no stipulations. Jack always wanted to tour, Bostaph was ready to work, Lee was ready to go, and Rob was hungry as fuck for it. We had five guys with nothing preventing us from getting out on the road and staying out as long as we could. And we were out there playing for hardly any money. But things started getting a *little* bit better. Rob Dukes, unfortunately, had to deal with some of the same stuff Zetro did when he replaced Baloff. Occasionally, we'd hear, *Get Zetro back! Fuck Rob Dukes!* There have definitely been factions in the Exodus fan base, but once fans gave Rob a chance and saw how he held his own, all that noise disappeared.

And we did start to see better audiences. The progression was there, for sure, but we still occasionally did horrible, fucking grim shows. But a grim show wasn't ten people, it was fifty. Hey, we were going somewhere. Things just started looking up because there weren't any situations that were pulling the band backward. Money was still a fucking myth, though. We'd heard about it. We understood that it was possible to make money doing music, but it was kind of like Bigfoot or the Loch

Ness Monster: mythical. There was some evidence that it was a real thing, but I hadn't seen it myself. We ended 2005 in Europe in November and December, co-headlining with Hypocrisy. It didn't start on a good note, because the promoter had had a falling-out with his wife, who yanked her financial backing from his company.

We showed up at SFO ready to fly to Europe, but we realized when we got there the promoter hadn't ticketed everybody in our party. Lee's brother jumped in with his credit card and bought us all new tickets, but on departure ten hours later than our original flight. Some of us went home, but some of us were just gonna wait it out at the airport. Bad idea. We spent all ten hours at TGI Friday's and commenced one of the most monumental episodes of alcohol consumption you've ever seen. We dirtied every shot glass and margarita glass in the place. We finally got the call to go to our gate, and before we got on, Lee pounded a three-finger shot of Patrón tequila and a Long Island iced tea. By some miracle, I boarded the plane fine—in spite of having consumed a ridiculous amount of booze—figuring I'd be asleep in no time once we took off. Lee, on the other hand, was gone. He tried to hug our sound guy, Thilo, and fell onto this lady who was sitting next to him, right on her chest, and not surprisingly, she went berserk. Rob Dukes, who's sober and had been for many years, was trying to defuse the situation by assuring the flight attendants who came over that he'd take care of Lee and that Lee would be asleep and no trouble in no time. The lady he fell on wasn't having it. She insisted he be removed. At this point, I realized something was going on—I was sitting in a different section—and I started cursing loudly, "What the fucking fuck is fucking going on?" A Russian guy with a kid was sitting behind me, and he got up and said, "Watch your language in front of my kid!" I turned and put my middle finger six inches from his face and said, "Fuck you!" He punched me hella hard, right in the nose. Bloody nose, and now it was a fucking police thing. I got hauled off the plane with Lee. The police asked me if

I wanted to press charges, but I was like, *Nah, I probably had it coming.* I have a picture of myself with one of the cops, who turned out to be a big Exodus fan.

This was just the ill-fated beginning to what turned out to be a poorly run tour. In spite of the logistical (and self-inflicted, alcohol-related) nightmares we encountered along the way, the turnouts at the actual shows were great, which was encouraging; we all came home with a little bit of money. And I mean a little bit. I'd pocket enough to pay my bills and rent for my crappy fourplex apartment for two and a half months. So the month I was gone, I paid for that and a little bit of gap in between until the next tour. But that meant we had to keep going. Time off is money going out and not coming in. Our trajectory was moving onward, slowly, but it wasn't going backward, and that was enough for me.

IN 2006, WE PUT OUR (NONEXISTENT) MONEY WHERE OUR MOUTHS WERE and toured relentlessly: Japan, Australia (our first time Down Under), US headlining, European summer festivals, the Monsters of Mayhem package tour. Some were better than others, and in those smaller markets, we'd still have the odd show that might require that Rob procure platters of shots while we were onstage to get us through the set. The White House in Niles, Michigan, definitely comes to mind. We weren't getting rich, but if I came home with a couple grand in my pocket, I was fucking stoked. I *felt* like I was rich. *Fuck yeah! I'm gonna go buy some new fucking socks! Epic!* We had a six-week tour headlining in Europe to close out the year, and I felt like we were poised to go out on a high note, because we'd been consistently doing well in Europe. For this one, however, we made a tactical error and hired a bus to tour in that was way overpriced. It also came with a driver, who shall remain nameless, this fucker with a world-class mullet. We fucking hated him. He passed out wasted on an overnight ferry one night, after trying to wrestle me

(I nearly choked him out!), and we gave him the greatest Sharpie job you've ever seen in your life. We colored his teeth in. His whole face was solid black. By the time we were done, there was no room to draw dicks anymore. Photographic evidence of this still exists somewhere, because of course we had to immortalize it!

Our final two dates were in Turkey—someplace we'd never played before—and the financial calamity of the tour finally set in. With just two shows to go, we knew we were going home with virtually nothing to show for six weeks' work. We were fucking depressed, like teary-eyed depressed. It was right before Christmas, and I wouldn't even be able to buy my kids presents. Thankfully, we tour with really good people in our crew. Some of them generously gave part of their salary back. Our drum tech / tour manager, Nick Barker, was like, *You guys paid me my salary the whole time; here's some money.* We got another Christmas miracle—and it's the only reason we came home with anything—when the airline we were traveling back to the States on didn't charge us any overage fees for all our extra bags. The guy in line before us got brutalized for his excess bags, so we thought, *This doesn't look good; we're screwed.* But that guy was being a dick, and the same person helping him let us have everything for free. So after touring Europe for six weeks, I went home with enough to buy presents for my kids and pay the rent and survive.

THOUGH TOM HAD LEFT EXODUS AGAIN PRIOR TO THE RECORDING OF *Shovel Headed,* as one of my closest friends, he and I remained in touch throughout his time away. He didn't want to give up on the band he'd formed with Kirk Hammett way back in high school in the '70s, but navigating the anxiety issues that seemed to occasionally hit him when we were touring was challenging. He loved playing live; it wasn't like he dreaded it at all. But he just couldn't figure out when a debilitating panic attack would hit him out of the blue. It probably felt safer to him to not risk experiencing that kind of thing when he was far from home, on the road with Exodus. I understood where he was coming from, but missed him being in the band. He and I went further back than the others, and that history and friendship meant a lot.

In early 2007, Tom and I met and discussed the prospect of him coming back after Paul Bostaph quit to rejoin Testament. Bostaph was great, but I'd always rather have Tom behind the kit. No offense to any drummer who's ever been in the band—and we've had some godlike, upper-echelon drummers—but Tom's the guy I played with since I was seventeen years old. This is my best friend, and this is the guy that speaks my language riff-wise. Tom's the best drummer for Exodus. Would Tom be the best drummer for Slayer? No. He'd be the first to tell you that. But for my band, he's the best drummer in the world; there's no one else. I wouldn't trade him for any other drummer on earth. It's Tom, then everybody else. It's just the way it is. So when he agreed to return and make a new record with us, it was fucking amazing. Tom was right where he belonged.

CHAPTER 23
GARDEN OF BLEEDING

S EVEN ALBUMS IN, WE'D RECORDED IN ALL KINDS OF STUDIOS, WITH A number of different engineers and producers—even produced some albums ourselves—but with our next album, we definitively figured out what worked for us and who we really liked to work with. Andy Sneap was our guy, and he'd shown his loyalty to Exodus by working with us under any circumstances we subjected him to, including our pranks and high jinks. He'd even worked for no money up front on our "comeback" album, *Tempo of the Damned*. First and foremost, he's one of the whole band's, and especially my, best friends on earth. So we're completely bonded. Number two, he understands the band better than anybody, and he understands me. He knows how to work with me; he knows how to work with Jack; he knows how to work with vocalists. Number three, we have a great time working together, because we're a fucking fun bunch to work with. Andy always said working with Exodus was like walking into a cartoon or an episode of *The Banana Splits*,

like when you go through a doorway and all of a sudden you're ani-
mated into the Exodus cartoon world.

Andy's like the sixth member of the band, and he knows how to get
the best out of me. I'll think something is really killer, and Andy will be
like, *You're rushing a little bit there.* Most people wouldn't catch it. And
Andy will push me, especially on the chuggy stuff. The superfast shit,
there's no room to push ahead, because you're already pushing as fucking fast as you can. But it's the "Blacklist"-type stuff (from *Tempo*) where
you really want those chugs to be just nailed to the beat. He's also not
afraid to look at me after I do a solo and I'm all full of myself, and say,
"You got sausages for fingers? You can beat that, come on. Don't fucking settle." He's all about getting the best out of the entire band.

And wherever we asked him to go to record us, he was game. It was
on *The Atrocity Exhibition: Exhibit A* where we realized that going into
a sterile studio, where we had set hours, wasn't our thing. That felt more
like a job—clock in, clock out. (We did that on *Shovel Headed*, and I
hated it. It was awful.) For this one, we tracked the drums at a proper
studio, Sharkbite Studios in Oakland, as we always did. But when it
came time to do the rest of the tracking, there was a vacant recording
studio in the place where we rehearsed. The person who'd built the
studio had moved out, with all their gear. So we moved into that, and
we built our own studio with Andy Sneap. We called it Flabby Road,
because it had a big wallpaper mural of the Beatles' *Abbey Road*, but we
were all getting a little fat, hence the name.

With this setup, we weren't locked into working specific hours, and
the creativity flowed a lot better. We were also able to get a lot more
done and work more efficiently. If my fingers were sore, Lee's amps
were set up, so he could do some solos. Or if he wasn't feeling it, Jack
could do some bass or Rob could do vocals. I think the results speak
for themselves, as far as the songs, performances, and sound. It's one of
my favorite albums we've ever done, and it's one of the best-sounding

records we've ever done. It's just crushing. And I love the songs—Rob Dukes is fucking just phenomenal; he really came into his own. And Lee, his contributions were just crushing, and Tom destroyed it, too. Some review I read about it said the guitars were almost too aggressive. Fuck, it's never aggressive *enough*; just everybody else is soft. Yeah, it's fucking aggressive and in your face.

After we'd wrapped up recording the new record, we had a short run of dates booked in Southern California. These would be the first time Tom had played live with us since the Megadeth tour, a couple of years previous. Before the first show, Tom was standing out back, looking kind of shaky.

"I can't go on," he told me. "Something's wrong; I feel like I'm having a heart attack." As he said this, he actually fainted and collapsed; it was fucking scary. In the past, when he was suffering from anxiety or panic attacks, I tried the gentle approach with him, but not this time.

"If you've got a fucking disease," I barked, "I hope I get what you've got because it's been killing you since the Headbangers Ball Tour in 1989! This is the slowest-developing thing ever, and I hope that's what I get."

He looked shocked at my reaction. I don't think he was expecting that.

"You're the strongest motherfucker I know! Snap out of it!"

He went and played the show and killed it. Ever since that day, he hasn't had any more episodes like that. The only other similar instance happened in London, at the start of our European tour in April 2008. We'd just finished an insanely hot set at the Underworld and were backstage getting a quick breather before our encore. I saw that Tom had that look.

"Are you all right?" I asked him. We were both sweating bullets, because the club was a fucking sauna at that point.

"Feel my heart," he said, looking concerned that it was beating too fast.

"Feel mine," I said. "This is normal." He was shocked that my heart was beating out of my chest, too. "We're not playing country music, you know. What we do is fucking athletic, it's work. By the time we get to the encore, it's like the fourth quarter of a football game. Yeah, we're all breathing like that." We never addressed the cause of his anxiety in full detail, because I don't think he knew exactly what was triggering it. He always would tell us that he loved touring and wanted to do it, but he didn't know what was going on. As time went on, though, he seemed to develop control over it.

THE SO-CALLED THRASH METAL RENAISSANCE WE'D BEEN ASKED ABOUT early in the new millennium actually started to manifest in a meaningful way around this time. It didn't mean that we were back to the Headbangers Ball Tour days of popularity, but there was definitely a groundswell, as evidenced by a whole crop of young bands like Warbringer, Evile, Gama Bomb, Havok, and a quartet of SoCal teens going by the name Bonded by Blood. These were new thrash bands playing old-school thrash and even wearing the old-school garb. It was super flattering, but we weren't ready to hand over the crown just yet.

So what better time for us to rerecord one of the cornerstone albums of the genre, right? Let me just say, for the record, that initially it was not our intention to do that when making *Let There Be Blood*. We did it to pay homage to Paul. At the time, there were a lot of tribute albums to various musicians, and we felt like Paul Baloff should have one. Our concept was to put out an album of nine different bands, each covering one track from *Bonded by Blood*. However, since we were undertaking this endeavor on our own—recorded and financed by our manager's friend Jonnie Zaentz (son of noted movie/record producer Saul Zaentz)—we had no budget to pay for other bands' studio time. So this concept never really got past the conversation stage, other than the fact that I ran the proposition by Abbath from Immortal when we were playing a festival in Europe, and he was super into it. He was like, *I want "Metal Command"!*

The next idea was that we'd record all the backing tracks, but have nine different people sing. Well, people still want to get paid, and we were looking at the added costs of studio time in nine different locales. So that was another nonstarter. Finally, our management and Jonnie suggested we just re-record *Bonded*, put a little money in our pocket, and call it good. We were super broke at the time, and I think Jonnie offered us a couple thousand bucks each, and he did all the recording in his studio and released it on his own label. So much for our good intentions of paying tribute to Paul. The reactions to it were pretty extreme when it was finally released. A lot of people hated it, and the prevailing sentiment was: *Why?* We got flak for the modern production, the fact that we were tuned lower (as we've been doing since '93), and even because some of the tempos weren't quite fast enough at times. Mea culpa on that last one, because the one thing I never did was A-B the two against each other. Otherwise, I would've been like, *Whoa, whoa! Tom, we need to play this faster!*

That said, I think the songs sound great. But was it necessary? No, not in any way. I haven't listened to it since it was finished. Live and learn. What I didn't understand was how *mad* people got that we did it. We didn't replace the original *Bonded by Blood*. We're not like Ozzy Osbourne, who re-recorded two of the original band members' performances (bassist Bob Daisley and drummer Lee Kerslake) using other musicians on later versions of his first two solo records. The original *Bonded by Blood* is still available, and it still sells very well. And *Let There Be Blood* doesn't—end of story. The people have spoken.

I did do one thing outside of Exodus to further the thrash cause, though. In early 2009, I agreed to produce Warbringer's second album for Century Media Records, *Waking into Nightmares*. I'd produced a record by a Seattle band called Panic back in the early '90s, and I'd been in that same role with Exodus, so I agreed to work with them at Shark-bite Studios in Oakland, where Exodus had tracked drums in the past. Sharkbite let them live in the lounge room, which was super unheard of. They weren't really equipped as a live-in studio, but they let War-bringer do it, which made it way easier all around, because we only had about a week to get it done. The budget was minimal. But they were easy to work with, and we had a good time. I just wish we'd had *more* time. This job also turned out to be a precursor to a lot more time we'd be spending together, because we'd soon embark on a North America tour, headlined by Kreator, together.

FOR THE FIRST TIME SINCE 1989, EXODUS WOULD RECORD A NEW ALBUM with the same lineup as the previous one. There had been continuous turnover and change through the decades, but we had a really solid lineup that I think was making some of the best albums of our career to this point. It was only fitting, then, that this album should be called *Exhibit B: The Human Condition*. Because *Exhibit A* had been pretty long, we held back a song Lee had written from those sessions, "The Ballad of Leonard and Charles," with the intention of opening *Exhibit B* with it. To further make the connection between the two albums, we teased the intro to it—with the million harmonies and acoustics—at the fade of the close on *Exhibit A*. And just to go full circle, we then faded the final song on *Exhibit B*, "Good Riddance," with the beginning of the first song on *Exhibit A*, "Call to Arms."

For the recording, we were committed to the idea of woodshedding together in a studio of our making, but this time, we left the Bay Area and headed into wine country in Sonoma County. The drums were recorded at Sharkbite in Oakland, but I found a vacation rental house near Guerneville that could accommodate all of us. The plan was that we'd all stay there together for an entire month. I was totally up front with the owners when I rented it and told them what we were doing. I said, *We're making an album. We're professionals; we're not going to wreck the place. We're not working through the night. Everything will be sound-proofed, and it'll be fine.*

Andy Sneap came over from England, and the recording was done on a laptop with a portable Pro Tools rig. Once again, we transformed the space we had into a studio. I slept in the room downstairs, which had its own bathroom, so we had a guitar cabinet in the bathroom and we ran speaker cables out of Andy's bedroom, where the amps and recording gear was, down the wall and into there. We dubbed our studio Camp Crunch. It was fucking awesome. When we weren't recording our parts, we'd be barbecuing on the grill. Lee did a lot of the cheffing, because he's an amazing cook. It was a beautiful, scenic environment that would occasionally be punctuated by Rob screaming like a mad-man when he was doing his vocals. It sounded like someone being murdered in the house. Poor neighbors. The guitars would get a little bit loud, but we had everything pretty well soundproofed, and Jack's bass was recorded direct, so we could just turn it down once it started getting late. We were super conscientious about the volume level. And when we'd finished, we left the place cleaner than we got it. The own-ers were so impressed, they sent us bottles of really fine scotch as a thank-you.

Maybe it's because we were finally making records in a way that suited us, or maybe it was because we were just older, better, and more experienced and had our shit together more, but both of the *Exhibit* albums are two of my favorites, without a doubt. I fucking love them. *Exhibit A* and *Exhibit B* are just monumental records, as far as I'm con-cerned. I'll put those albums—really any of them since *Tempo*—up against any of our contemporaries, and I'm talking my best friends. We were out there throwing fucking body blows, just punching people out.

Part of that was we were still wondering what success tasted like. We've never been slowed down by wealth and fame and all that free time wasted shopping for expensive new rides. We were fucking hungry because we were literally physically hungry, not making shit for money, and fucking starving. But we also had (and still do) a never-ending love of punishing riffs, and that shit's really fucking hard to play. It'd be easy to write stuff that would be totally acceptable to our audience, yet would be much simpler, much easier on the right hand. But we were pushing the envelope in ways we never did before. The *Bonded by Blood* material I can play in my sleep. I don't need to warm up, don't need to do anything. But this thrash requires massive dedication and commitment. And it might also challenge listeners.

Some people don't have time in their lives anymore for a journey. They just want instant gratification—*Give me three and a half radio minutes of some chugs and some lead guitar, and I'm happy.* When I get a new record, I want to listen to the whole fucking thing, the way the artist intended it to be heard. I don't want to listen to the single. We're trying to create a musical journey for people. Some people get it, but some people just don't have the attention span for that. I'm not writing for them.

CHAPTER 24
HELL AWAITS

A NYONE REMEMBER MySPACE? IT WAS KIND OF LIKE FACEBOOK before there was Facebook, but with music. I can't say it did anything for Exodus's or my musical career, but through MySpace, I connected with a woman, Lisa Perticone, who'd become my second wife. The thing is, I didn't *meet* Lisa on MySpace, because we already sort of knew each other, casual acquaintances, going back to the early days of the thrash scene. She was there at the first Metallica shows in San Francisco in the early '80s, and she also dated Sam Kress (RIP), a close friend of the band and one of the founders of Rampage Radio. So she was part of the early scene, but at some point, she left the scene and got married and had a daughter. Then through a mutual friend on MySpace, her name popped up. We'd seen each other a couple of times in San Francisco over the years, once at a Pentagram show, where I was like, *That girl's really cute. There's a big flower in her hair.* But I had a girlfriend at the time, so nothing came of it. Anyway, I was on tour supporting *Exhibit B*, and during our downtime, I started chatting with her via MySpace. This was around the time that Facebook was also starting to take off—yeah, I was on there for a minute—so we eventually moved the conversation over there and kind of fell in love without ever having to date. It was just fate, if you believe in that kind of shit. I was single, and she was single; everything just lined up.

Exodus had been touring nearly nonstop through 2010, so Lisa and I didn't have the opportunity to have a proper "first date" until the tour took us back to the Bay Area in September. We were scheduled to play at the Avalon in Santa Clara (which is now long gone) on September 12, so she came out to that, and we finally reconnected in person. The address of the Avalon was 777 Lawrence Expressway, so 777 has been our lucky number ever since, and we both have it tattooed on our knuckles. We both knew we'd found the right person, and we were married within a year (more on that later). She's one of the best things that ever happened to me. She's number one in the standings. I've been married twice, and I got it right the second time. I don't want to disparage my first wife. I was super difficult and a shit husband, and I made plenty of mistakes. I've got two wonderful kids from my first wife, and with Lisa, I have a third, her daughter, Frances. I don't plan on ever being married a third time or being divorced a second time. We're both committed to each other, and we try really hard to communicate. That was always a problem in the past for me, and I'm probably no different from most people in that regard. But we talk our way through things now, and we consider each other our last stop. She's my closest friend, and I trust her opinion more than anything on just shit in life. She's also my business partner. Half my side hustles are her idea. She knows how to market her husband, I guess!

I not only gained a third daughter when I married Lisa, we now have two granddaughters and a grandson. We both wish we could've met at a different time and had a child together. But at a different time, I wasn't the fucking best dude to be married to. We connected at the right time to where I'm not a shifty, fucking crappy husband but a guy who's committed to doing everything right. I'm fucking happy, and my family continues to get bigger and bigger. I guess it took me until much later in life to learn the lessons my father had always been teaching me, but I hadn't been listening to.

NEARLY A DECADE AFTER THE FATEFUL CALL WHERE I'D LEARNED OF Paul Baloff's fatal stroke—a decade I'd spent clawing my way back into the metal world's good graces—another life-changing phone call occurred. It was early 2011, and I was out with Exodus, along with Lisa, on the inaugural 70000 Tons of Metal cruise. Since this was the first of these big metal cruises that had ever been put together, a lot of my friends came out for it—it was a huge event. One of those people happened to be my primary tattoo artist and longtime friend, Bob Tyrrell. Bob got a text from Kerry King, asking him to have me call Kerry when I got home. I didn't think much of it at the time, but I did find it curious that Kerry didn't just text me directly, because he had my number. I think he just didn't want to bother me while I was gigging at sea.

When I got home from the cruise at the end of January, I rang him up, thinking (hoping) maybe he was gonna offer Exodus a tour supporting Slayer or something like that. We had a prior offer to do the Unholy Alliance Tour, one of the US runs, but we had to turn it down because we were fully committed to our tour with Arch Enemy at the time, and it would've really put those guys in a bind if we'd backed out so late.

"Yo, what's up, dude?" I said when Kerry picked up. The offer he had was a tour, but not for Exodus.

"We need someone to fill in for Jeff on Australian and European tours we have booked. His arm's really fucked up from a spider bite, and he can't play those dates. Can you do it? Do you want to do it?" he asked. Though I was committed to Exodus, and I remain so to this day,

I couldn't turn down the opportunity to play thrash at the highest level, with a band that came up with Exodus but hadn't been tripped up by their own mistakes. It was an easy yes, but my head spun just thinking about what this would mean. And obviously, I was concerned about Jeff's health, as well. Slayer had some big shows coming up, and if he couldn't play them, it must be pretty serious.

"Yeah, sure, I'm down," I confirmed. "My schedule is open." The timing was actually perfect, because I was planning on taking some downtime after the cruise. Exodus had been doing album cycle, tour, tour, tour, tour, and then straight back in the studio for four consecutive albums. I was starting to feel a little bit burned out. I didn't want to take time off, exactly; I just wanted to write. But I wanted to not be pressured into hitting the road immediately again. "There is one Exodus show that I can't miss, though. We're supporting Iron Maiden in Santiago, Chile, and that's a fucking big, big moment. I'm gonna do that show."

"No problem," he said. "We can try to find someone to fill in for a date or two while you're in Chile."

JEFF HANNEMAN WAS ONE OF SLAYER'S FOUR FOUNDING MEMBERS, SO I WAS temporarily stepping into some very big shoes. I wasn't worried musically, because I could learn to play the songs, no problem, but he'd been stage right in Slayer for nearly thirty years, and I considered him an old friend, so this was a huge responsibility that I, of course, took very seriously. Slayer were also operating at a whole other level than Exodus, so there were some things that needed to be taken care of before I could assume my role. First and foremost, I couldn't tell anyone about the situation I was stepping into. At this point, the public knew about as much about Jeff's situation as I did, which was absolutely nothing. The only thing I knew was that I had less than a month to learn the set and the first shows would be in Australia at the traveling Soundwave Festival at the end of February. At some point before then, the band would make an announcement regarding Jeff's illness—he'd received a near-fatal spider bite and the necrotizing fasciitis from it had required the removal of a huge portion of the soft tissue on his right arm—and that I would be filling in temporarily. Emphasis on *temporarily*. The expectation was that Jeff would rehab his arm, do physio, fully recover, and rejoin the band.

The initial response from fans to my filling in was generally super positive. People were like, *Get well, Jeff, but this is something to see*. A band like Slayer, with a guy whom people consider one of the forefathers of this kind of heavy metal, was a positive way to make the best of an unfortunate situation. People took it for what it was at that time: something really cool that you're only going to be able to see once. Little did we know.

I had less than a month to learn how to play the long list of songs they gave me, but first, I wanted to get to know the songs as a fan. I was more familiar with the *Show No Mercy* stuff than *Reign in Blood* and beyond because Baloff and I listened to that shit all the time back in the day. But they'd put out several albums since that I didn't really know at all. I immersed myself in the material—constantly jamming them in my car—just listening, so I innately knew where the changes were, so I could hum the riffs. No sense learning something that you don't know the arrangement to. I had to learn the material that way first. *Then* I learned the notes. I didn't even look at a guitar until after probably a couple of weeks just listening. I had to do all this while keeping it a secret from my own band. The only person who knew was my (soon-to-be) wife. I'd never played in another band, playing somebody else's material—other than covers or jamming with the Metal Alliance—but I looked at it like it was going to be a learning experience. I was gonna play some big-ass shows and go out there and just shred, and not have to be *the guy* or anything like that.

Slayer flew me down to LA for rehearsals, and I got to reacquaint myself with my old friends. They rehearsed in a really funny way for a band of their stature. It was a tiny studio where music lessons were taught, located in a strip mall. Exodus's room was five times as big. And Slayer could have afforded to build their own facility like Metallica did. But they used this little room with a drum kit, a small bass amp, and two half stacks. And in the next studio, someone might be taking a piano lesson. The first day, we ran through seventeen songs. I showed up prepared, and I was tight as fuck because I'd worked really hard. Kerry's guitar tech at the time, the late Armand Butts Crump, was sitting out in the lobby area listening, and he poked his head in just to see if I was even playing. He said the two guitars were so locked in, he couldn't tell it was both of us. Kerry also loaned me a little practice amp so I could continue to work on my own in my hotel room.

One day when we were rehearsing, Jeff actually came down to the studio to discuss some things with his bandmates. I felt really kind of weird at first, because he was the guy I hung out with the most back in the day, and now I was filling in for him. And I didn't really know the details behind the decision-making and whatever was going on behind the scenes. So I went out and talked to him and gave him a hug, and I asked him a question about a riff. He's like, *Right there, you got it.* He points out a couple of frets. I was maybe like one or two notes off or something. But he and the rest of the band were kind of having little meetings, so they all went off and disappeared together. It was strange being in a band setting and not being part of band decisions, but that was my new role as a hired gun, so to speak. And I *was* a hired gun, but I was more than okay doing that in a band like Slayer, playing thrash with old friends. For a guy who'd come from years of fucking heavy metal struggle and playing to eighteen people in Colorado Springs or ten people in Omaha, having a steady paycheck to take care of the rent and shit was fucking epic. It was a welcome change.

While I had to have the riffs and arrangements down tight, the band never asked me to play Jeff's solos note for note, not once. Which was good, because Jeff's style is so unique. It would've required me to remake myself as a guitar player. So what I did was just try to match vibe for vibe. If Jeff's doing all kinds of crazy whammy bar stuff in a song, then I'd do crazy whammy bar stuff on it, but I'd just do my own a little bit. If Jeff's playing real fast; I'm gonna play real fast. The solos where I match some of his stuff more closely were probably on the *Show No Mercy* things where he played with a lot of melody. So I would interject my own parts, but then he'd have a key melodic section—a little chapter in it, if you will. And I'd mimic that, not note for note, but just trying to keep those key melodies there. I've heard Slayer fans complain that I don't play Jeff's solos exactly the same, and I'm straight up honestly telling you, it's because I can't. Sorry. Playing his stuff to me is just as hard as if someone said, *You're going to go play in Dream Theater, and you have to play John Petrucci solos*. It's fucking ridiculous how different Jeff's style is from mine. His soloing was uniquely his and his alone. I just did my best job to keep the vibe the same. That was my approach to all of it, and Slayer were cool with it. It was liberating, because before I started jamming with them, I had no idea how many solos were in a Slayer set, especially for Jeff—a fucking lot! So in the end, I got to play the role of guitar hero—some songs I'd have three solos! So sick!

TRAVELING DOWN TO AUSTRALIA FOR THE SOUNDWAVE SHOWS WITH Slayer was an immediate upgrade from my lifetime spent in steerage, so to speak. I was always that guy at the bottom of the *Titanic*, and all of a sudden, I was Billy fucking Zane. Business class doesn't suck, and the hotels we stayed in were fucking amazing. Everyone in and around Slayer—crew, management, the band—treated me really, really wonderfully from day one. They made me feel super welcome. I think one of my best contributions to Slayer was that I totally got along with everybody, and I think I did a good job of keeping spirits up. I'm pretty good at making guys laugh. I hung out with the crew a lot because I felt like a crew guy. I was in truth an employee, like the guitar techs and everybody else. I got real close to Armand, since he drove me to a lot of rehearsals before we ever played a show, and I kind of learned the lay of the land from him, more than anybody, about what to expect.

Before the gates opened for the first Soundwave show, I got some time to play with Jeff's amplification rig because I'd never even touched it. The rehearsal studio just had a little half stack, so I needed to dial the sound a little more suited to my own way. I like a lot of gain; Jeff didn't. He had it pretty clean. I had to up the crunch and distortion to get it to where I was comfortable. My first performance was an outdoor festival in fucking front of tens of thousands of fans, and I wanted to make sure everything I could control was where I liked it. Even though this was a momentous gig, I wasn't nervous about it. I knew we were gonna be tight; I knew we were killer. All the first shows were fucking amazing. We had a great time. That was one of the few tours we did with the full Marshall wall, because we started running just the bottom line of cabs not long after that. It was awesome to just bow down in front of a wall of Marshalls.

We quickly went from the Soundwave dates over to Europe for a whole month of shows. Slayer knew in advance that I'd have to miss some so that I could play a quick run of gigs in South America with Exodus, including the one opening for Maiden, so they brought in Cannibal Corpse guitarist Pat O'Brien to cover for me. They flew him out early in the tour so we could coach him on a lot of stuff. It's super valuable to be able to observe when you're about to be thrown into the fire. Unlike me, Pat was super nervous about it, and he would practice until his fingers were like blistering. Kerry and I were like, *Pat, put the fucking guitar down. Have a drink. Just relax. Come on, you're all right. Just put that thing away for a minute. Let's fucking party.* We'd get him to relax a little bit, but I think he was nervous because I knew Pat, but I don't think he really knew anybody else. He was thrown into a super huge situation playing for fucking Slayer—which I was, too—but Pat hadn't known these guys since he was twenty years old.

I flew out of Italy on April 5, the day after our gig in Padua. Pat would finish out the final week of Slayer dates for me, but I would rejoin Slayer for a Big Four show in Indio, California, on April 23. Since Slayer paid for my flight to Chile, I flew better than the rest of my Exodus bandmates who came down together from California. Lisa also flew out for what would be one of Exodus's most epic shows ever. Playing with Iron Maiden in South America was a bucket list gig for all of us. Iron Maiden were supergood to us, too; they gave us an hour set, which was fucking unheard of. We didn't see the band, but the crew were very nice. Probably due to our excitement about everything, we went out and killed it that night. The crowd was so insane! There was a pit going, and people were really into it. So, of course, we had to watch Maiden's set. They opened up with a bunch of new shit that wasn't exactly rousing the crowd, and we were thinking, *We blew these dudes away, man!* That was until Maiden went into fucking "Hallowed Be Thy Name," and it was all over. Our egos just deflated—*You fucking dumbasses. You ain't blowing Iron Maiden off the stage anywhere on earth! What even made you think that for a second?* Sure, we had a pit, and they didn't, but when you hear sixty thousand people singing the opening of that song, it's game over. We were just a fucking bunch of guys with too much Jägermeister in them, knocked down to earth. It was funny as fuck.

Someone years ago decided that there were exactly four bands responsible for creating thrash—Metallica, Megadeth, Anthrax, and Slayer—and they were dubbed the "Big Four." Never mind Exodus were equally important in that whole formula, which also conveniently ignores all the early thrash bands from Europe like Celtic Frost, Kreator, Sodom, and Destruction. The Big Four really just became a marketing concept to reunite these four big and, inarguably, influential bands—the ones who also sold by far the most records—on one stage. Slayer did a run of these in 2010 for the European touring Sonisphere Festival, and now I'd get my chance to be onstage for the first American Big Four show, which was *only* the four bands.

Indio's located a couple of hours outside LA, so it was sort of in Slayer's backyard. Through his rehab and physio, Jeff had gotten back to playing guitar. He'd actually been rehearsing with Slayer leading up to the show, which I obviously wasn't there for, so I don't know how those went. I was there, however, for the initial discussion with Jeff about whether he would play the show. Jeff wanted to do it, but I think, having rehearsed with him, the band understood that physically, his right hand wasn't ready for a full set. That was expressed to him with me sitting there backstage in the trailer, which was super uncomfortable for me. I think at that point, he was like, *All right, I'm gonna do half of it*, and they said, *Why don't you do the encore?* Knowing my place, I left the trailer and let them sort it out. That's private shit.

I played the thirteen-song set with Slayer, and after I came off the stage and handed my guitar to my tech (who was actually Jeff's tech), Warren Lee, Jeff was there to give me a big bear hug. Because he had the right sleeve cut off the sweatshirt he was wearing, I could see for the first time how messed up his arm was. He put on his guitar and was met with an incredible outpouring of love and adulation as he was introduced and walked out onstage. The band blazed through "South of Heaven" and "Angel of Death," and I know it's a cliché, but they brought the house down, and Jeff played fucking great. Maybe he could've played the whole set. Or maybe once adrenaline and emotion wore off, his arm, which was heavily compromised by the spider bite, would have given out three songs in. I don't know. We'll never know. But what a moment. Watching him play with Slayer again, after he'd been close to death, was the biggest, most emotional moment of the entire show. It's a memory that's permanently burned into my brain.

I'll never forget it. I knew right then, following that for Metallica—or anyone—would be a tall order.

More than anything, though, it was a hopeful moment. It also, in my mind, crystallized the fact that my role in Slayer was temporary and that I'd only be filling in until Jeff was better. I mean, we all thought he would come back.

CHAPTER 25
DOUBLE DUTY

WHEN I COMMITTED TO SLAYER TO FILL IN FOR JEFF AS LONG AS they needed me, I also made it clear to Exodus that I wasn't jumping ship; my intention was to do what I could to keep things moving forward. We'd made two albums I was super happy with, we'd been touring nearly nonstop when we weren't recording, and we were definitely seeing the results. The tours were better, the crowds were bigger, and we had some well-needed stability in the band personnel-wise. Momentum was definitely going forward. So while the Slayer gig was a boon for me on a personal, professional, and financial level, it also affected Exodus, something I was acutely aware of and felt somewhat guilty about.

Thankfully, my brothers in Exodus were more supportive and understanding than I could have ever imagined. They would tell me, *You got nothing to feel guilty about. You deserve this and earned it, and you deserve to play these venues and travel the way Slayer does—no one deserves it more.* But that didn't stop me from feeling guilty about being away from the band.

It wasn't easy to navigate. But Exodus understood this was an opportunity for me to raise my profile and all that kind of shit, and I had their full support, which was awesome. They're my bros; they had my back.

Thankfully, Slayer also welcomed me as family from day one, which made my position in the band that much more comfortable. I was never made to feel like I was just a hired gun, even though I was well aware that's what I was. But there's a big difference between being one and being made to feel like one. I was always made to feel like I mattered. They treated me like I belonged there; they treated me like a friend, because we were old, old friends. In the tour books, when I first started playing with Slayer, it listed me as "Gary Holt, temporary guitar," but I never felt like a temporary, useless fill-in. They made me feel like family. And that has to do with decades of friendship, even if there'd been years and years since we'd seen each other and hung out. We obviously went way back, but their trajectory had been much different from Exodus's, so I soon discovered that the way they operated was on a whole different level from what I was used to.

Their shit was run well, from management to the crew. The road crew were a bunch of fucking hooligans, like fucking assassins, and none more so than Warren Lee, Jeff's guitar tech, who would be my right-hand man and closest friend in the Slayer camp. In addition to being my tech, Warren was the entire band's onstage bodyguard. He kept a cattle prod and a fucking hatchet in the fucking guitar vault, you know, just in case. If someone ran onstage, Warren would run out, tackle them, and drag them off. And if you fought as you were getting dragged off, then you were getting punched. Warren's a little guy, but he punches like fucking Mike Tyson in his prime. He knocks fools out. He routinely knocked dudes out who were twice his size. "Talk shit, get hit" was the motto.

I wasn't privy to all the inner workings of Slayer and their management, but from what I witnessed, there was never any amateur bullshit.

It definitely made me aspire to run Exodus smoother. I definitely saw how things could be better. There were times in the past when getting Exodus onstage, it was like, *Where's this guy? Where's that guy?* We couldn't even be gathered to go to the stage at the same time. Slayer headed to the stage like clockwork, like a fucking fighter going to the ring.

With the band's rigorous touring schedule, this level of professionalism was absolutely necessary. After the Big Four show in Indio, I spent most of the rest of 2011 on the road, between Slayer and Exodus commitments. Exodus had played some South American dates earlier in the year, but when I returned there in June with Slayer, the venues (and crowds) were bigger, and I was traveling at a comfort level much better than I'd ever been accustomed to, from flights to hotels. Unfortunately, I picked up something—a bug, a parasite?—while eating tacos with Dave Lombardo at the end of our Mexico dates that stayed with me for a long time and led to some very embarrassing incidents. On the plane ride home, I was up in business class—six rows of two seats on either side of the aisle—and I was sitting next to this guy who looked like Ricardo Montalbán. He was dressed really dapper and had on a white fedora. Well, I fucking let a fart go that was the most awful thing you've ever smelled in your life. I was pretending it wasn't me, because it was silent; I faked like I was asleep. I looked over, and the guy was holding a pillow over his face. I went to the bathroom, and black oil came out of me. It was fucking horrid, right? That wasn't even the end of it, because it seemed to come and go.

I barely had a week back home before we went over to Europe to play some big summer festivals and a handful of Big Four shows. Though there was a lot of hype about these Big Four shows, in some ways, they just felt like another festival to me, maybe because I still considered myself on the outside looking in and not really a part of the Big Four. I was just a guy holding Jeff's seat down for him, keeping it warm. I didn't feel like it really pertained to me. This was *their* thing. I was honored to be a part of the shows, but it didn't seem like it involved me at all. It didn't carry that much significance to me.

Don't get me wrong—the shows were hella fun and the vibe was killer. Everybody got along really well, and it gave me the opportunity to connect with Kirk again. Scott Ian missed all but one of the shows because his wife, Pearl, was giving birth to his son, Revel, so Andreas Kisser from Sepultura played in his place. Andreas joined me as one of two fill-ins at the shows. After our set in Gelsenkirchen, Germany, we had to leave early (I'm not exactly sure why to this day), and Metallica paid for a private jet for Slayer to fly to the next show in Gothenburg, Sweden. I'd never experienced anything like that in my life; it was fucking rad! Flying high, enjoying a glass of hefeweizen beer with a big steak, in total luxury.

After the show in Gothenburg, I went back to the hotel, and a bunch of us went to the In Flames bar, which was right around the corner. I had two beers and returned to my room to go to bed. I woke up the next morning, and it was like the scene in *The Godfather* when the guy woke up with a horse head in his bed, but this was a Rorschach test shit stain on my fucking sheets. I guess I farted in my sleep and, well, that was the result! I was desperately trying to figure out what to do, because I didn't want the hotel to know. I cleaned up as best I could, but I ended up being the last guy at lobby call (and I'm usually *first*) because I didn't want any maids going in the room while I was still on the premises. Jim Carroccio, Slayer's tour manager, was like, *What the hell's going on with you? You're fucking never late for lobby calls.* I said, *I just shit the bed. Let's get out of here!* I told him what was going on, and he said, *You need some real meds. Pepto Bismol ain't cutting it.* So I got some kind of anti-parasite meds, and that cleared things up. Now when I think about the Big Four shows in Europe, it mostly brings up memories of me shitting my bed in a five-star hotel.

After the run of Big Four shows, we played a handful of other festivals in Europe, one of which, Hegyalja Fesztivál in Hungary, was cut short due to progressively worsening weather in the area. We'd played the full set and one encore song, "Angel of Death," when shit started getting sketchy. There were some scary lightning strikes happening, and you don't really want to be holding something electrified on an open stage when that's going on. Tom Araya, Kerry, and I went back to the hotel, but Dave Lombardo wanted to stay at the venue. Dave didn't drink very often, other than like some beers here and there, but that night, he decided he was gonna party. He was drinking vodka and orange juice before we left. I got back to the hotel and went up to my suite, which had more square footage than most of the houses I've lived in in my life. It was massive. It was like a full-on huge apartment. I woke up the next day, feeling perfectly fresh after a good night's sleep. I opened the door from the bedroom and walked out into the main room only to find Lombardo sleeping on my sofa, a weed pipe next to him. *What the fuck happened here?!* I had no idea why Dave was in my room.

At some point, he woke up, still blind drunk, grabbed his weed pipe, and beelined out of my room. As the day progressed, I finally got the story. Dave got really fucking drunk at the venue and then rode back to the hotel with the crew. Someone in the crew actually had audio of it, because they kept having to stop the van so Dave could throw up. You could hear him vomit and fart at the same time at one point. Funny as fuck! They even got pulled over by the Hungarian police, because the police saw their Sprinter van on the side of the road and a drunk guy puking. When they got to the hotel late that night, they asked Dave what his room name was, because he didn't have his key. (We always checked in under assumed names—mine was "Michael Jackson.") He was so drunk, he couldn't tell anyone anything. The desk clerk gave him a room key, and they opened the door, only to see *my* luggage. At that point, they knew it was my room—my luggage was unmistakable—but they figured they'd just put him on the couch and get out of there. They wanted to get rid of him!

Later that day, when we met for lobby call, we started piecing together the evening for him. He pulled out his little digital camera, and it was just like the credits of *The Hangover*, where the guy's figuring out what he did the previous night based on his own photographic evidence. Dave didn't remember any of it. There was a picture of him spinning records at a DJ tent; he was onstage scratching records and shit, all this stuff. It was hella funny. He was totally wrecked. We had a private plane chartered for the next day to take us to Germany for our gig at Bang Your Head Festival, and he was definitely still feeling the effects.

One immediate benefit for Exodus that my playing in Slayer offered came to fruition not long after Slayer arrived back in the US: a support slot on the Hell on Earth North America tour headlined by Slayer (with Rob Zombie as direct support). While I was stoked to have my band out on the road with me, it meant I'd have to do double duty playing more than two hours of high-intensity thrash every night. I mean, physically, you could imagine. It was fucking rough. But I was proud of that shit because I never took either set off. I fucking went out and destroyed with Exodus, got offstage, changed my clothes and brushed out my tangled mess of hair, and waited through Rob Zombie's set to go do it again with Slayer. There ain't a lot of guys who could pull that shit off, and I was able to do it and do it at 100 percent each show. Obviously, I couldn't have my usual couple of beers before Exodus played and then a few during our set. So I would drink nonalcoholic beers until it was Slayer time. On the only outdoor show of the tour, Slayer let Rob headline because his stage theatrics wouldn't look like much in the daylight. So I literally got offstage, changed my clothes, brushed my hair, and went right back out. Thankfully, the tour only lasted a month, and we all had a blast, both my "families" out on the road together. This is also when I got to know Rob Zombie guitarist John 5 (now with Mötley Crüe), who remains a great friend to this day.

About a month after that tour ended, I nearly had the opportunity to do double duty on the final Big Four show in the Bronx at Yankee Stadium. Dave Mustaine of Megadeth had been having neck problems, and there were some questions as to whether Megadeth would be able to play this monumental gig. Out of the blue, Kirk called me.

"Is Exodus ready to play a show?" he asked.

"Yeah, what's up?" I wasn't in the inner circle regarding the goings-on with the Big Four shows, so I didn't know what he was getting at.

"Well, Mustaine's not playing the Yankee Stadium Big Four show," he said, "and Metallica want Exodus to play. Are you guys rehearsed?"

"We're always rehearsed," I assured him. "We're ready right now."

In total scramble mode, we figured out how we could pull this off on short notice. I'd play on my Slayer rig and we'd borrow some of Slayer's gear so we wouldn't have to bring in anything more than an Ampeg and a drum kit. Maybe word got out to Dave that Megadeth was going to be replaced, because he had a change of heart at the last minute and decided he was doing the show after all, so we were off the bill. I mean, that would have inspired me to get better if I were in his shoes.

It would've been very cool for Exodus to play, but the proper outcome happened—the Big Four did the gig, just as advertised. The part of me that would've loved to have played there with Exodus had to take a back seat to the true meaning of the show, which is it's the fucking Big Four, not the Big 4.5. I just appreciated the fact that when Megadeth originally thought they wouldn't play, it was Exodus that Metallica wanted. That meant a lot. Thanks, Metallica.

AS MUCH AS BEING PART OF THE BIG FOUR CELEBRATION WOULD HAVE been an amazing gig for Exodus to play, we had one coming up a couple of weeks later that was way better: my wedding reception. Yeah, Exodus played at my wedding, along with a bunch of my other friends' bands, including Death Angel, Heathen, Skinlab, Attitude Adjustment, and Jack's bluegrass band, Coffin Hunter (among others). I didn't have a lot of money at the time, and weddings are expensive, so Lisa and I decided to offset the cost of our wedding with the concert. If Exodus played, we wouldn't have to pay for the venue. So we held the festivities where we had our first date, at the Avalon in Santa Clara. Once you take the dirty headbangers out of the place, it was a really nice venue, with a beautiful bar. They had everything we needed to accommodate friends and family alike.

We decided to do the wedding in two parts. The first part was a private ceremony for friends and family—all very nice and beautiful and wedding-like. Coffin Hunter played the wedding because they provided the acceptable music that older folks could enjoy. Lisa's father, as his wedding gift to us, paid for the catering, so everybody ate well. After the ceremony and reception, the old folks and people who didn't want to listen to Exodus and friends play could go home. Then the Avalon opened to the public, and it turned into a metal show that we dubbed "Holty Matrimony." When it came time for Exodus to play, we were using Death Angel's gear. I was playing on Ted Aguilar's amps, and you know guitar players—we're comfortable on our own amps. If you're not comfortable playing, it's gonna be a struggle. Plus, I was wasted, just *ripped*. I told Tom, *Look, it's my wedding, I'm gonna be partying. Nothing difficult. Let's keep it simple.* So Tom kicks into "Iconoclasm," and I looked at him, he said, like a deer in the headlights, like, *What are you doing? I said nothing hard! No eight-and-a-half-minute epics!*

But the wedding was beautiful, and we had a fucking super memorable show. One of Lisa's oldest friends was so wasted during the metal part of the show, she was on the floor playing air bass, but it looked like she was masturbating, like her hand was thumbing around down south. The club threw her out. Undeterred, she climbed the fence to get back in. It was all too much for Lisa after a while. Poor thing found a place to curl up in the backstage area and fell asleep, exhausted by a long day, followed by the most metal reception ever.

Two thousand and eleven had been quite the intense and landmark-filled year as I bounced between two bands, jetted around the globe, and still managed to find time to get married. Even though Slayer wrapped up their touring in the fall, Exodus had our usual run of European dates lined up for November and December. This year, we were co-headlining the Thrashfest Classics Tour with Sepultura, on a bill that also included Destruction, Heathen, and Mortal Sin. Lee would get his opportunity to do double duty playing in Exodus and Heathen. By the time we returned home, the week before Christmas, I was gassed. I also came to the realization that I wouldn't be able to commit to all of both bands' touring commitments and also continue to make Exodus albums. Something had to give. Being a family man and having children and a wife, I had to allow myself some time at home. Part of me said, *Keep working. You're only gonna earn money when you're on the road, and the more you work, the more you make, and maybe someday you can entertain the idea of actually retiring.* But it was more important to balance the work life and homelife, so I had to make sure I was home sometimes. Though I didn't necessarily express this to my Exodus bandmates, they could see that Slayer was going to keep me busy as long as Jeff was healing and rehabbing (which was sort of an unknown timeline), and there might be scheduling conflicts in the future. So at some point early on in my Slayer tenure, Tom called me up and goes, *How do you feel about us going to Europe in the new year so we're not sitting around stagnant? What do you think? We could take Rick.* I don't know if he thought I'd be appalled, but I was all for it, immediately. I didn't want to prevent them from working and paying their bills, and plus, it kept the band's name out there. I was just doing my best to keep both bands happy. I had their full support, and they had mine. I said, *Yeah, of course. Fucking go for it.*

In early February 2012, we marked the ten-year anniversary of Paul Baloff's death with an all-star Exodus show, Bonded by Baloff, at the Oakland Metro Operahouse. This celebration of Paul's memory and legacy featured two stages of bands—Forbidden, Possessed, and Heathen, and we even got some of the Exodus alumni to jam with us. Rick Hunolt jammed on a few of the *Bonded*-era songs, and Jeff Andrews and Kirk Hammett came up and joined us on "Impaler" and "Whipping Queen." I missed Paul and really would've killed for him and other good friends I'd lost—Jimmy Lapin, Ronnie Schwartz, Toby Rage—to have seen me play the kind of shows I'd been doing with Slayer. I would've loved to have had them be part of that, a part of my fucking life. I could just imagine Baloff driving Kerry nuts backstage. It would have been fucking awesome: *Hey, what are you doing? What are you doing, man?*

Even though Slayer hadn't put out a new album since 2009's *World Painted Blood*, they were a touring juggernaut that packed 'em in wherever they went. And they went all over the world, to places I'd never been with Exodus, including India. So it was a big shift in gears for me to go between Slayer and Exodus, which I did frequently in 2012. Don't get me wrong—Exodus were playing bigger and better shows with every passing year, but we weren't anywhere near Slayer's level.

I didn't have any Slayer commitments in the spring, so Exodus booked a nice string of South American dates, where we typically did really well and the fans were passionate thrashers. That segued into early summer stints for both Exodus and Slayer in Europe, so Exodus went over with Rick Hunolt joining the band, just for the tour. The funny thing was, Rick didn't replace me; he just sort of reclaimed his former position in the band that Lee Altus took over. Which meant that, on that tour, Lee actually replaced me and played my parts. Confusing, right? Well, it was even more confusing for poor Lee, who basically had to learn all my solo sections, some of which were in different keys from his solo sections. Both bands were on the bill at the Graspop Metal Meeting festival in Belgium, so I joined Exodus for the set, and we went out with the three-guitar, Lynyrd Skynyrd–style lineup, which was a blast.

I barely had a week between my Graspop appearance with Exodus and the Mayhem Festival, with Slayer as one of the main-stage acts, launched in San Bernardino. When you're part of a tour package that has a dedicated Jägermeister stage, it's a pretty safe bet that bittersweet brown elixir is flowing freely. Jäger was the drink of choice for Exodus, and we always had it on our rider for many years, but when it's a cosponsor of a giant traveling metal festival, the availability is on a whole other level. Not only was it omnipresent on the Mayhem tour, we even had a little Jäger machine that dispensed it cold on our tour bus.

Because the Slayer dressing room was always open for other bands to come in and party, what started as kind of a joke turned into a ritual. Every day at a specific time, like 9:10 or whatever, people would show up for a shot of Jäger because we were done with our set, we were changed, and it was time to party. The gathering would last like thirty seconds. Everybody would pile in the dressing room, we'd pour like fucking seventy-five shots, and everybody shouted, "9:10!" or whatever, and then boom, down went the shots. The other bands knew where to come to have a drink and have a good time, and it was always our dressing room, because everybody was welcome to hang out. And many quite often crawled out.

On the night drives between shows, we'd sit on our bus and would just fucking pound shots. But it wasn't like a loud party. Everyone on the bus would be maybe quietly playing games on their phones, and then someone would lift his head up and go, *Shot?* And we'd all go, *Yeah!* We'd do a shot, cheers, and go back to whatever we're doing—the quietest bunch of drunks you've ever seen. Kerry *never* appeared drunk. He was like superhuman. He'd leave victims everywhere, and he'd just seem like he was fucking normal. I don't know how he does it. But he gets real quiet, so maybe the less you talk, the fewer clues you're giving away as to how drunk you are. But he was the fucking Bionic Man when it came to drinking. He would make an Absolut Mandrin and orange drink, but he would take a cocktail straw and gather enough orange juice to fill that cocktail straw and add it to a full glass of vodka. Mine would be like a smoothie. He just liked it *tainted*. A little colorization is all it was.

Other than the South America shows I did with Exodus in the spring, nearly every other gig I did in 2012 was with Slayer. We played in Europe, North America, South America, and Asia—nearly sixty dates in all. I didn't know how Jeff Hanneman's health was improving, but it seemed like he should have been good to go by this time. If he had been healthy enough to play two songs with the band at the Big Four in Indio in April 2011, surely he would have been able to play a full set at some point in 2012. However, wanting to keep my nose out of Slayer's inner-circle dealings, I didn't ask any questions, and nobody gave me any information. I just knew that they kept telling me when the next tour would be, no mention of a timeline for Jeff's return. The longer it went on, though, the more I wondered.

CHAPTER 26
RAINING BLOOD

YOU CAN SPECULATE ON INNER-BAND RELATIONSHIPS ALL YOU WANT, but from my first rehearsals with Slayer in 2011, everybody was all smiles. The vibe was good. Those guys had known each other for decades, and though Lombardo had been out of the band on a couple of different occasions, they seemed to have figured out how to make it work. Things are different in every band, but in Slayer, people were given their space. People kind of hung to themselves and did their own thing in their own world. In early 2013, though, all the space in the world wasn't going to fix whatever disagreement Dave had with his bandmates. This was all behind-the-scenes stuff, so the first I heard was when Kerry called me less than two weeks before Slayer were slated to go to Australia to play six Soundwave dates.

"Dave's not going to Australia," he said without much more additional explanation. "Do you want to come down and rehearse?"

"Well, you're rehearsing with a drummer, right?" I asked. I figured if he was calling me that I was sort of the last piece of the puzzle.

"Yeah, it's Jon Dette." John was a California guy and had been in Slayer on several previous occasions as a fill-in. He'd also played with Testament, so I knew he was a pro.

"Nah, I'm good," I said. "As long as you're tight with him, I play to you, so I'll be tight with you. I'm cool. I'll stay home. See you in Australia."

I played as much to Kerry as I did to the drums. In Exodus, I followed Tom; in Slayer, I followed Kerry. I always had a monitor on my side of the stage that had nothing but Kerry in it, and I followed what he was doing every bit as much as I ever did the drums. Kerry's such a fucking machine, and he's massively, savagely underrated as a rhythm guitar player. And his tone just rolls over you. It's hard to explain, but it's like an avalanche. He's as good as anybody in the world. His stamina is fucking second to none, and playing ninety minutes of thrash metal ain't easy.

Because there were things going on in Slayer that were outside my Gary Holt box, I wasn't privy to anything that went down that caused Dave to pull out of the Soundwave dates. I was hoping it wasn't permanent, but I didn't know. Dave and I were very close, we're friends, but he didn't talk to me about Slayer business. We'd toured together after he left Slayer in the early '90s and formed Grip Inc., and I was even close with his kids. I used to make paper airplanes out of giant concert posters when they were really young. Touring with him in Slayer, he and I used to go on missions to find döner kebab and just walk around on our days off in Europe. So, at the time, I didn't know if "Dave's not going to Australia" meant he was out of the band or this was something that could be worked out.

When we were in Australia, Dave put out a statement airing some of the band's dirty laundry, or at least his side of things. I think that was kind of a hard pill for Tom and Kerry to swallow, so it seemed like there was no going back. There might have been a chance at reconciliation if things had been handled privately, but I think Dave kind of sealed his fate when he went public. In a move that may have overstepped my bounds a little bit, I actually called Paul Bostaph via Skype from Australia and said, *You might want to call those guys. Dave's done.* Paul being an old friend and a former bandmate, I just gave him a heads-up. They'd probably already called Paul anyway, for all I know, since he had drummed for Slayer on four albums in the '90s and early '00s, but I just didn't think Jon Dette was ever really in the running for the gig, and I loved playing with Paul. I was gonna miss my ventures with Dave, though. We had a lot of fun doing that shit.

I didn't have too much time to ruminate on that unsettled situation, though, because not long after I returned from Australia, Exodus headed out with Anthrax and Municipal Waste on the North American Metal Alliance tour. I was more easily able to pull off US tours with Exodus, because there wasn't the extreme amount of travel that going overseas required. This was a really fun bill—yet another run with our good friends in Anthrax—but it had now been nearly three years since we released *Exhibit B*, and I didn't know when I'd be able to find the time to finally write and record a follow-up. At least if we were able to do quality tours like this, we could all continue to pay our bills, but we'd have to put out something new sooner rather than later to continue to build the momentum we'd slowly continued to gain. My being in Slayer definitely helped that momentum a bit, but we couldn't rest on that. Exodus was my first band, and I wasn't about to let that totally take a back seat. Slayer seemed to be able to tour nearly nonstop for years between albums, but I figured even they would also have to return to the studio sometime soon, assuming Jeff was ready to go. Kerry had apparently been working on some stuff, but with Dave leaving and Jeff's health issues (as far as I knew) unresolved, I was unaware of any plans for them to make a new album.

That became a moot point when I got a call from Kerry in early May, two days before my fiftieth birthday, telling me that Jeff had died as a result of alcohol-related cirrhosis of the liver. Like everyone else in the world, I was stunned by this news. I never, ever saw that coming. Up to that point, my understanding of why I was still filling in for him was the necrosis of his arm. They fucking surgically removed a chunk of his arm, and since this music is demanding as fuck to play with healthy arms, I figured I was only going to be filling in until his strength had returned and the rehab and physiotherapy got him back in shape to play. I had no idea that there was anything going on that would take him from all of us.

I can't imagine how hard it must have been to make that call and all the others Kerry had to make to break the news to everyone. I think he was still trying to wrap his head around it. He didn't have time to process it. He just had to get the word out and then he could grieve. There were probably a dozen people involved in the band doing the same thing. It was fucking devastating news to hear. I never expected it and always hoped Jeff would return. I've always been comfortable in my skin, and I was ready to have him come back at any time. It was his band and his seat I was keeping warm. It was a tragedy, gone way too soon. A lot of tears were shed. I had planned a fiftieth birthday party, but it turned into much more of a memorial for Jeff.

I don't know how Jeff went from playing a couple of songs with Slayer at Indio—and seemingly on the road to recovery—to passing away from liver failure two years later, but those years away from Slayer must have been very hard on him. I never spoke to him about that, so I can't address his state of mind, but if what I'd done my whole life was taken away from me, I'd be pretty fucking depressed. Nobody wants to have that decision made by an injury. You want to walk away on your own terms. Being able to do it and choosing not to is different from not being able to do it.

Jeff's widow, Kathryn, couldn't bring herself to be at Jeff's memorial at the Hollywood Palladium, but she wrote a note that was read by

Kristen Mulderig from management. Part of Kathryn's note included an anecdote about when Slayer first told Jeff that they were going to tour with a replacement. Apparently, Jeff looked really bummed, and he hung his head down and said, *Who is it?* She told him, *Gary Holt*, and he looked up and went, *Fuck yeah.* Having that affirmation and belief in me, that me replacing him would be a cool thing, meant everything to me. This was the first time I ever knew that Jeff had ever expressed any opinion at all on my participation in Slayer. And it was one of the heaviest moments of my life. I fucking cried real tears of gratitude. It was an emotional blow during a very emotional night. I'll carry that with me forever. Jeff approved. He didn't say, *Cool,* he said, *Fuck yeah.* I had his seal of approval.

I later found out from Armand—Kerry's guitar tech—that, back in 2010 when Exodus played a full *Bonded by Blood* set at Hellfest, where Slayer were also on the bill, Jeff came to the stage to watch the show. Jeff notoriously kept to himself when touring with Slayer, so this was a revelation to me. Armand said, *Jeff never watched any other bands, none of them. He'd play a festival, it didn't matter who was playing, he wasn't watching any. He must really like you guys.* He came out of the dressing room or off the bus to watch the whole set.

After Jeff passed, I had a conversation with Slayer's manager, Rick Sales, and it was one of the most casual conversations he and I ever had. We talked about just random stuff, but there was never anything like, *Do you want to continue?* or *Do you want the gig?* One thing that was understood was that they were definitely going forward despite Jeff's passing—with Paul Bostaph as the new drummer—and I was gonna be part of the plan. I'm sure there were internal discussions about whether they would carry on, but once again, that was out of my realm of responsibility. I was never privy to their decision-making and never asked to be. They knew they just had to tell me where to be, and I was there; it didn't matter. I didn't need to be involved in that kind of shit.

That was kind of the beauty for me of being in Slayer. When I was in Exodus, I had to wear so many hats, and in Slayer, I had to wear one. Just go out and fucking shred and play angry. I didn't have to worry about anything else, and I didn't wanna know. I wasn't a partner, never was, and never asked to be. I was an employee, and I was just like a crew guy, except I got onstage instead of in the truck. And I was perfectly fine with that. The only change was in the tour books, where it no longer listed me as "temporary guitar." It said: Kerry King, guitar; Tom Araya, bass, vocals; Paul Bostaph, drums; Gary Holt, guitar.

Through two years of touring with Slayer as Jeff's replacement, fans had largely embraced my presence in the band. I think people understood that Slayer didn't get some shred dude from nowhere who wore his guitar as high as his necktie and was over there fucking shit up. I was a thrash metal peer from back in the day, one of the forefathers of the style. Fans took it for what it was at the time: *This is something really cool, and you're only going to be able to see it once.* I was always respectful of the band's (and Jeff's) legacy and their fans. I always tried to bring a positive stamp to the show. Typically, the response I got was super positive, but not always. There was one guy on the first tour in Europe, a guy with a really awful skullet. He was just fucking flipping me off constantly. Eventually, I felt like I wanted to do something about it. There was a time in my life when I might've jumped down and confronted him, but I motioned to our production manager at the time, John Lafferty, and he got on the radio. I think the guy saw people looking at him while they were on their radios, and he knew he was gonna get thrown the fuck out, so he took off. Years later—I'd done so many Slayer shows by this point—we played a show in Milan, and a guy was dead center, front row, and he was flipping me off and hollering, *Fuck you, motherfucker!* at me the whole fucking show, like really, really fucking pissing me off and being real aggressive. At the end of the show, I think he was a little surprised when I went right off the front of the stage and onto the subwoofers, which are in the front of the stage, between that and the barricade. All of a sudden, I was a foot and a half away from him, and he didn't have shit to say. I can't understand that kind of shit. If you really are that opposed to me being there, why'd you buy the ticket? He was the only one who *really* got to me. But I was fucking lucky. Slayer fans were overwhelmingly supportive, and they're notoriously defensive of their band. It could've been horrible.

People definitely had their opinions about Lombardo versus Bostaph, as well. There's only one Dave Lombardo, but there's also only one Paul Bostaph. I think in many ways, it's unfair to compare the two, because they both have very different styles. Dave has like a jazz player's mentality that I think in a lot of ways is what carries those earlier Slayer songs. There's this element of danger and looseness where it felt like the unexpected could happen. And Paul's a machine, a robot—not in a bad way. If you built a robotic human capable of just pummeling with maximum force, you'd have Paul Bostaph. Paul's drumming on *God Hates Us All* is just fucking phenomenal, the whole record. Dave obviously played on the classic early records, and he's always gonna be renowned as the guy who did that double-kick break on "Angel of Death." Any band that has had both those guys is fucking lucky. *Wow, we went from Dave Lombardo to Paul Bostaph—that's pretty fucking cool, not really a drop-off.* Paul's discography with Slayer, Forbidden, Testament, and Exodus is phenomenal. His track record speaks for itself. He's a fucking god on drums, and as much as I missed Dave in Slayer, I was thrilled that Paul was the guy they got to replace him.

While I spent the summer with Slayer in Europe, Exodus lined up their own European tour, this time with Lee's axe partner in Heathen, Kragen Lum, filling in for me. As much as we all love Rick Hunolt, it was a huge inconvenience for Lee to have to switch over to playing my parts when I couldn't tour with Exodus. Kragen's an amazing guitar player and just a generally super schooled musician. He does all of

Exodus's tablature books, so filling in for me was an easy transition for him—he could really nail the parts well—and Lee could perform his role in the band as per usual. So just like I was listed on the Slayer tour books as temporary guitar, Kragen sort of wound up with that same role in Exodus when I wasn't available to tour Europe.

Because I never really saw Exodus play a show without me—if our paths crossed at a festival, of course I'd perform with them—I never really thought too hard about it. But I was at a festival in Europe with Slayer one time, hanging out with Brent Hinds from Mastodon, and he goes, *Yeah, I just saw Exodus the other day.* It was so weird hearing someone tell me they saw my band play the other day at a festival and I wasn't part of it, hearing someone speak about my band as if I weren't in it. It kind of tripped me out. It was probably just as weird for my Exodus bandmates to see me play in Slayer. I'd always get them out to our shows when we were in town. It was great to see them, but I think they might have felt a little weird. Lee once said it was like watching someone have sex with your wife, in a bad way! I can understand that.

After Exodus's summer tour with Kragen filling in, we didn't have anything else on the immediate horizon, so I knew I needed to get to work on new material. I had Slayer commitments until the end of November 2013 and no tours confirmed until May 2014, so my hope was that I could write and Exodus could record during that window. I actually started writing while I was on tour with Slayer at the end of 2013, because I knew I needed to get the songs done in this compressed time frame. Slayer graciously set me up with a sort of practice room in the backstage area. I had a half stack, and I'd go in and work on riffs.

While the backstage area was a good place for me to write when I had the time, Slayer also attracted a pretty interesting cross section of famous fans who would find their way back there, especially when we were in places like LA or New York. One time in October 2013, when we were playing a couple of shows at the Hollywood Palladium, I discovered Roy

Frank "RJ" Mitte III, who played Walter "Flynn" White Jr. in *Breaking Bad*, in our dressing room, completely wasted. Lisa, who was at the show that night, hadn't come backstage yet, because the wives usually gave us a little time to get dressed. I didn't even bother changing, I just ran downstairs and grabbed her: "Flynn is in my dressing room!" He and I talked about guns for a long time. It's kind of scary when a guy you just met wants to talk guns for an hour, but also cool as fuck!

I LOVE EVERY ALBUM I'VE MADE WITH EXODUS, NO QUESTION. AND SOME have been easier to make than others. But after three really great albums, two recorded by Andy Sneap, *Blood In, Blood Out* was a struggle pretty much from the start. It wasn't my ideal to have to write the album the way I did, working while I was on the road with Slayer, away from my Exodus bandmates. Having looming Slayer commitments dictating my time frame to write, rehearse, and record made it that much more fraught. And because our specific time frame didn't work for Andy Sneap, he was only able to record Tom's drums at Studio D in Sausalito and later mix and master the album. The guitars, bass, and vocals were all tracked by Jack on his Pro Tools setup in Tom's sweltering rehearsal room (a converted laundry room) on the goat farm in Briones, where he worked. We did it on the cheap instead of booking a really nice studio and burning through the budget, so we could keep some of the advance to pay our bills. I knew that I had shows to do in the spring with Slayer—a quick surprise appearance at the Golden Gods Awards in LA in April to play a new song, "Implode," a quick week of double duty with Exodus and European dates in May—so I had my back up against the wall. I had to record my parts and go. That was difficult for me, too, because I prefer to work when I'm feeling motivated and not like, *Fuck, I got two more solos to do, and I gotta leave. Let's get these done.* I didn't have the option to, let's say, live with them for a while and maybe tweak here and there. I also wouldn't be there to help record all the vocals, which I usually did, since I wrote most of the lyrics. On every other Exodus album, I had been there from start to finish, and I couldn't be this time.

For a number of different reasons, many of the same ones I've laid out above—lack of time to rehearse, not having Andy Sneap involved, me being gone—Rob was having a really difficult time with the material. He was going through some things, changes in his own life that I don't think impacted him negatively, just maybe his focus wasn't there. He struggled with the *Blood In, Blood Out* stuff. And because we didn't have the luxury of rehearsing like we did for the previous albums with him, he had to learn the songs as he went, and I think that process was difficult for him. When I was touring with Slayer in Europe, I was getting reports that it just wasn't going well. It wasn't an acceptable quality, and it just wasn't getting there. I'll take some of the blame for not having been there for all of it. But the band kind of got to the point where everybody thought maybe we should have Zetro come in and do a couple of takes. Maybe the thought was that it would kind of scare Rob a little bit.

Rob's such a super capable singer, and everybody was almost convinced to keep him. He'd come into Exodus like a blank slate and turned into my ideal modern-era Exodus singer, no disrespect to Zetro or Baloff. He did a great job on *Shovel Headed* when he was just learning this art, but *Exhibit A* and *B* are masterpieces, fucking phenomenal. But I kind of felt like since I was out on the road with Slayer when all this was going down and I hadn't been around for as much of the recording, it almost wasn't my decision on who would sing in the band. I voted for Zetro, and everybody else did, too. Tom broke the news to Rob. It was fucking hard; it's still hard. I'm still stinging from it. I fucking love Rob. And when he was gone, I missed the guy, missed his sense of humor. And maybe if I'd been with Exodus more and not missing tour after tour after tour, I might have fought harder to keep him. Rob fought with us to restore Exodus. He joined a band that had fucking zero prospects, but a bunch of hunger. And he deserves all the credit in the world for how we turned the band into this modern thrash fucking gargantuan and became eminently heavier than we ever had been in our lives.

There have been times in the band's history when things weren't always smooth between everybody. There was definitely tension between Zetro and me for years in the original run. There was the "founding guitar player dude, original songwriter/guitar player, and the guy who's not Paul Baloff." Which was obviously never fair to him. There were a lot of things that he did that rubbed me the wrong way and led to the band going on a hiatus in 1993. The difference between Exodus and a lot of bands is that we've learned to really appreciate what we've done and what we continue to do and what we will do. We've grown. Some people don't ever fucking change. We know not to take any of this for granted.

No one would have imagined that after the way things ended with Zetro after *Tempo* that he would ever return. But once again, he showed up when we needed him and he killed it. This was not an easy album to make for any of us. But his experience and expertise—and his impeccable timing (of course)—were a crucial part of *Blood In, Blood Out*. Zetro's always had an innate ability at timing. You'd think he was a drummer. You just tell him, and he'll get it. Sometimes his timing might be different from what I envision, and sometimes I like it better. He's got real rhythm, and on *Blood In*, Zetro really stepped up. There were things I would've done differently, but it was pretty difficult to explain what I was really looking for via fucking phone conversations and five-thousand-mile distances and emails. I couldn't discuss it with Zetro face-to-face. It got to the point where all the other guys in the band were saying they loved the album, and I was like, *Well, there's things I want to change.* But because of all the impediments of me being in Europe, it wasn't worth the trouble to try to fix a couple of parts I wasn't as happy with. I think because I wasn't there when so much of the album was put together, I'm maybe not as attached to it. On every previous Exodus album, I'd been there from start to finish, and I wasn't this time. Zetro did a great job, and I still think it's a killer album, but I can be hard on my own records. I love the hell out of them at the time, but I always feel like, *I can make it better. I can do better.* It's what pushes me to come up with better stuff and not rest on any laurels the band might have.

CHAPTER 27

FINAL CAMPAIGN

W HEN *BLOOD IN, BLOOD OUT* WAS RELEASED IN OCTOBER 2014, IT actually charted in the top 40, which was huge for Exodus. Despite whatever mixed feelings I had about the album and the way it came together, I was very proud of that. Exodus celebrated this achievement with another dose of double duty for me: a month of North America dates with Slayer and Suicidal Tendencies. This required a feat of strength from me to pull this off, because we were doing Exodus headlining shows on off days, too. So I did a fucking shit ton of shows back-to-back-to-back-to-back-to-back. The pace was so insane that I smoked some weed on that tour to help me relax. I couldn't drink before my Slayer set, so I'd take a couple of hits from my weed pen just to keep me from stressing, because it was a lot of fucking work.

Slayer had slowly been working on a new album (without me, it should be noted) when we weren't touring in 2014, and it was getting close to being finished. I knew that I wasn't going to be heavily involved in the record, but at one point, Kerry contacted me and asked me if I was ready to come in and bust out some leads. He had already done all the rhythm guitars and his leads. Before I went down to the studio in LA, they sent me some files of the solo sections, because I hadn't even heard most of the songs yet. We'd played "Implode" at the Golden Gods Awards, but everything they'd worked on since was all new to me. Since I wouldn't be playing solos on all the tracks, I set aside one day to come in and play my parts, not something I'd normally do. But honestly, this was all new territory for me—just contributing solos to a band I'd been playing with for three years now.

I also was trying to maximize my home time, which was so precious during this era of nonstop touring and bouncing between bands. I figured the quicker I cut my solos, the sooner I could go back home. Terry Date—a great guy and a legendary producer—was working on the album, and I walked in with my Kemper preamp and patched it in without going through the process of working on the tone, which is normally my favorite thing in the world to do. I wanted to move things along as quickly as possible. I didn't want to cut corners, but there wasn't a whole lot of solo work on the album for me anyway. On the older Slayer stuff I played live, there were so many different leads. But on *Repentless*, there were songs without *any* solos, which is cool as fuck. There are also some that I didn't solo on at all.

Kerry and Tom were both there in the studio, and they were stoked and happy with what I did. Tom would go, *That's fucking killer. Love it, dude, that sounds amazing.* They had a 49ers football game on the TV above the mixing console, and I'd watch the game and drink beer while I was recording. As I was doing some of the final solos, I felt my wrist kind of getting fucked up. At that point, I figured I probably wouldn't be able to play the next day even if I'd wanted to, and I didn't want what was supposed to be a day or two of work to stretch into four or five days I was away from my family. I could still play, so I just pushed through to finish them. The next day when I woke up, I couldn't move my left wrist. I blew my hand out so bad soloing that I literally couldn't move my hand at the wrist itself. I couldn't grab my backpack. I was relieved that I had finished, because I wouldn't have been tracking that day.

Ultimately, I think the album came out great. Kerry did an amazing job, and Terry Date's production sounds like a ton of bricks. Paul and Tom were killer, too, and I did some pretty good solos on it. I'm never *completely* happy with my lead work. That's an Exodus thing, too, so it has nothing to do with Slayer. I think if I'd given myself more time, maybe a couple of days, I'd be more satisfied with what I did. And not having any stake in or time spent with the songs like I normally would, I kind of feel a little detached from *Repentless*. Don't get me wrong— I'm still super proud of the record and my contribution to it, but it was the first time in my life I didn't write something on an album I played on. I would love to have written some songs on it, but I understood why I wasn't asked to. This was a Slayer record, and they deserved to handle their band however they chose to, however they saw fit. Kerry was writing tons of stuff, and he had it covered, and I was writing for Exodus at the time as well. Still, I took some pride when *Repentless* charted in the US at number 4. And I have two gold records—from the Czech Republic and Poland—that have my name on them, which I'll probably be buried with. I may not have written any music for Slayer, but playing live, I put my stamp on things, for sure.

My wrist wasn't the only physical casualty of playing for years in two very active thrash bands. I was fifty, and a life spent thrashing started to catch up with me a little bit. I'd had back pain since I was a kid, going back to my skateboarding days, but a long part of my tenure in Slayer was marred by severe back problems. It didn't keep me from playing live, because I'd do the show even if I could barely get through the set. I looked angry, but the reality was that I was in fucking agony. I'd limp to the stage, and I'd limp off. On days off, I didn't go out, because I couldn't comfortably walk anywhere. I was going to see doctors in urgent care or clinics between shows and getting trigger point injections in Europe where they prescribe stuff like tramadol, Toradol, and other pain meds. I was eating like 2,400 milligrams of ibuprofen a day. And I've had three epidurals, even though I've never given birth. At one point, I finally got an MRI, because I thought I needed a hip replacement—that's where the pain was centered. The doctor I was seeing broke the news to me.

"Your hip is fine, but your back's broken, basically," he told me. "And by the way, you have a horseshoe kidney."

"A *what*?" Never mind he just told me my back was broken.

"A horseshoe kidney," he repeated. "You have one big one. Instead of two separated, they're connected. You can't really disconnect one. You'd better take care of that thing."

Oh yeah, and about that broken back, I had a broken L5 disc that was causing the painful sciatica. The solution was to travel with an inversion table so I could hang upside down and decompress my back and create space in that disc. Slayer were super accommodating. They knew my back was really fucked up, so my inversion table was brought into the dressing room every day. Kerry said I looked like a vampire bat, hanging upside down by my feet. It also helped that Slayer traveled in style and comfort, which made it easier. I'd have a lot of days off to rest and treat my back. The tours might have looked long, but we weren't doing five shows a week. It was pretty chill.

As my Slayer commitments ramped after the release of *Repentless*—more than two hundred dates around the world from 2015 through the end of 2018—I did fewer and fewer tours with Exodus. Exodus were really concentrating on Europe, where they were doing good business supporting *Blood In, Blood Out*. Kragen Lum became not only my longtime fill-in—jetting off to South America, Australia, Japan, and Europe when I couldn't—he later helped with band management. He's got a great business mind, so he took on that role for a bit, even when he was no longer playing in the band.

For me, going between the two bands was never a problem musically. It was a lot of material to remember, but I always had a good mind for that. Early on in my Slayer tenure, I was sitting in a dressing room getting ready to go on with Slayer, and I was playing one of the riffs. Kerry looked over at me.

"You're not playing that right," he said flat out.

"Show it to me."

"I'll show it to you later," he said. "Sounds fine."

"No, show it to me now," I insisted. He did, and I went out ten minutes later and played it perfectly. I was able to look at it and remember it. Even if the set was an hour and a half long and the song was fifty minutes in, I could remember the tutorial from sixty minutes earlier. My musical memory helped me immensely in Slayer, since, unlike Exodus, these were not songs I wrote. I could still hang on to them. Show me something and I'll play it—wherever it is in the set—exactly like that.

I guess I never completely, however, got over moving from stage left (Exodus) to stage right (Slayer). Slayer were shooting the video for "Repentless" at a prison in East LA not long after I'd done some Exodus dates. When we took our places for filming, I went to the wrong side. We were just set up in the prison parking lot, but I went to stage left, which is where Kerry normally is, but it's where I've been in Exodus since Kirk Hammett left and joined Metallica. Kerry walked up and kind of waved his thumb and goes, *You're over there, buddy!* Things like that I had to adjust to, like, *Oh yeah, I'm going back and forth from one side of the stage to the other.* But musically, it wasn't hard. When I'd be back in Exodus, though, they'd give me shit, like, *Welcome back to the ghetto, fool.* Happy to be back!

In January 2018, Slayer made a surprising announcement. I was told they had decided it was time to bring the band to a close and that there would be a farewell tour. At the time, there wasn't any date on *when* it would end, but it didn't really matter to me, because I was committed. I'd been there for more than seven years already, so I figured, *Let's finish this thing, and then I'll go back to the life I've got waiting.* I was also kind of relieved that the end was in sight because there were many times when the guilt around my absence from Exodus would get really bad. But at the same time, I understood what my playing in Slayer did for raising Exodus's and my profile in the metal world. Remember how I was once a footnote in thrash? So even though I had been itching to try to find some time to write and record a follow-up to 2014's *Blood In, Blood Out*, I knew the farewell tour would put the brakes on that indefinitely.

As to why Slayer decided to "retire," I can only surmise. I was never part of inner-circle decisions, but I'd been around the band enough to get a sense of the mixed feelings some members had toward touring. I think the travel over the years had been rough for Tom, who, like me, has a family. Tom also had some serious issues with his neck in 2010, which probably contributed to his desire to wind things down. And I know Jeff, while still alive, had expressed his lack of enthusiasm for touring. In my tenure in Slayer, we toured our asses off. As we all got older, it even increased. Maybe if we had slowed down a little during those earlier Gary Holt years in Slayer, we would've continued, because we wouldn't have maybe felt as burned out. When I first joined Slayer, it wasn't uncommon to do three or four shows in a row. Toward the end, we never did more than two in a row. It had become an easier schedule. It was easier on Tom's voice, and we were getting older. All that said, I think Kerry felt Slayer were ending too soon, but better to go out swinging than go out punch-drunk from some bum who'd never held a heavyweight title knocking you out. We were going to go knocking fools out. We were still wearing the belt, and we were going to retire with the fucking belt.

DURING MY YEARS PLAYING IN SLAYER, MY FATHER'S HEALTH HAD PRO-
gressively deteriorated. He'd been a lifelong smoker, so he'd had a
quadruple bypass surgery and different things with his lungs. At age
eighty-five, he was in hospice care, and as 2018 wound down, I was
receiving multiple updates from my family about his well-being while
I was on tour in Europe with Slayer. He wasn't going to have any more
procedures, no more surgeries. I knew that I would have to go home at
some point, and it had to be before he passed. So I took a chance and
picked my exit. I decided that I would fly home after the Berlin show
on December 2, before the band went to Scandinavia for four dates. It
seemed like a perfect spot to break away. Every day leading up to that
was nerve-racking as fuck, though. I kept wondering, *Am I delaying this
too long?* Slayer arranged for Phil Demmel to fly over and fill in for
me. He spent about a week in advance of my departure learning the set
with me and watching the shows. It's super valuable to be able to watch
the set in real time before you're thrown into the fire. Phil, under the
gun, learned a lot of songs quickly. He wasn't ready at first, but he had
a big advantage going into it in that he was a lifelong Slayer fan. And as
I've said, the key to learning any song by another artist is knowing the
arrangement first. You can learn the notes easily once you know where
every change is. There were times when I didn't know if I was making
the right choice staying for the extra days to make sure the band was
ready to play a show without me, but it worked out in the end. Through
this, I had the full support of Slayer. Everyone knew that I had to do
what I had to do. They were total brothers, which is all you can ask for
at a time like that.

Leaving when I did worked out, as I was able to spend time with my
dad. I was there for one of his last good days, where I could talk to him
and stuff. My daughters were able to see him as well. I even fed him his
last meal, the day he passed at home, December 17, with my mom and
all his kids present, knowing he was loved and respected. It was rough.

He was the wisest, most amazing man I'd ever known. It took me a long time to internalize that, though. He was always Dad, and he was always a really good father to all of us, but as I got older, I realized how much wisdom he dropped in my lap that took me forever to grasp. When I was young and stupid, it was just like, *That's Dad being Dad.* But he was just being *right.* He taught me everything I ever needed to know about being a man. Those were all lessons that took a long time for me to realize the truth behind. The Christmas holiday was tough for our extended family that year.

Slayer weren't planning to get back out on the road until early March 2019, when we had dates scheduled in Australia, New Zealand, and Asia, so I had a couple of months to grieve my father's passing and spend some much-needed family time before I was called back for duty. Though it wasn't announced to the general public until later that summer, I knew before then when Slayer's Final Campaign would end, with two dates at the Los Angeles Forum at the end of November 2019. I could finally start thinking about what life and my career would look like after nearly a decade in Slayer. I didn't, however, dwell too much or focus on those final dates. I wanted to soak up every moment, every show in these last nine months.

Because we were headlining bigger venues and the dates were spaced further apart, every off day in Europe, I tried to go out and do something fun with my guitar tech, Warren Lee, or whoever was up for it. Tom and I went out a lot on days off because Kerry would go out so late. He wouldn't eat dinner until 9:00 p.m., and I'd have already eaten at 7:00 and be ready for bed when he wanted to go out. On beautiful summer days in Europe, I liked to go out and drink some beer. I'd find a little outdoor beer garden and just sit there and fucking watch the world go by and pound some wonderful Belgian beers or whatever the local brew was. Tom was always down for doing that with me. We got pretty hammered in the middle of the day a few times on that final tour, pretty fucked up. We'd get back to the hotel at 3:00 in the afternoon and were fucking weaving.

Slayer had obviously played some big shows during my stint with the band, but when it was announced that this would be their final tour, we were playing—and selling out—the kinds of venues I associated with the biggest touring acts of my youth, full-on arenas, every night. I grew up going to arena shows. I played some arena-ish shows (more like large theaters) in the '80s on the Headbangers Ball Tour, even some fucking places where I saw a lot of shows as a kid. But with Slayer, we were playing the fucking Shark Tank (SAP Center) in San Jose, which has a concert capacity of nearly twenty thousand, and sold it out. We sold out the Oakland Coliseum Arena (also close to twenty thousand capacity) where I have seen countless shows, from the Who to Janet Jackson to Madonna. When I was there with Slayer, I spent a lot of time just walking around taking pictures and trying to soak it in. And when I'd walk out onstage at a place like that and look at the crowd, it's remarkable. Playing that kind of uncompromising music for a fucking sold-out arena is mind-blowing. And I'll remember it until the day I die, until Alzheimer's kicks in, whichever comes first. I hope I'm still remembering that shit when I'm crossing over.

Another thing that was a childhood dream come true that the scale of this tour provided was incredible stage pyrotechnics. That was my teenage wet dream. It was fucking everything I'd dreamed about after seeing my rock heroes as a kid who probably just had some flash pots, nothing like the firestorm that Slayer were hauling from city to city. As a kid, I was like, *Maybe someday, I'll have that.* I couldn't have fathomed what Slayer's stage production would be like. What teenage me probably also wouldn't have fathomed is the inherent danger in being surrounded by all this firepower on a nightly basis, especially when you're running all over the place and playing ripping thrash. Before every tour, we'd have a production day to go over everything, and our set lists always had all the pyro cues on them. Before every show, the local fire marshal would come in and inspect it. His job was to approve it and approve how big we could go with it because you could dial it up and down. I always loved it when we were allowed to go big. One of the biggest thrills was to go out for the pyro testing and just lie back on the stage, leaning on the monitor wedge with my phone ready to record a video, like, *All right, go!* I started lots of fires as a kid, and here I was being part of the fires. It was fucking great. Instead of setting stuff on fire myself, people were paid to do it.

As suits their music and image, Slayer didn't go cheap on the pyro. There were fucking walls of flames, and it was fucking hot. Friends who had been in the crowd would comment that they could feel the heat twenty rows back from the barricade. Try being fucking five feet from it. It'll dry you out. You could be all soaked in sweat, and it'll dry your shirt. I'd come offstage kind of dry because I worked in what amounted to a giant, propane-powered dryer. But it was so fucking spectacular to be a part of. It was bringing Slayer the way Slayer should be, fucking everything on fire. Hell awaits. It should look like hell, right? We fucking brought hell to a town near you.

I never got torched or burned, but I had a couple of near misses, especially when we added the downstage flamethrowers. I had one go off in a place I wasn't expecting it. I had to check to see if I still had any eyebrows. That shit would destroy you if it hit you. But the stuff back by the amp line, I knew where my limits were. I knew how close I could get. I would put the headstock of my guitar in that shit, walk up and fucking sweep my guitar right through it, real quickly. Fucking Bostaph had it worse than anybody. He was stuck in the middle of all that shit and couldn't go anywhere. I could at least vacate the premises if it got too hot.

The final tour also brought out some surprising, unexpected Slayer fans. We were playing Budapest in June 2019, and our tour manager

came up and told us that the actor Jason Momoa, who was in town filming *Dune*, was coming to the show. I'm a *Game of Thrones* super fan.
I've watched the whole show, every season, front to back, at least five or
six times. And when I'm done, I have to fight the desire to do it all over
again. It's not about Aquaman for me, it's all about Khal Drogo. Needless to say, we were stoked to meet him, and it turned out he was a super
rad dude. He's about as down to earth as you can imagine. We got the
message that he liked to drink Guinness, so we had a cooler of Guinness for him, and we partied. During the show, over the massive volume
of a Slayer show with pyro and everything, I could hear him yelling,
"SLAYER! WOOOOOHH!"

One of the other iconic moments for me on the final tour was playing a sold-out Madison Square Garden on November 9, 2019. If you
can sell out the nineteen-thousand-plus-capacity Madison Square
Garden, you are at an elite level as a musician. And for Slayer to do
that as headliners really spoke to how they were able to bring uncompromising thrash to such a high level. The venue does a really cool ceremony to acknowledge that achievement. They gathered us up before
the show and presented us each with these little turquoise-blue Tiffany's boxes. Each one contained a sterling silver replica ticket, with
the New York skyline on it, from the show. Apparently, they do this
for any act that sells out the Garden. That thing is a prized possession
for me. I was pretty fucking amazed when they handed it to me. I'm
sure bands who sell out the Garden all the time are like, *I'll put it with
the other ones*, or *I'll give this one to my brother. I've got three.* But I'm
never getting another one. They don't give them out to the support
band. That's assuming I'd ever get lucky enough to get on a tour that
sold out the Garden. But as a headliner? That's not gonna happen
with Exodus. I'm a realist. And I'm happy with my lot in life; I'm not
thinking one day we're gonna all of a sudden sell millions of albums
when we never have before. But yeah, I love that ticket; I cherish it.

That show also had a one-off laminate, just for that show, and I keep it inside the Tiffany's box with the silver ticket.

I will never forget standing on that Madison Square Garden stage, in front of nineteen thousand screaming Slayer fans—raging thrash diehards—and feeling the intense heat briefly engulf me as the stage pyro sent twenty-foot flames toward the ceiling. This fire, more than a decade removed from my last hit from a meth pipe, was not a destroyer. It offered a rebirth. I had, against all odds, gone from being a washed-up, meth-addicted thrash guitarist nobody wanted to touch to improbably touring the world playing in one of the most fearsome and important metal bands of a generation. This was my renewal. This was my redemption. I'd survived, and even though Slayer was winding down, I knew that *I* wasn't going to stop.

After Madison Square Garden, we were just weeks away from the final shows. Rather than focusing on something coming to an end, we were just living in the moment—sold-out arenas everywhere—and enjoying the camaraderie of the other bands on the tour and our crew and each other. We were just all having fun, not really discussing the end. When we got there, we were there. Maybe we were just in denial, but it really didn't seem like we were heading to the end of anything; we were just appreciating what a killer tour it was. It wasn't until we got to Southern California that I felt this was it. We were to play two nights at the Los Angeles Forum. First night was no problem, other than one little snafu. Before we went on, I was standing on the side of the stage with Tom waiting for the intro to go, and what started playing after the normal "Delusions of Saviour" opener was not what I was expecting. It segued into the beginning of "South of Heaven," and the crowd went crazy. Not me—I was freaking out! We were supposed to be doing "Repentless"!

"It's the wrong intro, it's the wrong intro!" I'm yelling. "What are they fucking doing? It's one of the biggest shows of my life, and someone's fucked it up!"

"It's all right," Tom said, laughing. "It's the right one, we forgot to tell you we were gonna change it up for these LA shows. It's all good."

"Thanks for letting me know. I'm fucking freaking out here."

Night two is when it felt weird in an emotional way, that this is it, this is the last one. I have a photo, it's the last ever photo shoot of the band, that was taken on our way to the stage. It looked like we were on our way to our own funeral because we're fucking nervous. We were trying to be tough or straight-faced, but you can tell there are a lot of nerves going on there. To a man, we looked like we were fucking about to stand trial for murder. We didn't look fucking confident, we looked scared. That's the only way to really describe it—a lot of nerves. The show was epic, though, and it flew by. The emotion never really hit me until my ending solo lead break in the last song, "Angel of Death," where I always hit the one whammy bar note and held the guitar above my head. When I was doing that, I was fighting back tears. That was an emotional moment because I'd been doing that stunt, trick, gimmick, whatever the hell you want to call it, for a long, long time with Slayer, and I knew I was doing it for the last time. That's when it hit. And then watching Kerry do the chain drop at the end of the show that was signifying the end of an era, and we were all super emotional.

To celebrate (or mourn) the occasion, I'd bought two bottles of Mad Dog 20/20 fortified wine—the same shit Exodus celebrated our first real record contract with—because Slayer's manager, Rick Sales, liked his wine. I came from the ghetto, so I figured I'd get him some ghetto wine. I walked into the production office where he was sitting, presented them to him, and said, "Rick, I wanna thank you for everything. You guys treated me like family. So I brought you a couple bottles of wine." Then I showed him exactly *what* wine I'd brought him! He cracked one open—no corkscrew needed!—and took a drink. Both those bottles got drunk. They did not sit around like a gimmick. I passed them around, and everyone took a pull.

For some, Slayer's final tour seemed like an unexpected and abrupt ending. I think a lot of people didn't understand why they hung it up then. I was asked a lot if I thought that this was indeed it for a band that seemed to still have a lot in the tank. Or maybe there would be a reunion at some point? I didn't see it happening. I saw November 30, 2019, as the last time anybody was gonna see Slayer live onstage. That said, if Slayer wanted to return, and they were all ready, I'd be there with them. If we felt we could still play this shit and everybody wanted to do it, I'm down. They know I'd do it. I just don't see it ever happening. I'm sure the way the concert industry works, they've probably been offered gobs of money to come back since probably four months after the last show, during the pandemic. But my sense was that the band had moved on. But what a career it was. I was honored to have been a part of it, to help keep Jeff's music alive, and to play the songs that Kerry, Jeff, and Tom wrote and that Lombardo and Paul played on. I'll carry that shit with me my whole life. It was an amazing time.

The end of Slayer really underscored how lucky I was to have two musical families: Exodus have been my family since I was seventeen, and Kerry, Tom, Dave, Paul, and Slayer's management made me feel like family from the very beginning. They never treated me like I was a hired gun. They treated me like I belonged there; they treated me like a brother from day one, and it's all you can ever fucking ask for. They never made me feel like some fucking bum, like, *Let's whisper when that guy's in earshot because we don't want him to hear what we're saying about him.* They were all really, really wonderful people. I love them all.

But now it was time to move on to my next chapter.

CHAPTER 28
COLLATERAL DAMAGE

T HE END OF SLAYER WASN'T AS TRAUMATIC FOR ME AS IT MIGHT HAVE been for other members of that band. I could just go right back to my other musical family, Exodus. I didn't have to try to start a new band. I felt very lucky to have what I have and to have it waiting for me. Not a lot of guys are that fortunate. Though there were many tours I missed while I was away with Slayer, we still managed to make a killer Exodus album together, and those guys kept the band moving forward and kept our legend alive when I couldn't be there. I have nothing but love for all of them, even the three more-right-leaning dummies! Ha ha ha! I'm the minority, politically, in Exodus, and I'm the principle lyricist, so I look at it like, *I get to have my say, so fuck you guys*. Ha!

Zetro and I are closer now than we ever were in the '80s and early '90s. It took three go-rounds in Exodus for us to become bros. It's kind of fucking weird, right? He's in the band, we break up, he's back in the band after Baloff dies, he's out of the band again, and the third time's the charm, they say. We've done great work together, but now we have fun hanging out, too. He's been an awesome bandmate. I'm also still supergood friends with Rob Dukes. He's my brother and always will be. That's kind of the way it is with Exodus. There are no bitter ex-members. We're all friends. Even Robbie McKillop, who left after *Impact Is Imminent*, back in 1991. I still talk to him and send him his royalty checks. Of course I talk to my former H-Team partner, Rick Hunolt, all the time, too. We're all a tight family, from guys like Johnny Tempesta, to guys who didn't even play on an album but maybe helped us out when we needed it, like Nick Barker. We're a gang; you don't ever get out.

I absolutely enjoyed my time in Slayer, and as much as I love those guys, the band vibe was different from Exodus's. They were maybe less of a gang. So when I knew there was an expiration date on my Slayer gig, I was ready to get back to it with Exodus. Bring on the backstage showers in dirty backstage fucking bathrooms, where you have to wear shower sandals so you don't get athlete's foot. I was happy as fuck to do it. And I was willing to do as many shows in a row as Zetro was up for because he's the singer and it's harder on him. If my fingers got sore, big deal. But Zetro's one of those guys who'd do fucking ten in a row. So a little over a month after Slayer ended, Exodus played on the 70000 Tons of Metal cruise, a nice full-circle moment, since that was where Exodus were playing when Kerry first contacted me to join Slayer in early 2011. After that, we had a great package tour, Bay Strikes Back, booked in Europe with Testament and Death Angel for early February. I was jumping back into full-time Exodus mode with no hesitation.

I'm for better or worse a voracious reader of the news. Every day, I start my day with coffee and I read the news and see what's going on in the world. As January progressed, leading up to our European tour, I'd been reading a little bit about the coronavirus that had apparently started spreading out from China. We were set to fly to Denmark on February 2, so we had a few days to prepare for our first show in Copenhagen on February 6, and there didn't really seem to be any cause for alarm. We proceeded with our usual mayhem with typical results over there. Zetro was smoking weed in the back lounge of our bus when we were crossing into Switzerland—he didn't realize we were leaving the EU and crossing a border—and this Backstreet Boys–looking border guard didn't like that. Lee was hammered at the time and he kind of became a full-on ugly American toward the guy. So the Backstreet Boy and his cronies decided to strip-search us as kind of a fuck you. I don't think they thought they were going to find anything. But they were like, *This guy's awful mouthy. "Get in this room and take your clothes off."*

One of our ferry rides on that tour was so brutal I thought we were all going to the bottom of the sea. Full-on storm, boat rocking up and down, just the worst weather to be caught in while on the water. But it was amazing to be back in Europe with Exodus, and I loved it. And the fans welcomed me back as well. At one of the shows, someone made a banner that said, WELCOME BACK TO THE MOTHER SHIP, GARY. I brought it home, and it's hanging up in my office.

As we continued on our tour, coronavirus started running rampant across Italy, so our February 25 date in Milan was canceled. It seemed like it was nipping at our heels as the tour went on. We'd play a city, and at midnight the night of our show, they would reduce capacity of public events to the point where the show we just played would not have been possible. Like we played Paris to 1,500 people, but by the next day, those types of crowds weren't allowed. The more this happened, the more concerned we got. You have to remember that, this early in what became a pandemic, people had no idea exactly how it was spreading or how to prevent getting it.

We didn't have hand sanitizer, but we had so much Grey Goose vodka on the bus, we were using that instead. We had enough vodka to stock a bar for months because we'd get a bottle every day as part of our rider, and we weren't drinking a bottle every day. I never drank vodka;

I only drank beer with the occasional little Jäger shot. Vodka was Lee's thing. So we'd shake hands with fans and walk on the bus and go to the sink and start pouring Grey Goose on our fucking hands to kill germs! It was weird and crazy—and kind of scary—to be in the middle of what was unfolding. We managed to stay ahead of the lockdowns and venue closures until our final show of the tour—which was scheduled for Hanover, Germany, on March 11—was canceled. Traveling in our tour bus on the way to put our gear in storage in Germany (something we did at the end of every European tour), Lee woke me up.

"Gary, get up," he said with a panicked tone. "I just read that they're closing the airports in Germany." I bolted upright. We were scheduled to fly out the next day.

"Holy shit, can we even go home?"

"I don't know, man," he said. "The headlines say, AIRLINES SHUTTING DOWN TO FLIGHTS TO AMERICA, so we'd better figure that out *now*."

We soon found out that the airport closure was for non-US citizens. We were okay. And the closure wouldn't take effect until midnight the following day, and we would hopefully be long gone by then. Our flights were booked. It was just a matter of if we were ever gonna get on these things or if we were stuck there until we passed some sort of protocol, which none of us would've, because we were all currently getting sick. We just didn't know what it was—a cold or something much worse? The night before flying out, we and Death Angel all went out to dinner, and I remember not feeling very good at dinner. I felt like maybe I was getting a cold, which is not unusual on a winter tour in Europe. Austin, Death Angel's lighting designer, was also feeling like shit that night, and I was like, *Ah, shut up, there's nothing wrong with you.* Turns out, he had COVID. Most of us did. Those who seemed fine were probably just asymptomatic. I was okay on the flight home, until I landed. I made it through customs, and then in the car on the way home, I started feeling kind of shitty. It just progressed. I tried to go about my business, like,

Ah, I've just got a really bad cold. Then I got really sick, and it felt like I had the deadliest flu ever; I couldn't eat, and I slept like twenty hours a day. It was the sickest I've been in my life. I tried and tried to get tested, but it was so early in the pandemic that testing wasn't readily available. I was told go to the ER. I was like, *I'm not going to the ER. I shouldn't go out anywhere unless I absolutely need to be carted into an ER. I shouldn't be walking into one; I'd infect everybody.* By the time I finally fought my way into getting tested, it took seven and a half days to get the results. By then, I was already on the mend. It took me a couple of months to feel normal, though, and I lost sixteen pounds in the eleven days I was laid up. I'd feel healthy and fine, then go out and try to use my leaf blower to clear the driveway, and I'd be exhausted in five minutes just carrying the blower.

A lot of the bands and crew on the Bay Strikes Back came home with bad cases of COVID, but none more so than Death Angel drummer Will Carroll, who ended up intubated in a coma and almost died. During the first few weeks after we got home, we'd reach out to each other to check in. Testament singer Chuck Billy and his wife, Tiffany, both got it. My guitar tech had it. Surprisingly, there were some who didn't or they just didn't feel sick. Tom spent a lot of time in close quarters with Will Carroll on that tour but didn't seem to get COVID. But those of us who felt like shit, we were just checking off the boxes, positive, positive, positive, trying to help each other with testing. It may seem odd to say, but we ended up getting lucky with how the Bay Strikes Back tour worked out, all things considered. We only had to cancel two shows and we were playing to big, violent crowds at every stop. If that tour had started a week later, it would've been a financial death knell to us because of all the canceled shows, unsold merch, and fucking unpaid bills. Yes, some of us got seriously ill, but we survived, and at least we went into what became a very dark and challenging period on a high note.

In early 2020, pre-pandemic, Exodus didn't have any summer tours booked. The plan was to finally write, record, and release our follow-up to *Blood In, Blood Out* in 2020, something that would have been feasible in that time frame under normal circumstances. Typically, we try to balance making new albums around tours and festival offers and making money to pay our bills. But like pretty much every industry in the world, the unfolding pandemic created uncertainty and panic within the recording industry. Albums that were previously set for release were put on hold, recording sessions in studios were canceled, and record-pressing plants even temporarily closed up shop. I could still write a new album, but the rest of it was a giant question mark. Creativity, as Tom would say at the time, was the only thing we could control. We couldn't control where we could go, whether we could cover our faces or not, but we could write some thrash. So I started writing riffs, putting together songs, and sending them off to Tom, my writing partner. He'd get little rough recordings I did on my iPhone and a couple of things I'd done on my laptop.

When we got home from the European tour and the lockdowns hit, he'd decamped to his house in Lake Almanor, in northeast California, that he and his wife owned. Since recording at a studio wasn't going to be viable for Exodus and we had some experience recording in unorthodox places, we concocted the idea that we'd set up a studio at his place, which was pretty isolated from the world, and record our new album, *Persona Non Grata*, together there. Before that, though, Tom and I needed to get together and bring the songs to life. So I went up to Tom's place with a ton of riffs, some completed songs, and some ideas. It would just be a matter of teaching them to him—he had his drums there—and completing the songs, and maybe write new stuff along the way. Tom and I were doing this super old-school, just jamming out. We didn't have anything set up to record or capture any of it. We spent at least a couple of months in early spring writing together, during what turned out to be an unusually warm and dry period. I'd go up there for a week, come home for a bit, and then go back up. Because I was going back and forth and it was a three-hour drive each way, I couldn't bring my twenty guitars up there. I had to narrow it down and bring what I thought I really would use. There was no need for the other members of Exodus to come up until we were ready to record, because it was such a long haul. At one point, when we had a good catalog of stuff—enough to share—I was like, *All right, time for you guys to come join us.*

Once Tom and I felt we were ready, we arranged for our gear and the recording equipment to be sent up, and the rest of the band and engineer Steve Lagudi followed as well. The plan was to isolate together and stay there until the album was finished. We obviously had no other work we could do, so we could focus all our time and energy into creating a killer record. It was a luxury to not have to live a normal life while recording. With past albums, we'd be tracking all day, and then we'd go home and have to do all our home shit. But up at Lake Almanor, I could just play guitar all day long, every day. Tom, Steve, and I stayed at Tom's place and Lee, Zetro, and Jack lived at an Airbnb owned by Tom's cousin that was about a mile away, but during the day—before we got into the recording—we spent time learning the songs. The first day Lee came up, I was like, *Grab a seat*, and Tom and I started crushing him. He also finished the song he wrote for the album, "Slipping into Madness," while we were up there. Once Jack was settled, I went over the riffs with him; and as I started writing lyrics, I'd show those to Zetro. Because of the lockdowns and early panic of the pandemic, I hadn't seen hardly anybody for months, and now we were all hanging out, cooking steaks, playing metal, and getting drunk at night. It was rad.

If the pandemic gave us anything positive, it was time. Time together and time to make an album that we were super proud of. It was a relief not having to stare at a deadline or worry about what we'd do if we needed to record something more after we'd taken the gear down. Steve, who came out from New York to make the album with us, was like, *We'll book my flight home when we're done.* He was totally into it. It was exciting being there when the truck rolled up with all of Steve's recording equipment. And I mean, he had *a lot* of shit, not just your typical home-based Pro Tools rig. When all was said and done, we had two studios—with drums in each one—set up in Tom's house, with a shit ton of tracks at our disposal. In the past, we'd usually recorded the drums in a studio because you need so many inputs, a proper room, and a lot of mics. Everything else—guitars, bass, vocals—could be recorded in a bedroom. At Almanor, because Steve had all the gear shipped in, we were able to set the two drum kits up and keep them set up the whole time. This way, Tom could come back to a song a month later if he thought he could maybe play it better.

The creative environment never ended that summer. I'd be working on stuff in the evening after we'd consumed some steaks. Six beers later, I was still sitting there with an acoustic, noodling on various Jimmy Page–wannabeisms. We just lived it. It was a beautiful summer by Lake Almanor in the mountains, other than some serious smoke moments. The year 2020 was the largest wildfire year in recorded California history, and we definitely felt it at Almanor. During a period of high winds, the state cut power to our area to prevent downed power lines from starting more forest fires. And there were times during the recording, when Tom was pounding away and inhaling the heavily smoke-laden air, when we were like, *We can't stop recording and wait until the wind clears the smoke. Let's keep going!* It was the smokiest environment I've ever experienced, and Steve Lagudi would stand outside smoking cigarettes. It was unhealthy for us to even *breathe*, and he was making it way worse for himself by puffing on a Marlboro on top of it.

Going back to the days of near-constant touring in Slayer, I had started to experience some pain in my elbows, like tennis elbow. I used to joke that Slayer's riffs were so heavy they destroyed my arm! It started in my right elbow, and it would get incredibly sore. To get past that, I went to a doctor, and he recommended I get a cortisone shot. That worked amazingly well, and I'd be pain-free for six months. Then the pain would come back and I'd get another shot. After several of those, the left arm joined the pain party. Next thing you know, I was getting shots in both elbows, and all they were doing was masking the underlying condition and turning my tendons to mush. It got to the point to where sometimes I'd get the shot and it didn't work so well, and then the next one would work great. Just to be safe, I got one before we started rehearsing for the new album, which worked fine until we were tracking "The Beatings Will Continue (Until Morale Improves)" and the down picking blew out my right elbow. I eventually made it through the album, but I knew if I wanted to keep playing thrash, something had to give. My elbows were locking up; I'd sit and work on riffs, and my left arm would just want to stay stuck in that bent position. I couldn't even play for ten minutes. I thought that might've been it for my career. I've known enough guys over the years who got carpal tunnel and stuff like that that just causes nightmares for their playing ability, and here I had this elbow problem in both arms, with no idea where it was gonna lead me.

The fact that all the tracks for *Persona Non Grata* had been recorded gave me some peace of mind. We still had to mix it, but there was no hurry, because we weren't even close to figuring out a release date. Still, if I didn't figure out my elbow situation, there'd be no touring for me once things opened back up again. Eventually, I was able to get MRIs on both elbows, and I sent them to a really close friend of the band's who's a San Francisco Giants hand surgeon, Dr. Scott Hansen. Looking at the MRIs, he said, "You have injuries that look like you've been throwing ninety-mile-an-hour fastballs your whole life, like you're shredding those tendons." After my consultation with him, I made the mistake of googling what the recommended treatment is—worst thing you could ever do—and it said I'd need Tommy John surgery. If you're not a baseball fan, that procedure was named after a pro baseball pitcher who was the first guy to have his elbow tendon replaced with a cadaver tendon. The recovery time for pitchers is typically more than a year. I was horrified and thought, *Fuck. My shit is fucked. If they have to do this on both elbows, I'm not even gonna be picking up a guitar for a year, who knows!* Dr. Hansen sent the imaging to the Giants' elbow guy, and he said, *No, he can avoid surgery; he just needs therapy.* Whew! So I did a lot of physical therapy online, because of the pandemic, with my doctor and a lot of little exercises with one-pound weights and things like that. I can't get any more cortisone—even if my elbows hurt—I just ice them because that pain's telling me something. I still get little flare-ups, a little soreness, but it goes away on its own, and it's rare that I do have to ice it down. Basically playing thrash for so many years gave me an extreme case of tennis elbow. As long as I take care of them, I'll be okay. Still it's an uncomfortable feeling to start staring down your metal mortality. Without the ability to play, what would I do?

CHAPTER 29

THE BEATINGS WILL CONTINUE

W HEN WE FINALLY WRAPPED UP THE RECORDING OF *PERSONA*, AFTER
months spent up at Lake Almanor, we knew the album was sick
and we were very proud of it. Anytime I go on Instagram and
say something like, "Writing new shit and it's super crushing," some
people inevitably respond with "Dude, that's what they all say." But I'm
saying this as a fan of the band, and that's not coming from ego. I'm still
this band's biggest fan. If I write something that I'm jacked up about, it's
because I'm fucking excited. We knew *Persona* was killer.

Andy Sneap couldn't come over and record it, obviously, but we did
get him to mix it. And mix it. And mix it again. He must have mixed
it about thirty times because . . . we could. Andy was sequestered at
home in England in his studio, so he indulged our various efforts. Plus,
it's not uncommon for us to try multiple different mixes. There's what
I call the "Joey DeMaio" (of Manowar fame) mix, where Jack's bass is
really loud. It sounds great, but it makes the guitars a little bit softer.
Not volume-wise, but the crunch gets eaten up, because he has a very

crunchy bass. And then we also do the "guitars are ridiculously too loud mix," which I'm—surprisingly—the first to say that the guitars are too loud. It's just a matter of dialing things in. We thought we had the right mix dialed in, but a month after Andy did the final mix and mastered it, I went back to him and said, "I know you're gonna hate me, but what do you think about *this*?" It was a midrange-frequency thing on the guitars that no one else would notice, but I noticed it, and Andy agreed. Andy said that we had the time, so we did one final mix. Nearly a year after we'd started the process, *Persona Non Grata* was finished and in the can; it was just a matter of waiting. Vaccinations were slowly starting to become available, and there was some glimmer of hope around the corner, it seemed, but we had no idea when it would be released.

During the recording of *Persona*, Tom (as well as the rest of us) noticed he was losing some weight. He was pummeling his drums like always, but he was getting a little bit lighter. I just thought it was because we were playing so much in a hot room, but he was also experiencing some gastric issues. For a long time, Tom had had stomach issues, but it never seemed like anything major. So there was no great concern about it at the time; we just figured it was a bad case of GERD or the start of an ulcer or something. He got some tests done while we were recording, but you're talking about mountain doctors. It wasn't until we were done with the recording and he saw some city folks that he finally got the *right* test and they figured out what was going on.

In early 2021, I got a call from Tom with news I didn't want to hear. He had squamous cell carcinoma (SCC) of the stomach. There was a big tumor that they were going to start treating immediately with chemotherapy and he'd need his entire stomach removed after that. I broke down. It was fucking hard. I took it badly. I couldn't handle my best friend giving me this horrible, tragic news. He faced it, though, with a level of positivity that was remarkable. We all like to think that we'd have this kind of PMA, but it's easier said than done. It would be really easy to have a lot of dark days. He probably did on his own, but with us, he kept the positivity. He knew we all had his back.

Back home and isolated, after a fun summer spent with my bandmates, I started to succumb to depression. I felt like I couldn't do anything—couldn't play guitar, couldn't tour, just stuck at home. My elbows were fucked and required a lot of therapy and rehab, Tom was fighting through cancer, potentially fighting for his life, and all I wanted to do was get drunk. Until the pandemic, I wasn't really a hard drinker anymore. On tour, I drank beer and might occasionally have a little shot of Jägermeister, but I was always the first guy in bed. I always made sure I got my sleep, even in the Slayer days. But I was developing a fondness for 12 percent ABV triple IPAs that come in twenty-five-ounce bottles. I'd say I only drank five beers, but each of these was equal to two beers by volume and had three times the alcohol. In the past, if I was drinking by myself, it meant that I'd open one or two beers while I was watching a football game. Or maybe if it was a beautiful summer night and I was grilling, I'd crack a beer. I'd never sat around by myself and gotten hammered. But all of a sudden, I found myself doing that a couple of times a week.

We'd had a get-together with friends one evening, and afterward, I discovered a whole cooler full of White Claws were left behind. I'd always made fun of my friends who drink White Claw; it's not a real drink! But I eventually drank every last one of them, because there were nights when I got too drunk to go get more beer and the only thing I had around the house was the leftover White Claws. I'd crack one open—mandarin lime or some shit—take a taste and go, *This tastes horrible.* And then I'd drink it all—*glug glug glug.* I'd crack open a blackberry pomegranate and taste it: *Terrible!* I'd pound it down. One day, Lisa came to me and said, "Why are there a bunch of White Claw cans by the hot tub?" It took me a minute to remember that I had been sitting in the hot tub—a super old-school, '70s-style tub—pounding

White Claws by myself at like midnight. I was also becoming miserable to be around. Some days, I'd be happy. Some days, I didn't drink. But some days, my wife would be hiding in a room from me, because I'd be standing outside being a passive-aggressive, miserable fucking cunt. I was becoming kind of an asshole. And it was out of self-pity. Half of that pity was for someone (Tom) who was going through something way worse than I was. But he wasn't turning to alcohol. And once again, I wasn't liking the person that I saw looking back in the mirror. I started becoming dark. Dark Holt. I could see the signs that my drinking was a problem, the signs that I was a pretty fucked-up person when I had a buzz on. It was time for a change. It was time to stop wallowing in self-misery and do something positive, so on June 15, 2021, I got sober. I haven't touched alcohol since.

In the same way that quitting meth restored my lost creativity, quitting drinking had some immediate benefits as well. I play better than ever, my skin cleared up, I'm more focused than ever before, and I dropped some weight. And yeah, I'm a better husband. *Keeping* the weight off has been sort of a challenge, though, because there's a lot of sugar in beer, so when you cut it out, your body starts craving it. I've never been a dessert guy, but I sort of developed a sweet tooth. I'm trying to keep my weight down because if I'm twenty pounds heavier, it's like putting a twenty-pound metal fucking weight-lifting plate on my back and carrying it around. It's bad for me, especially with my past back issues, which have mostly stabilized. There are times I miss drinking. I miss the camaraderie. But I don't miss getting drunk. I have a certain group of friends, whom I don't see that often, but we used to pound the beers when we'd get together. Thankfully, there are amazing nonalcoholic beers out there now, because I still like the taste of beer. So I'll drink those, but I won't drink ten of them; I'll drink one or two. I can hang out with the guys in the band who still drink, and I laugh at them because they're fucking ridiculous.

Not long after I stopped drinking, Tom underwent a total gastrectomy to remove his stomach tumor. In prepping for the surgery, they actually discovered he had a second type of cancer, as they found some nodules of mesothelioma in his abdomen walls. They were able to successfully remove both types of cancer, and Tom started his road to recovery, with the goal of eventually getting back onstage with Exodus, so we could promote *Persona*. It would be a process, though, to regain both his stamina and strength for playing a full set. He'd lost a lot of weight, and chemo takes its toll as well. And when you undergo the kind of major surgery he did, that alone requires a lot of healing. He had a long road ahead, but he had nothing but hope and positivity.

That summer, we also finally got a confirmed release date for *Persona Non Grata*, November 19, 2021, and were booked to play at two festivals, Psycho Las Vegas in late August and Full Terror Assault in early September—our first live performance in nearly eighteen months. Finally! Tom obviously wouldn't be ready to perform with us at those, so we asked Johnny Tempesta to fill in temporarily until Tom was at full strength. We'd actually had the opportunity to do a US Bay Strikes Back tour in late 2021, around *Persona*'s release, but we postponed because there were a million pandemic-related rules that bands had to follow that were gonna make it really difficult to even make a tour happen. It was gonna be a nightmare. And Tom was still recovering from his cancer, so we decided to wait until the timing got better.

Tom returned to the Exodus fold on October 7, at the Aftershock Festival in Sacramento, and he fucking killed it. He was playing so fast in "Strike of the Beast," I could barely keep up. He was the star of the show. This was Tom's moment. He just pummeled it. It was so phenomenal. He came back and summoned up these pent-up reserves of aggression and just destroyed. It brought a smile to all our faces. That said, getting him back in the fold permanently was a process. Initially, he had his struggles with stamina, but Tom Hunting at 75 percent is still way better than any other drummer on earth, at least for Exodus. There were certain songs he didn't want to play at first because he didn't feel like he was there yet. And because he was still rebuilding his core strength after the surgery, sometimes he'd mention that he didn't feel like his balance was back. But when we finally kicked off the US Bay Strikes Back tour with Death Angel and Testament, he was ready to go.

We did ourselves a favor by postponing this tour until April 2022, not the least of which was getting Tom back as close to full strength as possible. But doing it a little deeper into the pandemic, when more people were vaccinated and there were fewer restrictions, just made it a little easier to dip our toes back in the water. We hadn't full-on toured in more than two years, and on this one, we'd have to deal with completely new challenges beyond just shaking the rust off. It was fitting that we were sort of picking up where we left off by resuming the Bay Strikes Back lineup, which went over so well in Europe. Now that we had a new album out—finally!—we were ready to start grinding to make up for lost time. COVID was still out there, and as we now know, you can still catch it even if you're vaccinated.

Sure enough, Tom and I both caught it on that tour. I'd see other bands during this same time where one guy would test positive, and they'd decide they couldn't play, and they'd isolate. We were like, *Fuck that. We're not doing that.* I believe in the vaccine, but I don't believe in hiding. If you're gonna tour, you're gonna tour. You're literally sharing a bus with your merchandise guy whom you hope is taking lots of people's money all day long. He's touching their money. Money's one of the dirtiest things in the world, and then he gets on your bus. Unless you put *that guy* in a bubble and isolate him, what's the purpose in isolating? You can't isolate from it on tour. You can't. What are you gonna do? If you believe in the vaccine, like I do, you believe it's done its job and that it reduces the severity to a nasty cold. I saw other bands doing their meet and greets from thirty feet away up on the stage with the people in front of them and a merch guy. The same fan you're afraid to take a picture with is touching you by association anyway when he interacts with the merch guy. We hoped *all* the fans touched the merch guy, because we depend on merch money. We want those dirty twenty-dollar bills flowing! Keep 'em coming! You just have to be smart about things. Don't pick food out of your teeth after shaking hands. Shake hands, and when you're done, go and wash your hands or sanitize. All the food in catering, all our bottles of water were placed there by human hands. There's just a chain of fucking contact with the fucking virus. If it's there, it's gonna find you. It's just part of life.

The spring run of the Bay Strikes Back tour in the US did extremely well, which was super encouraging. It was a good way to ease back into things because we didn't have to carry the load ourselves as far as its success or failure. We went out and crushed and had a great time. And it went over so well that we did another run with the same three bands in the US in the fall. In between, we took Exodus back to Europe to hit all the festivals and even went to South and Central America in late summer. We worked pretty much every month in 2022. It was a good year, a really good year. After all the uncertainty of the pandemic and my years away from the band when I was playing with Slayer, it felt amazing to be back in the mother ship and to feel the fire from the fans. It was like reuniting with family.

My parents always preached family above all, and they were fucking right. It took me a long time to truly understand that and how I could apply it to a life that necessitated me being away for long stretches of time. My father and mother were role models in so many ways—hardworking, reliable, supportive, loving—but my chosen profession made it hard for me to see how the lessons they tried to teach me fit into *my* family situation. So yeah, I made a lot of mistakes along the way.

But when I met Lisa, I found an understanding and loving partner who helped me navigate being both a family man and a professional working musician. It's still hard, and it will always be hard to be away from family, but I've found the balance that hopefully works best for all of us.

It helps to have understanding bandmates, many of whom have their own families. When I was in Slayer, I knew that my daughter Chelsea was graduating from college—the first in our family to achieve that—so I asked far in advance if I could have the time free to attend her graduation ceremony. They graciously booked the tour around that so I wouldn't miss such an important milestone. When I was younger and was a little bit more selfish, I didn't think about that kind of stuff. It was more like, *I gotta miss this birthday. I'll buy them a better gift than I might normally have, spoil them a little bit, make up for it with incentives.* It's what we do, and I'm not alone in it. We miss out on a lot of shit doing this. I know how to make time better now.

As my career ascended through both Exodus and Slayer, my family with Lisa grew. When I married her in 2011, I not only gained a wife but a third daughter—our middle child, Frances, who's within two years of both Chelsea and Sophie. I'm not her biological father, but I'm considered Dad. My father always treated and my mother still does treat Frances as one of their own, just like he raised my mother's four kids from another marriage as his own. Frances has given us two granddaughters (Freyja and Layla) and a grandson (James).

People say that grandchildren offer you the chance to learn from your mistakes as a parent and to do it right. When my first granddaughter, Freyja, came along, it changed my entire life. I bonded with her from the time she was a newborn. She came home to our house and lived there with us and her mom, of course, for most of her early years. It changed my entire life. Everything I do is centered around getting home and spending time with my grandkids. They make me so fucking happy. And they make me feel young because I get to be as stupid and silly as I want, and they love it. It's the best; it changes everything. When I'm not on tour, it's an obsessive thought to get home to see them. I have pictures of my grandkids on my amp rack. On my guitar work box, I have drawings from Freyja that say she'll miss me. I'd love to have more grandkids, but that's obviously not up to me. Maybe Sophie and/or Chelsea will one day make our extended family even bigger.

Chelsea lives in Hollywood these days. She's done so well for herself. She's an incredible artist, and she's working as a storyboard artist now. She's done stints at Nickelodeon, worked for Warner Bros., and even worked on the rebooted *Rugrats*. She's living her dream. Sophie was living with her mom during the pandemic, and she and I would meet up for socially distanced lunches, which always brightened the dark days of that period. She now lives about ten minutes away from Lisa and me in a condo we bought as a rental for her. She just pays the mortgage, and we're happy to have her close by.

My mom, age eighty-nine, is still living in the house my father built, where she raised all her kids, where her children, grandchildren, and great-grandchildren still visit. My brother Steve lives there, too, and looks after her. Living a little bit removed from the Bay Area now, I don't see her as much as I'd like, but she's surrounded by her loving extended family—my siblings and their children—in a home that has seemingly always been filled with children of one generation or another since it was built. I want the same thing, maybe on a slightly smaller scale. Some of the greatest moments of my life are centered around my kids and grandkids these days. Music is not the sole focus of my life now. The music is a means for me to do something that keeps me happy, but it also allows me to spend the downtime with my family, and that makes me *really* happy. I don't have to go work a day job, and I'm fucking lucky. Money can be tight, but we get by. Exodus always loved to party, and wherever the party was, we were going to be the center of it. Now my party is spent hanging out with my family. It's the most important thing to me—taking my granddaughter to school and picking her up, and spending time with my kids and grandkids.

EXODUS IN THE TWENTY-FIRST CENTURY IS A VERY DIFFERENT BEAST NOW from the band Kirk and Tom formed, or the one that put out *Bonded by Blood*, or even that hell-bent crew who wreaked destruction on the Headbangers Ball Tour. We've evolved into a far more dangerous animal, a ferocious fucking beast. Our fangs have grown, and we have a thirst for blood. We're not in any way, shape, or form a bunch of tired, nearly sixty-year-old dudes. We go out and smoke people. We will make your band look bad. And our albums are crushing and sick. When we play big festivals, there are multiple pits in the audience, and the punters are just going berserk. Onstage, we've got smiles from ear to ear; we still live for that shit.

And we're hungrier than ever because we're still fucking struggling musicians. We haven't achieved anything. We own zero gold records. We're not part of the so-called Big Four. I still feel like we have to prove ourselves. None of the guys in the real successful thrash bands ever had to look at their career and say, *Man, after ten good years, I was a footnote. I was in the where-are-they-now category.* They've always been out making money and doing big tours. I was fucking shoveling dog shit for a living on an RV lot. I don't look back and dwell on the what coulda, shoulda been. I'm not rich and never will be. But I'm still here and still making music. What do I have to complain about? Nothing. I'm lucky. I don't take where I am today for granted. I still love it. I still wanna bang my head. If I stopped, it would kill me. It was a grind to get here. But I think Exodus are finally getting our respect now. It took a long time. Better late than never, right?

And I've long since given up trying to make the old-school people happy who want us to sound like it's 1985 forever. That's impossible. I can't do it. Trying to sound like twenty-year-old Gary Holt would be the fakest thing I could ever do. I'm a different guy. Music is different. *Bonded by Blood* will always be the greatest album I've ever been a part of. But I want to explore different musical landscapes within thrash, and why not do a twelve-minute-long song? Who says I can't? Metal's not supposed to have rules. That's what blows me away when people start putting rules on it. Thrash was created to break rules. Fucking no one thought an album like *Bonded by Blood* was socially acceptable at the time. It was fucking dark, evil, horrible stuff that people didn't like. I still have magazines, fanzines from '85, just ripping on *Bonded by Blood*, saying it was a half-rate *Kill 'Em All* rip-off that would be forgotten in a year. Guess they were wrong.

Sometimes it takes decades to find who you really are, and Exodus are fucking killers. We're not Tom Cruise in *Mission: Impossible*, we're fucking John Wick. We're here to kill you, not sneak in past your laser security and steal something. There's nobody more aggressive than we are. We're not gonna fucking give up. We push. We push and keep fucking going hard. It's the only way we know how to do it. I know someday it's going to have to slow down, because I'm already dealing with arthritis and tendonitis and all this shit. But when I can't play thrash metal is when I won't play thrash metal.

EPILOGUE

AFTER THE SEVEN-YEAR GAP BETWEEN *BLOOD IN, BLOOD OUT* AND *PERsona Non Grata*, I swore fans wouldn't have another long wait between Exodus albums. We were back together and crushing people with impunity once the pandemic eased up. *Persona* was received well (it reached number 20 on the Billboard album chart), our tours were packed with enthusiastic fans, and the hard work we'd put in over the previous two decades had paid off. We were on a roll—and closer than ever personally—and could map out our own future without being subject to Slayer's schedule or other outside factors. So what's that cliché about the best-laid plans?

As great as 2022 was, the following year had some challenges. Exodus had to cancel a European tour, I dealt with neck issues, and we had to make a decision regarding what label would be putting out our next album. We did all this while still managing to tour the US with our good friends in Anthrax and Black Label Society, play some dates in Asia, and finish out with a late-fall US run. I even managed to get a start on the riff writing for the *Persona* follow-up, which will be released on our new label Napalm Records. We love Nuclear Blast, so it wasn't easy to make the decision to go to Napalm. It came down to one thing only: turnover. I only knew one person who remained at Nuclear Blast (the label was sold in 2018) from when we first signed, and if he ended up leaving, I'd have nobody there. The whole band felt like we didn't want to put ourselves in a position where we didn't have allies there anymore.

On the plus side of the ledger, Tom was deemed clear of cancer by his doctors in 2023, so that means he and I will continue to punish mother-fuckers together for the foreseeable future. Writing for the next album started slowly because working on the first song always takes forever. The next thing you know, though, I'm randomly stumbling onto new songs in the dark. Album to album, at this point in my life, I'm gonna write what I wanna write and hope people like it. I'm a big fan of writing thrash riffs that play on different rhythmic concepts from what other people are doing and trying to create textures without melodies some-times. I love melody, but I'm really into the rhythmic aspect of things. The rhythm guitars, I want to do things that are a little bit different. People never learn my riffs right, because there's always weird things going on that people don't understand. The new shit is fucking punish-ing. It's fucking ridiculous how heavy it is. We're on a mission to be the heaviest band in the world, and if not the heaviest, the most aggressive. When we'll record the new album and when it will be released are up in the air, but you may be listening to it while you're reading this.

And that thing I thought might never happen, happened. As I write this, three Slayer appearances at US festivals were just announced for fall 2024. I found out about them just before the general public did, when I was asked to resume my position on stage right. I think people are going to be happy to see Slayer again, and I love playing those songs. Some of them are part of my DNA, too, now. But if Kerry and Tom want to play "Ghosts of War," I'm gonna have to start woodshedding! These Slayer shows will have zero bearing on anything Exodus have scheduled, whatsoever. It's not going to affect us at all, not a single show. Do I think Slayer will ever tour again? No, I don't think so. But I've been proven wrong before.

SELECT DISCOGRAPHY

EXODUS

Combat Tour Live: The Ultimate Revenge: Exodus/Slayer/Venom Video (Combat) 1985

Bonded by Blood LP (Torrid) 1985

Pleasures of the Flesh LP (Combat) 1987

Fabulous Disaster LP (Combat) 1989

Impact Is Imminent LP (Capitol) 1990

Good Friendly Violent Fun LP (Relativity) 1991

The Best of Exodus: Lessons in Violence LP (Relativity) 1992

Force of Habit LP (Capitol) 1992

Another Lesson in Violence (live) LP (Century Media) 1997

Tempo of the Damned LP (Nuclear Blast) 2004

Shovel Headed Kill Machine LP (Nuclear Blast) 2005

The Atrocity Exhibition . . . Exhibit A LP (Nuclear Blast) 2007

Let There Be Blood LP (Zaentz) 2008

Shovel Headed Tour Machine: Live at Wacken & Other Assorted Atrocities (live) LP (Nuclear Blast) 2008

Exhibit B: The Human Condition LP (Nuclear Blast) 2010

Blood In, Blood Out LP (Nuclear Blast) 2014

Persona Non Grata LP (Nuclear Blast) 2021

British Disaster—The Battle of '89 (live) LP (Nuclear Blast) 2024

SLAYER

Repentless LP (Nuclear Blast) 2015

The Repentless Killogy DVD (Nuclear Blast) 2019

The Repentless Killogy: Live at the Forum in Inglewood, CA LP
(Nuclear Blast) 2019

ACKNOWLEDGMENTS

I WOULD LIKE TO THANK ADEM TEPEDELEN FOR BEARING WITH ME WHILE I replayed my life—the good, the horrible, and the great—in as much gruesome detail as I could muster. You dug deep, opened a few wounds, and we had a lot of laughs. To Laura Mazer and all at Wendy Sherman Associates for your guidance in making this book a reality. To Ben Schafer and all at Hachette Book Group for believing that my tale was worth reading in the first place. Thank you all.

To my bandmates, Paul Baloff (RIP), Tom Hunting, Rick Hunolt, Robbie McKillop, Steve "Zetro" Souza, Mike Butler, Jack Gibson, Lee Altus, Rob Dukes, and Paul Bostaph (and all the guys I played with but never recorded with) for making my riff fever dreams reality. Brothers for life. It's been my privilege to have played music with the former members and to continue playing thrash with the current. Special thanks to Jeff Andrews: You were part of the band when I was brought in, and you were one of the coolest, funniest dudes I have ever known. Rob Dukes, you helped usher this band into a new level of heaviness—my deepest gratitude for all your work and all the laughs you brought me. Lee, Zet, Jack, and Tom, you guys never cease to amaze me and push me to take this music we love further than ever. And together, we just fucking flat-out destroy fools! My gang of heavy. Posers must die!

To the memory of Paul Baloff, the greatest thrash front man of all time. To this day, every riff must pass the "Pavel test": Is it heavy enough for you? I think so. I will continue to crush on your behalf.

To Kirk Hammett, for that day he said, "Hey, wanna learn to play the guitar?" Changed my life forever, bro. Thank you. Gravy boys for life!

Especially to Tom Hunting and Rick Hunolt, as much brothers as my own blood. The memories we made I'll carry with me until the end. Playing thrash with you guys, I consider myself blessed. In a most unholy way, of course! As Pavel would say, "Why so heavy!"

To Zetro, thanks for helping to make some of the sickest records in thrash, especially *Persona Non Grata*. Totally epic. Good times indeed. Cheers!

Jack, I've played longer with you than anyone else, and you've always brought the thunder to the band's lightning. And early on, you brought the white lightning! Glad I never drank that shit!

Lee, I've known you longer than almost everyone who's ever played in Exodus. We go back to the beginning of this thing called thrash, from the Old Waldorf and beyond. It's been sick as fuck playing alongside you.

To my Slayer family: Kerry King, Tom Araya, Dave Lombardo, and Paul Bostaph, my other brothers. You made me feel like family from the jump. It was an honor for me to play these songs with you guys and to honor Jeff onstage every night. And thanks to Ayesha, Sandra, Paula, and Amy, their other halves. To Rick, Kristen, Stu, Ernie, and all at RSE Group, thanks for being so awesome to me, start to finish. And to Jeff and Kathryn Hanneman, for giving me the thumbs-up to play Jeff's songs. It meant more to me than you'll ever know.

To the entire Slayer crew, especially Warren Lee, my security guard as much as my guitar tech of almost nine years of Slayer. Brothers for life. Love you, bro. To Armand Butts Crump (RIP) for being the guy who prepared me for the Slayer machine. To my Exodus crew, Brian "KISS" Quinlan, Frenchy Pete, Vasilis Sarakinos, Nick Barker, Mike Hamilton, Ross Erkers, and more; there have been many bodies in the camp over the years, and you're all appreciated, especially Steve Brogden, my right hand in my left-hand path of metal, and Robin Mazen, nobody worked harder for us.

To Kragen Lum, for being the best stunt double a guy could ask for. Thanks for holding down the fort for me.

To my siblings, Kathi, John, Butch, Steve, and Charles, I love you all. Family is what matters most. You have had my back through the good and bad. Kathi, you had to tolerate sharing a room with your baby brother, and I was a pest! And all of us brothers survived some nasty shit; I am proud of us all. The rest of my family, there are just too many of you to thank here, but know that I love all of you.

To my mother-in-law, Teri Perticone, for being the coolest, best second mom I could ask for.

To my childhood friends, James Maxwell, Ronnie Schwartz (RIP), and James "Moose" Mangrum, Richmond High for life! Where's the kegger? Meet out back to match a doob? "Got my ticket to Day on the Green, did you?"

To my blood brother and friend for nearly forty years, Matthias "Vodka" Prill. From head of the Venom fan club to resident rat pack fan and consumer of fine distilled spirits . . . and legendary fisherman. More handsome than ever! Cheers, my friend!

To all the Slay Team, Lonnie Hunolt, Andy "Airborne" Andersen, Alexis Olson, and Toby Rage (RIP). We may have brought the thrash, but you brought the blood.

To Brian Lew and Harald O., for your friendship and for capturing all the mayhem.

To all the old friends from the early days on, Adam Segen, Pam and Craig Behrhorst, Connie Taylor, Fred Cotton, Lààz Rockit, Anvil Chorus, and far too many to list here. Friends to this day.

To Toni Isabella and all at Bill Graham Presents, for being a surrogate family to a bunch of insane maniacs throughout the good ol' days.

To all the fans who have supported me since day one and remained there through the worst of the worst and the best of the best. Exodus fans, you destroy all!

AND MOSTLY TO THE FOLLOWING:

To my parents, June and Bill Holt: Dad, not a day goes by I don't miss you and think of you and all the lessons you taught me, that took so long for me to hear. I am always listening now. Mom, you've been my biggest fan since the day I brought a guitar home, and you have shown me a level of support that knows no equal. A better mother there will never be. Love always.

To my daughters, Chelsea, Frances, and Sophie: Every day, you make me want to be a better father—proud girl-dad right here. I love you all so much; you mean everything to me. More perfect children don't exist in this world. And I will continue to work on being the best dad you could ever have. The pride I have for all of you, it's extreme.

To my grandchildren: Freyja, James, and Layla. The joy you have brought to my life is indescribable. The inner child in me lives forever through the three of you; there's nothing I'd rather do than spend my time hanging out with you kids. You're all my true happy place.

And to my wife, Lisa: My best friend, my doorbell-ditch partner in crime, my other half, my last stop, my all. After Forever. That's the love I have for you. You've always believed in me and have always told me there's nothing I can't accomplish, but none of it is possible without you. You're my muse, my true love, watcher of shitty reality TV partner, the only person who connects with me in every way. I love you.

FOREVER REMEMBERED, FOREVER MISSED

Toby Rage

Jeff Hanneman

Ronnie Schwartz

Ty Schwartz

Scott Franklin

James Lapin

Mike "Kneeslides" Street

Bob Johnson

Dan and Lynn Northcut

Frank Hastings

Randolph Mangrum

Debbie Abono

Wes Robinson

Sam Kress

Jon and Marsha Zazula

Cliff Burton

Adrianus Van Oudheusden (Fozzy)

Armand Butts Crump

Bill Graham

INDEX